Plato's *Laws*

EDITED BY

GREGORY RECCO

AND

ERIC SANDAY

Plato's *Laws*

Force and Truth in Politics

INDIANA UNIVERSITY PRESS

Bloomington and Indianapolis

This book is a publication of

Indiana University Press
601 North Morton Street
Bloomington, Indiana 47404-3797 USA

iupress.indiana.edu

Telephone orders   800-842-6796
Fax orders   812-855-7931
Orders by e-mail   iuporder@indiana.edu

© 2013 by Indiana University Press

♾ The paper used in this publication meets the minimum requirements
of the American National Standard for Information Sciences—Permanence
of Paper for Printed Library Materials, ANSI Z39.48-1992.

Manufactured in the United States of America

Library of Congress Cataloging-in-Publication Data

Plato's Laws : force and truth in politics / edited by Gregory Recco and Eric Sanday.
    p. cm. — (Studies in continental thought)
Includes bibliographical references and index.
ISBN 978-0-253-00178-8 (cloth : alk. paper)
ISBN 978-0-253-00182-5 (pbk. : alk. paper) — ISBN 978-0-253-00188-7 (ebk.)
1. Plato. Laws. 2. Political science—Philosophy. I. Recco, Gregory. II. Sanday, Eric.
    JC71.P264P54 2012
    321'.07—dc23   2012019903

1 2 3 4 5   18 17 16 15 14 13

Contents

Acknowledgments

Thank you to *Proceedings of the Boston Area Colloquium in Ancient Philosophy*, v. 26. for permission to reprint sections of chapter 13 by Sara Brill.

Plato's *Laws*

Introduction

This volume embodies a cooperative, intensive, and comprehensive interpretation of Plato's *Laws*, a single, massive dialogue that challenges even the hardiest reader. In general, it is useful to focus on a single dialogue because of the sort of thing a Platonic dialogue is. While Plato's works certainly deal with common themes in common ways, each dialogue also has something like the integrity of a work of art; it has, so to speak, its own rules. An elaborate dramatic conceit, unique and well-drawn characters, novel images and arguments, all contribute to making the individual dialogue an appropriate object for study. It seemed to us especially appropriate in the case of the *Laws*—whose mere length sets it apart, as do its unique setting, principal speaker, and fresh take on politics— to undertake a reading in common calculated to bring out what is distinctive about the dialogue.

Sharing the end of reading in common, our essays cover the whole dialogue book by book, and several reflect on it as a whole. Forgoing the aim of complete commentary, the authors were invited to highlight whatever aspects of the text they judged most salient and fruitful. Finally, before final versions were due, authors had access to draft copies of one another's essays and, to greater or lesser degrees, incorporated responses to one another's work. All these features, we think, lend the volume an even higher degree of cohesiveness than would come from merely working from a common text. The authors come from diverse backgrounds and even disciplines: philosophy, political science, classics, history, each charting a different path through the vast wilderness of the *Laws*. While their essays are at least as diverse as their backgrounds, there is nonetheless a theme common to most if not all that can serve as a starting point for introducing the material in this volume.

Partly by comparing other dialogues of Plato (most notably the *Republic,* of course), and partly through thinking about our own times, the reader of the *Laws* is bound to consider the idea of a free, rational, non-coercive politics in accordance with the good, which the dialogue at times seems to present as a real possibility and at others as a hopeless delusion or a far-distant promise. Throughout all the dialogues, Plato is attentive to the elusive nature of the good and of our relationship to it, paying special attention to how certain ways of relating to the good uproot us from it, leaving us prey to tyrants within and without; the passions, opinions, and errors that hold sway in our common life and discourse tend to make political life a bloody contest or a bitter disappointment. In the *Laws* in particular, we see Plato puzzling once again over the task of instituting a community in such a way that it is open to the good, even if it begins as one that might well be harmed by philosophical openness and that in any case has not been well prepared for it by the traditions and practices of its erstwhile progenitors.

As for the *Republic,* even its Athenian dramatic setting did not provide the most auspicious prospects for a free and rational politics, and Socrates' late appeal to a "pattern laid up in heaven" attests to the remoteness of that hope. The *Laws'* Cretan setting and its aged and hidebound interlocutors—one a somewhat undistinguished Spartan, the other an internally conflicted Cretan, neither naturally well-disposed toward Athenian political innovation—do not appreciably brighten one's hopes. Nonetheless, the nameless Athenian Stranger has been invited, with only a little in the way of subterfuge, to discuss the founding of a new city, and so long as he is there in that capacity, his view of the matter may have some beneficial effect on the progress of the conversation.

But just what truth about politics does the dialogue bring to light? Better: what understanding of political life does the Athenian bring to this conversation? One possible view of the Athenian Stranger is that he behaves more as a rhetorician than as a philosopher and as someone who in some sense fundamentally endorses Kleinias's account of politics as war among people and within the soul, although perhaps the Athenian holds this view reluctantly and sometimes in frustration. Another possibility would be to take the Athenian Stranger more as a philosopher, and see the dialogue as a call to move beyond the occasional endorsements of Kleinias's vision of politics as coercion and deception to embrace a politics of reason and truth. A third possible view would discover in the ambiguity between rational politics and coercion a kind of truth all its own, and in the strife between reason and force something that is simultaneously a threat to and resource for the healthy functioning of laws. In different ways and to different degrees, all of these views are present in the essays collected here, and the collection allows the reader to pose anew both the interpretive questions concerning the Athenian's or Plato's ultimate views and the general philosophical question of what understanding of politics ought to guide the founding and functioning of our commonwealths.

According to the first of these three types, the Athenian Stranger is willing to put forward a vision of non-coercive politics, but what he ultimately accepts as the underlying truth of the matter is the force and deception that protect political community from its own self-destructive impulses. This is to attribute a degree of strategic deception to the Athenian, whose actions are read as manufacturing political community by coercive means. For example, on this view, the preludes to individual laws and to the laws as a whole are interpreted as bordering on manipulation, even though the Athenian presents them as persuasive speeches intended to educate the community on the need for the laws and their obedience. The preludes have the function of maintaining the community within the parameters of a workable although not ideal, and distinctly not philosophical, political space.

Conversely, one might see in the *Laws* the promise of a philosophically rigorous politics of free, non-coercive persuasion. This perspective sees the Athenian Stranger as upholding the value of openness demanded by reason and valuing various rational practices in everyday political life. By prioritizing the spontaneity of play and emergent order over the violent submission to external authority, the Athenian Stranger might be taken to have in view the ideal of self-moving soul articulated explicitly in Book 10, which would be echoed in the procedures for training judges and forming the Assembly, which are described in Book 12. Insofar as the Athenian Stranger does make use of coercive means, therefore, they can be seen as provisional or even provocatively ironic measures taken in service of promoting the freedom of the citizens. This stance reads all concessions to externally imposed order as a kind of facilitating constraint.

A third possibility is to view the Athenian as rightly acknowledging the priority of spontaneity over coercion and yet also recognizing the necessity of force, violence, and deception not only as a provisional measure, but as responding to the implacable limitations and ambiguities of human freedom itself. On this view, what comes to the fore are what could be called "sub-political" forces, such as geography, economic and erotic practices, etc., as both violent and potentially liberating. It is surely partly because of the unprecedented level of administrative detail found in the proposals of the *Laws* that such matters have greater prominence than in other writings on politics, but this third view is also to be explained on the basis of what is internal to the question itself. For the embodied, desiring being who comes from somewhere in particular, freedom is not to be found in the mere negation of these determinacies, nor in their remainderless transubstantiation into the universal. Rather, they must be understood in their necessity and in the indelible mark they will leave in the heart of any future community, however well managed. On this third view then, political life would subsist in the tension between freedom and coercion.

Having given this general account of the possible interconnections of freedom and coercion, let us pass on to some more particular ways in which this theme gets played out in the dialogue and in the essays in this volume. As will become clear, this is not intended (and would not succeed) as a summary of all that is to be found in these rich explorations, but it will enable us to highlight some of the contributions they make to developing and sharpening the question.

In a different way, the relationship between coercive and rational politics can be seen from the framing structure of the dialogue as a whole. Framing decisions, which are not brought up within the dialogue for explicit discussion, are examples of the way the dialogue itself might be read as manipulating the reader, leading the reader without her consent, or at the very least demanding that the reader be alert to decisions that do not seem open for discussion. To call these decisions coercive or manipulative is just to point out that all rhetoric draws substantial power from its ability to posit a starting point and grow momentum without asking for permission, and it is to claim that Plato's *Laws* is an example of a particular kind of rhetoric.

The *Laws*, for example, picks its frame in a very specific way. One notices a lack of explicit reference to the Good or the Forms generally, or to mathematics, as Mitchell Miller points out in his essay. One might surmise, by virtue of this excluded content, that the *Laws* takes place entirely within the domain of *pistis* (trust) of the citizen, borrowing Socrates' term for the sort of opining that deals in stable, recognized objects (*Republic* 511e). That is, the *Laws* and its many individual discussions are directed ultimately at the citizen's trust in the inherited ways of the city and its unspoken structures of authority, rather than at the citizen's understanding the reasons behind the city's ways. We might interrogate the text with this question in mind, namely, whether the city makes paths available for its citizens to step out of its defining framework. The discussion does at times explicitly provide a route out of *pistis* for individual citizens, such as judges and members of the Assembly, but these are provisions for a relatively small number of citizens, and the procedures involved are not a matter of public scrutiny, perhaps not even for those enlightened few. For the citizenry in general, the rule of law is first and foremost predicated on an explicit recognition that the claims made on us by pleasure and pain are inescapable, and that therefore there is a material limit to the kind of freedom and rationality possible for the body politic. For both types, ordinary and extraordinary (or privileged) citizens, the mere fact that the city is something founded places the manner in which political questions are framed somewhat out of reach, and so to speak, forces it upon them.

Just as Pericles had famously set the stage for fifth-century Athenian politics with his call to fix one's eyes on the power of Athens and become her lover (ἐραστής), so too here in the *Laws* we see a kind of rhetorical gesture meant to inaugurate a political orientation. Without deciding the dramatic dating of the *Laws*, the controversy surrounding which is discussed by contributors in this volume, we might still notice the rhetorical impact the *Laws* would have as a fourth-century Athenian political document. The mid-fourth century was a time, centering around 355 BCE, in which Athens turned decisively away from the Periclean vision of empire toward the ideals of peace and wealth, as Mark Munn points out in his essay. The retrenchment of Athens within its own territorial boundaries might shed light on the insular character of the regime imagined in the *Laws*. Seeing the *Laws* as a kind of inverted Pericleanism might help the factive reader to extricate many of the defensive military proposals considered by the Athenian Stranger, for instance, from their apparent contingency and, most jarringly, their apparent irrelevance to fifth-century Athens, in which the other dialogues seem so happily nested. Noticing these kinds of parallels answers the very familiar call of Platonic dialogue to dig up its unstated framing assumptions and bracket their rhetorical impact for the sake of thinking about them.

The lengths to which the *Laws* goes to assert its framework without discussion or appeal to the reader's rationality is in itself a provocation to do the work of excavating those assumptions and to transform the rhetoric of the *Laws* into philosophical discussion. But at the same time we might be bending the dialogue a little too far. The *Laws* may not allow the reader comfortably to employ the strategies that are solicited by other dialogues, and therefore one might gain some relief from the idea that the text does not demand to be read as an endorsement of a philosophically grounded constitution. Following this supposition, one would want to examine seriously the evidence that this is a more manipulative text, or at least a differently manipulative text, than anything else written by Plato.

The text will not let us ignore the wide berth the Athenian Stranger offers coercion and deception in the education and maintenance of the citizenry, which might lead one to conclude that the Athenian is placating his Spartan and Cretan interlocutors with regard to their political assumptions and winning their trust in order to supplement those assumptions with non-coercive elements, such as we find in the preludes to the laws. However, this view cannot exclude the possibility that, to the contrary, the Athenian is extending and perfecting the coercive methods of his interlocutors precisely by clothing these techniques in the garb of freedom and rationality. There is, again, a kind of relief in being able to entertain the thought, often and with good reason considered taboo for the interpretation of Plato, that the *Laws* at least only adopts non-coercive political practices (or the rhetoric of such practices) in order to extend and perfect coercive techniques. As Michael Zuckert points out, the strategies necessary for introducing the Spartan and Cretan interlocutors to the practice of giving preludes to the laws indicate the larger truth that politics cannot be pacified; command and coercion will not disappear into persuasion. Michael Zuckert's essay forces one to wonder whether politics, which on his reading is inextricably tied to war, does not render the ideal of a free community into another technique of coercion. This general view seems supported by key indications in the text, for instance, the claim that the subject they are considering, human political community, is the "truest tragedy" because it requires us to be exceptionally serious about matters that are comically shameful, i.e. human matters, as David Roochnik's essay details.

One finds throughout the text a good measure of "coercive freedoms" and, in general, support for the view that the political measures they are discussing are intended as serious techniques grafted on to silly, or worse, irrational and self-destructive, communities. The very stuff of political community in Aristotle's view—political friendship—appears at times in the *Laws* to be founded more on self-consoling discursive practices concerning the distribution of authority and responsibilities than on the intuition of a shared good or the real production of a kind of equality that navigates between the extremes represented by monarchical and democratic constitutions. Gregory Recco's essay develops the idea that the Athenian Stranger's proposals for responding to tensions concerning equality seem to favor, as well as embody, salutary rhetoric. There are other similar examples of "enforced freedom." Most obviously, the type of virtue promoted among those citizens who cannot be made virtuous, or that part of the soul that cannot be turned toward the good, seems to be very much like the kind of shame–virtue described by Socrates in the *Phaedo*, that is, virtue based on a vice, such as courage that is motivated by fear. More specifically, for those citizens who are irremediably warlike, the law code encourages the thought that we are governed by beings higher and stronger than ourselves, as if the love of strength could not be corrected, but it could be forced to resemble virtue.

Robert Metcalf, in his chapter, argues that the preludes operate at the level of *pistis*, appealing not to established authority but to the judgment of the citizen.

However, this appeal most often provides rhetorical, not philosophical, reasons for following the law and accepting its authority. Again, it seems that the appeal to the independent judgment of the individual extends coercive practices rather than supplanting them with a vision of independent judgment. In these examples and others one sees the laws aiming to manage, rather than transform, vice. The "penalties" (δίκαι) detailed in Book 9 acknowledge a degree of violent enforcement of social constraints for the sake of a successful community, as Catherine Zuckert makes clear. The sober realization of the impossibility that the lawgiver's task will be completed with any degree of sought-after perfection, as well as the recognition of intractable limitations faced by lawgivers, all point to the community's dependence on exceptional human nature and extraordinary measures if there is to be any improvement of the human lot.

There are two places perhaps more than any others in the *Laws* where it seems that the Athenian's coercive deceptions will enable citizens to live within the social order while managing their own disordered lawlessness separately. First, the Athenian's treatment of eros, which elsewhere in Plato is a force harnessed for its potential to embody virtue and transform the individual soul, strongly suggests institutionalized transgression or inversion of the law, permitted because the shame it engenders makes citizens more easily coerced. As Francisco Gonzalez shows, eros is an "outlaw," i.e., something outside the law that becomes an institutionally accepted perversion of law that the law is in a position to control more than educate; the aim is precisely not to educate desire. Similarly, in Books 11 and 12 we see problems inherently associated with the possession of private property. By pointing to several of the restrictions prohibiting citizens from the type of interpersonal association and institutions that uproot them from genuine political possibilities, for example, commerce and innkeeping, Eric Sanday shows that there are practices and institutions of the same sort that are essential to the functioning of the city—not just its economic function but its self-preserving management of perverse elements that resist being brought under the law and educated. Private property provides a place for the uneducable parts of the soul to house itself, a relatively safe arena in which unmoored and untrained desire can indulge its impulse and potentially exhaust itself relatively innocuously, at least with respect to the city's good. Similarly, Gregory Recco shows how the Stranger appears to make room for the disappointment of political ambition not by educating it, but by presenting its necessity in a quasi-ritualized and mystifying form, so as to neutralize it.

It should not be concluded from these indications, however, that the city described in the *Laws* employs only coercion, manipulation, and deception, or that it is animated only by the norms of order and stability. In fact, the manipulative stratagems aimed at apparently uneducable elements of the city and citizenry have in some instances the ultimate aim of holding the city to a vision of the human good that needs time to take root. In other words, what is uneducated today may not always be. Indeed, if the city is really to last, perhaps its stability must not be a brittle rigidity, but something more supple and responsive to unforeseen and unforeseeable developments. The city must thus make provisions for its own development into a self-conscious, self-moving, intelligent whole. It must contain at least some elements capable of coming to know and empowered to make that knowledge effectual. The institutions concerning education and deliberation, therefore, cannot merely be tools of indoctrination and control. Eric Salem explores the art of introducing new and more liberating institutions in his study of the Athenian Stranger's opening exchange, in Book 1, with the Cretan and Spartan interlocutors, where we see an interest in the unfamiliar being seeded and nurtured in their discussion of the initiatory power of Athenian drinking practices. Throughout this volume, essays attest to the Athenian's recognition of this necessity and to his making provisions, however incomplete or inchoate, for real freedom within the confines of the proposed Cretan colony.

For example, the story the city tells about itself is not an accurate description of its historical origins, but it need not be historically accurate in order to do justice to the city's animating principle. The city founders are sober-minded about what is possible for the city to accomplish, the degree of freedom and rationality that can be realistically attained in political life. They carve out a myth of origins that does justice to the city's potential for achieving freedom and virtue, much like Socrates' story of the "priests and priestesses" in the *Meno*'s account of the soul's prior existence (*Meno* 81a). The prior life of the city tells a story of cyclical cataclysms, emergence, and development through stages of political constitution, from dynasty to aristocracy, descent from the mountains into the plains, and the founding of historically specific cities: Ilium, Sparta, and Athens. The goal for this strand of political rhetoric is freedom, i.e. the reconciliation of the very widely divergent principles of Athenian freedom and Spartan coercion into a workable unity. As John Sallis points out, the Athenian sees in music and musicality a paradigm by which freedom and necessity might be woven together within the context of establishing the proper beginning, the beginning that the lawmaker needs in order for the city to achieve what it is capable of being.

One should also consider the possibility that it is not the egalitarian ideal of the city as a whole that motivates the Athenian, who seems in some instances satisfied (or constrained) to provide for an environment in which a few exceptional human beings can flourish according to a godlike ideal. The development of a few heroes of the human community would in this view have a transformative effect on the community as a whole, even if that community can at best achieve a condition in which it simply preserves itself and provides the proper conditions for a few to excel. Toward this end, and in some sense challenging this characterization, all citizens are exposed to the transformative potential of play in their education; they are all initiated into the practices on which self-legislation is founded. There is a sense that all citizens idealize self-moving spontaneity and freedom during maturation, but some fail to safeguard that principle and in their adult lives turn their back on a higher promise. Although it is not thematized explicitly in the dialogue, the repeated references to the problems associated with the young, especially the three types of atheism described in Book 10, strongly suggest a second birth and a second education in human development, similar to the one rooted in childhood experiences. The second birth of human education takes the form of transforming certain, potentially inevitable, views concerning the cosmos and divinity, which have to be reoriented away from the simply self-sufficient materialist attitude that is either necessary or in some sense unavoidable. Sara Brill clarifies this inevitable shift toward atheism and the corrective "prosthesis" in her essay focusing on the ambiguity of the human soul, which is rooted in nature and simultaneously beyond nature, both "exceeding nature" and being "exceedingly natural." Brill draws attention to the legislative cosmology with which atheism will be excised from the soul, in which the laws themselves are the prosthetic limb that brings order to the disordered soul.

From the point of view of educating free individuals, the lawgiver cannot force people to be free, only provide the conditions in which such a promise can be fulfilled. It is then up to the individuals to freely embrace, or freely renounce, their freedom. The young who demonstrate a particular facility with their education will be led through an educational path that fulfills the promise of the human capacity for play and autonomy. John Russon makes it clear that in principle, through the educational practices proposed by the Athenian Stranger, the city embraces an ideal of spontaneity and self-legislation, and that this ideal is purposefully instilled in the citizens from the beginning of their maturation. This comes through exposure to other ideas and practices, which they will be sent out to study, and companionship with uniquely talented individuals—experiences which constitute an education of the best citizens. As Patricia Fagan makes clear in her account of the ancient Greek literary context in which the *Laws* is placed, there is a double imperative for a non-Cyclopean politics in which the strangeness of one's own inherited ways is manifest through encounter with what is strange, both outside oneself in the world abroad and within oneself in one's own spontaneous impulse toward play. It is worth noting, however, that even these "best" citizens are not able to rule autocratically without becoming corrupt, which may explain the Stranger's attention to the geographic and more broadly material foundations of the city. In the end the *Laws* as a whole values the organization of many citizens and of institutions over the rule of the king.

These questions and quandaries concerning freedom, truth, and coercion are not likely ever to be definitively dispelled by philosophical, political, literary, or historical interpretations, however ably carried out. Nonetheless, in a spirit of thanksgiving for the intellectual generosity of our contributors, we offer this collection of essays in the hope of furthering the conversation concerning what is widely regarded as Plato's last great work, whose obscure byways and troubling indications led us to call on friends new and old for assistance. The hope for a free, rational arrangement of our political lives founded on shared insight into the human condition is paradoxically well-served by this ancient conversation among old men already living near the end of the age of the polis, striving to understand from what sources, human or divine, they might draw in order to found a new city. Unlike founders of a city, who live apart from the citizens-to-come and perhaps have less reason than they to share in a spirit of trust concerning the city's all-too-human institutions, we readers of Plato's *Laws* find ourselves, as readers, in a position to be envied by founders and citizens alike; to read is already to have as one's explicit task to understand the alien logic and unfounded structure before one and to make one's peace with it, in freedom from all constraint, violence, or necessity.

1 Reading the *Laws* as a Whole: Horizon, Vision, and Structure

Mitchell Miller

My project in this essay is to orient—or, both more precisely and more modestly, to mine the text in order to provide some suggestions as to how one might orient—a reading of the *Laws*. To that end, I will offer three sets of reflections, guided by these questions: (1) To begin from the negative, what fundamental dimensions and motifs does Plato *exclude* from the dialogue, indicating that they lie beyond the horizon of relevant possibilities for thought that delimits the Athenian Stranger's conversation with Cleinias and Megillus? (2) How, positively, does Plato define this horizon itself? That is, with what basic terms, in what basic relations—and conveyed by what allusions, in this case to his earlier major works on polity—does he have the Athenian establish this horizon? (3) Finally, what is the basic force he intends the text of the *Laws* to have, and what is the structure he has the Athenian Stranger give his discourse as a whole in order that it might have that force?

Trying to get such a holistic purchase on a text as monstrously massive as the *Laws* is a daunting, not to say hubristic, undertaking. On the other hand, its very massiveness makes the effort all the more, not the less important. If there is in the Platonic corpus a forest that is hidden by the heterogeneity and bulk of its many stands of trees, the *Laws* is it. Fortunately, there are several passages in the dialogue that seem intended to give us bearings, and we will pay close attention to them. But, of course, to single these passages out risks being just another way of losing sight of the forest. At the day's end I take solace in the thought that providing something that is at least worth disagreeing with will itself have some orienting power for those who share the ambitious project of taking the measure of the *Laws* as a whole.

I. What lies excluded, beyond the horizon . . .

Asking what has been excluded must seem a peculiar way to begin. I am motivated by an experience that I suspect I share with many readers of the *Laws*, the mounting surprise, as one reads, at the fact that Plato does *not* invoke almost any of the motifs and projects that in earlier dialogues we have been led to think of as defining the depths of philosophy. He leaves un-introduced, seemingly beyond the reach of the Athenian Stranger, eros as the drawnness of the soul to the face of the beloved and the Beautiful—and, so, to the transcendental horizon of the forms—that we know from the palinode in the *Phaedrus* and Diotima's ladder in the *Symposium*, respectively.[1] Nor is there any mention of the "greatest study," the pursuit of the Good, that is the deepest project of the *Republic* and sets the goal of the "longer way" that proceeds through the development of dialectic in the *Sophist* and the *Statesman* and that climaxes, on my reading, in the *Philebus*.[2] (Nor, it goes without saying, is there any indication of the arguably still more basic notions of the One and of the Great and the Small.[3]) We *do*, however, get a reminder of the mathematical studies of *Republic* VII both at the end of the Stranger's discussion of education in *Laws* VII and, albeit in very compressed form, in the discussion of the "more precise education" (965b) that the members of the Nocturnal Council will need. But this is one of those exceptions that prove the rule: the highest of the mathematical studies explicitly proposed for the members of the Nocturnal Council is astronomy, not harmonics—yet in the *Republic* it is especially the passage from the study of figure in the geometrical studies, including astronomy, to the study of ratio in harmonics that bridges the philosopher-to-be into dialectic.[4] In the *Laws*, it seems, astronomy, not harmonics and, so, also not dialectic, is the highest study projected for the members of the Nocturnal Council.[5]

But ought we to have been surprised to find all this—above all, the Good and the forms and the depths of eros and mathematics that open the soul to them—excluded from the world of the *Laws*? In fact, in the stage-setting opening pages of the dialogue, the text as much as tells us that precisely this is what, in setting its highest aim, it will leave out. There we learn that the elderly threesome are on a walk in the countryside, with lovely shade trees to provide places for rest and relief from the Cretan heat; thus, as in the *Phaedrus*, they are not only at leisure—they are also outside the city and free from the restraints that propriety puts on exploring the critical and unseemly and perhaps subversive. What's more, the path ascends to a height, the recurrent Platonic symbol of the Socratic/Eleatic quest for the forms, the orienting bounds of the perceptual and political given; and at this height we will come to the sacred source of the laws and the state. But here, of course, is the manifold rub: the height we aim for is a *cave*, the site not of the light or ether of an upper realm but, rather, of the very absence of such light and clarity, and the source of the laws is the *birth*-place of, therefore, what is precisely *not* timeless, hence not the site of the forms and the Good but rather of what is in time and subject to cultural representation, namely, *Zeus*, the chief of the anthropomorphic Olympian gods. Thus the opening page gives fair warning, at least on reflection, that in the *Laws* we will be operating within the bounds of the sense of reality not of the philosopher but rather, at best, of the acceptant πίστις, the metaphysical "trust," of the thoughtful citizen.

II. . . . and what marks the horizon: "the god" and the "first" and "second-best" cities

"Is it [a] god or some human being (Θεὸς ἤ τις ἀνθρώπων), strangers, that you take to be the cause of the establishing of your laws?"[6] With these, the opening words of the dialogue, the Athenian Stranger indicates the double boundary of this pre-philosophical sense of reality.

On the one hand, there is "god" or "the god." This figure is left both indeterminate and fundamental: only loosely associated with both Zeus and Cronus (see (2) below), he is the presiding power in the world. In the opening words of his imagined prelude to the assembled Magnesians the Athenian puts him first as the god who "holds the beginning and the end and the middles (μέσα) of all that is" (4:715ef.); he "is always attended by Justice" (ibid.); and he is the "measure of all things" and the being who, in order that we "become dear to him, [we must] do all in [our] power to become like" (4:716c–d). These elevating references leave him shadowy, however. Only in the digression on atheism and the gods in Book 10 will he receive a sharper—and suddenly quite unconventional—portrayal as the good soul possessed of intelligence that, self-moving, sets all else, above all the sun, into motion.

On the other hand, there is the city that is ruled by law. Here we face a thicket of well-known—if not allusions, then at least—pointed resonances of the *Republic* and the *Statesman*, in the course of which the Athenian Stranger establishes the status of Magnesia as a "second-best" city. There are four passages to note.

(1) εἰς ταὐτὸν . . . συμπέσῃ (". . . coincide in the same . . . ," 711e8f.) In a reflection on the interplay of god, chance, and art in Book 4, the Stranger argues that the conditions that would make for "the swiftest and easiest" (712a,

cf. 710b, 711c) transformation of an existing city into "the best and with the best laws" would be the partnership of "a lawgiver who knows the truth" (709c) and a young tyrant of moderate character. Still better would be when these are one and the same man, "when the greatest power coincides in the same [man] (εἰς ταὐτὸν . . . συμπέσῃ), one with intelligence and moderation" (711e8–a2). Can one who knows the *Republic* help but hear the resonance of Socrates' paradoxical declaration that the "smallest change" (473b) that would allow his just city to be realized would be for "political power and philosophy [to come to] *coincide in the same* [man] (εἰς ταὐτὸν . . . συμπέσῃ)" (473d2–3), the philosopher-king? But by the very association that Plato provokes in the *Laws* by his repetition of the language of the *Republic* he gives us occasion to notice that the Athenian hopes for something pointedly different from what Socrates did: the "truth" that the Athenian's "lawgiver" "knows" is not what Socrates' figure of the philosopher seeks, the Good and the forms, but rather "the best laws": and so the tyrant the Athenian fantasizes, rather than becoming a philosopher, will make himself the agent who establishes those laws in his city; and since, as the Stranger argues, it is by the example the tyrant sets for his subjects that he can best bring about the transformation of his city, to establish the best laws requires that he begin by subjecting himself to them. Accordingly, while Socrates' philosopher-king rules from above the law, the moderate tyrant will bring it about that all, himself included, are subject to the rule of law.[7]

(2) ἐπὶ Κρόνου (". . . in the time of Cronus," 713b2). Only a few speeches later, at 713a–714a, the Athenian sets the stage for his prelude to the Magnesians by introducing the "myth" of the age of Cronus. Readers of the *Statesman* will recognize this as Plato's return—but, again, with several interesting differences—to the great myth that he has the Eleatic Stranger present in that dialogue.[8] Long ago, the Athenian now says, we humans lived under Cronus in a paradisiacal condition, free both from material scarcity and internal strife. How did Cronus manage this? He knew that, "human nature" being what it is, no man can be an "autocrat" over the rest without falling into "hubris and injustice," and so just as we now put ourselves in charge of cattle, he put δαίμονες, "divinities"— that is, beings of a higher species—in charge of us; these divinities, in effect our shepherds, provided us "peace and respect for others (αἰδῶ) and good laws (εὐνομίαν)[9] and unstinting justice (ἀφθονίαν δίκης)" (713e). "Good laws" and "justice" are absent in the *Statesman* myth, where human beings in the age of Cronus are earth-born, and their herdish lives, lacking both "polities" and "the possession of women and children" (*Statesman* 272a), are thoroughly apolitical. The Athenian Stranger, accordingly, is now reading the presence of "good laws"

and the political justice they establish back into the time of Cronus. The general point of this adaptation, the Athenian makes plain enough. We humans can hardly gainsay the god's knowledge of our nature. Accordingly, no one should risk trying to rule autocratically over the rest; instead we must all "imitate" the life we had under Cronus and his divinities by subordinating ourselves to that "within us that partakes of immortality," namely to "the dispensation by νοῦς (mind) that we call νόμος (law)" (*Laws* 714a).

But if the general point is clear, in its specifics it sets the stage for the rest of the dialogue by raising big questions. Among them: what is it that the god knows about "human nature" that dooms to injustice any man's effort to rule autocratically? What is the sense of "imitation" in accord with which we are "imitating" the rule of Cronus and his divinities by resisting autocracy and holding to the rule of "good laws"? In what sense is "[what] we call νόμος" a "dispensation by νοῦς"? And how may we get our bearings in order to attempt to achieve—and, now as we read the *Laws*, in order to determine how well the Athenian actually does achieve—this "dispensation"?

(3) ... ὅτι μάλιστα κοινὰ τὰ φίλων ("... as much as possible, ... things in common," 739c1–2). We get some help with these questions from the third resonant passage, at 739cff. Here Plato has the Athenian's words echo Socrates' formulation of the principle of the best possible polity at *Republic* 423e–424a: where Socrates declares that the rulers of his just and good city "will easily discover ... how all ... must be governed as far as possible (ὅτι μάλιστα) by the old proverb (κατὰ τὴν παροιμίαν) that friends share things in common (κοινὰ τὰ φίλων)," the Athenian declares that "the first" and "best" city will be that in which "the ancient adage (τὸ πάλαι λεγόμενον) is realized throughout the city as far as possible (ὅτι μάλιστα)," namely, that "friends share things in common" (κοινὰ τὰ φίλων) (739c). And in his detailing of this sharing, the Athenian reiterates Socrates' vision in each of its key aspects: women and children and "every sort of property" will be "common"—that is, there will be no private family or private property—, and this will enable the extraordinary spiritual unity that Socrates celebrates[10] in the *Republic*, the "community" of pleasure and pain: "everyone," says the Athenian, will "praise and blame in unison, as much as possible delighting in the same things and feeling pain at the same things" (739d).[11] As before, however, so here, and much more explicitly, Plato reminds us of Socrates' city in the *Republic* in order to mark how the Athenian's project differs from it. A city in which all things are "in common" would have to have, for its inhabitants, "gods or the children of gods" (739d); Magnesia, by contrast, is to be inhabited by human beings and so can only be the "second best" city.

This notion of "second-best" (739a, e) marks the aspiration as well as the limitedness of the city that the Athenian now begins to design, and this double aspect, this sense in which Magnesia is, while only *second*, nonetheless *second-best*, is the key to his notion that human polity must "imitate" the rule of Cronus and his divinities; now, however, it is the city of "all things in common" that he declares to be the "model" (παράδειγμα, 739e1) that we must "hold to" and "seek to realize as fully as possible." Accordingly, even while the Athenian accommodates the humanity of its citizens, their non-divine "birth, nurture, and education" (740a), by accepting private property and separate family units, he also subordinates the private to the common. The land, he declares at 739e, must be divided into separate lots and farmed not in common but by different households; but it is family lines, not individuals, to whom the land is assigned, and this assignment is inalienable and inalterable "for the rest of time" (740b). "Each man who receives an allotment should deem it to be at the same time the common possession of the whole city" (740b), given in irreversible trust. Thus, in this and many other ways, the Athenian sets out to construct a mean, a political order that, even as it falls short, expresses the fullest possible human approximation of the divine.

(4) δίο δὴ τὸ δεύτερον αἱρετέον, τάξιν τε καὶ νόμον ("for this reason one must choose the second-best, ordinance[12] and law," 875d3). At 874e–875d, Plato has the Athenian interject a reflection on the status of the rule of law that cannot help but remind one who has read the *Statesman* of the Eleatic Stranger's subtle and dialectically balanced position on that question—but, again, with telling differences. The Athenian, about to turn to the class of personal injuries in all their inexhaustible empirical variety, acknowledges that law cannot, as true understanding can, address the specificity of each situation; it can only speak ἐπὶ τὸ πόλυ, addressing particular situations "for the most part" or "on average" (875d4). And just before saying this he declares that "no law or ordinance surpasses[13] knowledge, nor is it right that mind (νοῦν) be subservient or slave to anything else—on the contrary, it should rule over all things, provided it is genuine and really free to be itself." On both counts he reiterates criticisms of the limitations of law that Plato has the Eleatic Stranger make in the *Statesman*—but with striking differences in each case. Whereas the Eleatic embeds his criticism of law's directedness to the average within the context of endorsing its usefulness to the true or knowing statesman, the Athenian undermines this whole argument by his bottom-line declaration that "such understanding, genuine and really free to be itself, . . . in the present day does not exist anywhere at all, except in fragment." Thus the Athenian declares *as a basic truth* what the Eleatic instead *credits to the ruled*, the subjects of con-

temporary democracy and oligarchy alike, namely, the deep and pervasive suspicion that their rulers do not possess true knowledge of the ruling art and instead pursue their own interests. Accordingly, where the Eleatic, though hardly confident, nonetheless himself remains open to the possibility that a knowing statesman may appear, the Athenian is closed to it and concludes, without qualification, that "for this reason one must choose the second-best, ordinance and law."

In noting these differences, I do not mean to beg the question of Plato's position, nor do I mean, in characterizing the Athenian as closed, to suggest that he is dogmatic or unreasoning. On the contrary, in reaching his position the Athenian goes deeper than the suspicion of the ruled, and he provides the elements of a subtle psychological analysis. To the ruled, as the Eleatic reconstructs their position in the *Statesman,* their ruler or rulers lack knowledge *and instead* pursue their own interests; to the Athenian, by contrast, *even if one should somehow manage the immensely difficult task of achieving knowledge,* nonetheless, he should not be trusted to rule accordingly. For although he would know that "the common binds cities together whereas the private tears them apart" (875a6–7), "his mortal nature (ἡ θνητὴ φύσις) will always drive him toward getting more for himself and [advancing] his private interests (ἐπὶ πλεονεξίαν καὶ ἰδιοπραγίαν), causing him to flee pain irrationally and to pursue pleasure and to put both of these before what is more just and better" (875b6–8).

Earlier, reflecting on the Athenian's tale of Cronus's imposition of the rule of divinities, we asked what it is that the god knows about "human nature" that dooms to injustice any man's effort to rule autocratically. In accepting private property and separate families, the Athenian appropriates the same divine knowledge—or, we could say equally well, in first crediting it to the god he declares as a noetic insight—that the community of pleasure and pain lies beyond our capacity as human beings. But while we cannot transcend the claim the private makes upon us in the form of the inescapable power of our own pleasures and pains, we can acknowledge this claim and attempt to put it in check. This brings us back to the double aspect of the idea of the "second best." For the Athenian Stranger, adopting the rule of law is itself the expression of this acknowledgment and so (at least if we can follow through and craft good laws) a "dispensation of νοῦς." Appreciating this should give us our bearings as, moving from tree to tree to tree in the forest of the *Laws,* we attend to the Athenian's law-giving. In each case we need to ask: has he struck the mean between the divine and the human, achieving the fullest possible internalization, in the order and life of our inescapably human community, of the rule of the god and the ethical priority of the common?

III. Toward an understanding of the force and structure of the text as a whole

How may we get our bearings toward the third task, grasping the force and structure[14] of the *Laws* as a whole? The text provides one obvious starting point: when, at the end of Book 3, Cleinias announces that he has been appointed to a commission charged with making laws for a new colony and asks the Athenian and Megillus to help him by "construct[ing] a city in speech" (702d), he sets the project that will unify the remaining nine books of the dialogue; and in the suddenly formed retrospect, the first three books take on the function of stage-setting reflections for this project, laying out the orienting ideas of virtue, of musical psychagogy, and of the extremes of freedom and despotic authority that frame its context of constitutional possibilities. Accordingly, we can narrow our focus to Books 4–12 and the project of writing the laws for the colony of Magnesia. Within these books, in turn, there are at least two signal passages in which, however indirectly, the text itself seems to give us direction, and we can use these to make a beginning. Let me comment as succinctly as I can on each of these passages, then let them guide us in a first effort to make out the force and compositional structure of the Athenian's exegesis of the Magnesian constitution.

A. 811c–d: the poetic force of the discourse as a whole

The first passage to consider is the exchange at 811c–d in which the Athenian reports with a sense of delight that his speeches, considered in retrospect, suddenly look like divinely inspired poetry. Cleinias has just asked the Stranger what "model" (παράδειγμα) he might offer for the sort of "literature" (τὰ γράμματα) he would recommend for the young. Here is a translation of the passage:[15]

> AS: It may well be that I've had a stroke of good luck.
> K: In what regard?
> AS: When I now look back at the reflections (λόγους) we've been working
> through from dawn to this very moment—and not, it appears to me,
> without some inspiration from gods—they seem to me in every way
> to have been spoken like a work of poetry (παντάπασι ποιήσει τινὶ
> προσομοίως εἰρῆσθαι). No wonder, then, that a feeling of delight comes
> over me as I gaze at our own speeches (λόγους οἰκείους) gathered, as it
> were, in close array (οἷον ἀθρόους); of all the many discourses I've listened

to or studied, whether spoken in verse or in a free flow (χύδην) like ours, these appear to me the best measured, really (μετριώτατοί γε), and the most fitting of all for the young to hear.

What can the Athenian mean by his characterization of his λόγοι as "spoken like a work of poetry"? He is of course not referring to their diction, for he immediately contrasts them with λόγοι "spoken in verse." If we look instead to content, we will be struck by the Athenian's claim a bit later that "the [Magnesian] constitution is constructed as an imitation (μίμησις) of the noblest and best life, and this, we declare, is really the truest tragedy" (817b). But this, even while we will later see that the notion of the best life may indeed be relevant, is the wrong place to focus. In the passage itself the Athenian draws attention to the way, first, the discourses "are spoken" as, second, this presents itself in retrospect to him as, now, a reflective auditor; what's more, he stresses that they now seem to have been "inspired by gods." Shouldn't this encourage us to think that Plato intends the written text to present itself with the force of good poetry, that is, as having the power to waken and inspire in its reader a certain vision that alters and reorients his sense of the way things are? But, to be stressed here, this force emerges *not* in the particulars—the syntax, for instance, or turns of phrase[16]—of the Stranger's speeches but rather *in the way, seen in retrospect, they fit together as a whole*; it is only when the Stranger steps back and lets the *full set of the day's discourses come to view together,* "gathered, as it were, in close array," that he is moved to appreciate their poetic force.[17]

B. 768d6–8: the interplay of structure and the process of understanding

If we are to share this appreciation, we too must try to step back and see the whole. But how? To see a text whole requires recognizing the distinction and fit of its parts, and at least initially, the immense reach of the conversation resists such structural judgments, making them seem capricious. This difficulty makes the second of our two passages crucial: at 768d6–8, midway through Book 6, Plato appears to give us guiding language for the way in which the conversation, at least from the moment the Athenian takes up the project of founding Magnesia, should be seen in its compositional totality. As we shall see, this language has a dynamism about it that makes it puzzling at first; but this dynamism, I will suggest, proves to reflect the phases of the process by which the text brings the reader to just that sort of visionary experience and retrospective understanding of the whole that the Athenian speaks of at 811c–d.

We should begin by locating 768d6–8 in its surrounding context: the Athenian has twice stressed that a constitution has two fundamental "aspects" (εἴδη), related as part and counterpart: the "offices" (ἀρχαί) of the state and the "laws" (νόμοι) by which the officers regulate the various practices that fall within their spheres. (See 735a and 751a.) The primary task of Book 6 is to identify the "offices," and at 768c the Athenian is nearing the completion of this task; he has just given a sketch of the system of courts and is about to turn to "a sorting out of [the] δίκαι (suits and prosecutions)" that each court will hear. But then he stops himself. Since δίκαι proceed on the basis of the "laws," it would be better, he suggests, to suspend discussion of them until "the end of the law-giving." He then gives us what I take to be the key sentence for identifying the dynamic structure of his execution of the project of founding Magnesia.

> In regard to each and all of the specifics of the entire constitutional ordering of the city, it isn't possible for the whole in its precise structure to become clear until our exegesis has proceeded *from [the] beginning* and, taking up *the things second in order* and *the middle things* and *all [of its] parts*, reaches *[the] end*.[18]

On first hearing, the Athenian's designation of the parts through which one moves from the "beginning" to the "end" is puzzling. His phrase τὰ δεύτερα, "the things second in order," suggests a linear movement "from the beginning" through enumerated stages—but if that were the whole story, we would expect to come next to the third things, not to τὰ μέσα, "the middle things." And again, τὰ μέσα suggests a three-fold composition, with the initial movement "from the beginning" to "the middle things" balanced by a final movement from "the middle things" to a final set of parts that compose "the end"—so it is a surprise to come instead to "all [the] parts," not, that is, to a final third but, rather, to the whole *ensemble* of all the parts together.

What these moments of surprise give us occasion to recognize is that the Athenian, rather than simply distinguishing parts, speaks with reference to the process of moving through them. To mark the most obvious sense in which this is so: ἀρχή, "beginning," connotes a source or what is primary, and τέλος, "end," is not just a terminal point but, rather, a goal or target that gives us a sense of direction along the way; to depart from an ἀρχή is to begin with an orienting sense of what is most important, and to move toward a τέλος is to approach completion or fulfillment. More deeply, the Athenian appears to be distinguishing the phases of this process by marking the changing sense or aspect under which the discourse itself and its contents will present themselves to us as we move through it. His language suggests we should expect two moments of transformation. In the first, as we move on from "the things second in order," "the beginning" and "the things second in order" come to stand together as the first of the three equally weighted and balanced moments of "beginning," "middle," and "end." In the second, as, presumably, we move on from "the middle things" to the "end," the latter will somehow give way to πάντα μέρη, "all [the] parts," that is, again, the whole *ensemble* that the many "parts" make up together. Thus the Athenian points ahead to a moment when, to recall and interpret his initially opaque language, τὸ δὲ ὅλον καὶ ἀκριβὲς . . . γενέσθαι σαφές, "the whole and the precise"—that is, the discourse as a whole in its precise structure—"will become clear."

C. *The structure of the "exegesis" and the vision of the whole that is its aim*

If we let ourselves be guided by these two passages, 811c–d and 768d, we will find ourselves faced with two related challenges. First, can we discern in the Athenian's "exegesis" of the Magnesian constitution each of the three phases that we have just distinguished? Second—and this will be to complete this first project—, can we identify the visionary experience of "the whole in its precise structure" that the Athenian intends the exegesis, "spoken like a work of poetry," to occasion?

Let me begin by distinguishing the first two of the three phases. (1) *The nested hierarchy of movements that lead from ἡ ἀρχή to τὰ δεύτερα, from the basic to the secondary.* We have already begun to see the sense in which a movement from ἡ ἀρχή to τὰ δεύτερα structures the first phase of the Athenian's founding. As throughout the text, there are a number of digressions and, so, stops and "second starts" (723e) along the way, including, most notably, the reflection on preludes at 718a–723d; but this latter digression both provides the occasion for understanding the Athenian's opening address to the assembly of Magnesians as itself a "prelude" to his law-giving (723d, 724a) and sets in relief the hierarchical structure by which, before and after the digression, he orders the content of the laws. He first works through a remarkable series of those beings to whom virtue requires we attend, beginning with "the god" and "justice" (715e–716a) and descending in order from there through the Olympians, chthonic powers, δαίμονες, heroes, ancestors, and our parents (see 717b); then, resuming his prelude at the beginning of Book 5, he expands his focus to mark as "second" the soul (727a), as "third" the body (728d), and (presumably) as fourth, "money and property" (728e), and then, turning outward from children (as, presumably, one's ownmost property), he moves from friends to fellow citizens to strangers, especially suppliants. Next, drawing on the superiority of the gods that he has just established, he moves from the "divine things" (732e), that is, those qualities of living—enumerated, once again, in a hierarchical series— that make for a virtuous life, to the "human things," pleasure and pain and desire (732e), that should be subordinated to the divine, and he enumerates four pairs of lives, virtuous and vicious, that are and are not structured by that subordination. Finally, again characterizing this whole reflection as a "prelude" (734e), he turns to the material organization of Magnesia, offering a set of reflections on purges of the citizenry, division and allocation of the land, allowable ranges of private wealth, and so on. The whole complex of relations he has thus traced fits together, I suggest, as a kind of nested hierarchy: the ranked series of beings that begins with the god and justice provides orientation for the turn from divine to human things; this turn then provides orientation for the account of virtuous and vicious lives; and, finally, this whole prelude on the subordinative order of moral and ethical life provides orientation for the final turn to the material organization of the city.

(2) *Reaching τὰ μέσα, "the middle things": the constitutional order of "offices" and "laws."* The Athenian's reflections on the material organization of the city, in turn, complete the context for his exegesis of the two fundamental "aspects" of the constitutional order of the city, the "offices" (ἀρχαί) of the state and the "laws" (νόμοι) by which the various groups of officers are to govern in their designated domains. Under the heading of "offices," the Athenian includes the several caretakers of the legal order, at the level of the city as a whole the Guardians of the Laws and at the level of the tribes and classes the Council; the ranked hierarchy of military commanders; those charged with directing religious rites and festivals, the various custodians, priests, and mantics; those charged to monitor the several place-specific spheres of communal life, the Field and Market and City Regulators; and the Supervisor of Education. This first part of the exegesis takes up the opening section of Book 6, 751a–768d, breaking off with the Athenian's decision at 768d to defer a full account of the δίκαι, the suits and prosecutions that will occupy the courts, until "the end of the law-giving." (For key reasons that we shall consider later, the Nocturnal Council is not introduced until Books 9 and 12.) The exegesis of the "laws," in turn, runs from that point on up to his promised return to δίκαι at the beginning of Book 9. By contrast with his treatment of δίκαι in Book 9, which focuses on violations of the moral-ethical order and lays out negative laws and appropriate punishments, the exegesis of the laws in Books 6–8 is essentially positive in character, laying out the normative practices in all the spheres of communal life—of education,

religious ritual, military training, agriculture, the crafts and commerce, and so on—that the various officers have just been charged to oversee.

For a host of reasons, it seems evident that it is these exegeses of the offices and the positive laws in 6 and 6–8, respectively, that the Athenian has in mind when he speaks of "the middle things" at 768d. As a balanced pair, they are a collective plural—hence τὰ μέσα, "the middle things." As the positive core of the Magnesian constitution, they are central to the Athenian's project, not "secondary"—indeed, they provide the specifically political content of his exegesis and stand as the proper complement to the moral-ethical content of the first phase. And, of course, they occupy the middle place in what they thereby mark as the threefold unity of his full discourse, standing between the orienting moral-ethical "prelude" and the treatment of δίκαι in what, taking our cue from the Athenian's deferral at 768d, he now appears to project as the third and final part. In this final part we may expect to learn of the various violations of these normative practices and of the juridical penalties by which potential violators are warned off and actual violators are corrected. This, then, as it appears at this moment, is the threefold unity of the "beginning," "middle," and "end" of the exegesis of the Magnesian constitution; whereas the middle part's specification of the normative practices of communal life and of the duties of those charged with directing and maintaining these practices fits together, on the one hand, with the moral-ethical prelude as, roughly, a positive and specific explication with the general principles to be explicated, the middle part also fits together, on the other hand, with the (projected) treatment of δίκαι as, roughly, the positive and normative with the explication-to-come of its negation and restoration.[19]

(3) *Remaining in step and/or breaking stride? The structural function of Books 9, 10, and 11–12.* Or so, certainly, it seems, as, following the Athenian, we move into Book 9. But we have noted Plato's warning to us, through the Athenian's initially surprising language at 768d6–8, that the final phase of his exegesis will not just provide the last part of its threefold configuration but, beyond that, will in some way bring into view πάντα μέρη, "all [the] parts," and, so, τὸ δὲ ὅλον καὶ ἀκριβὲς, "the whole in its precise structure." To put ourselves in position to see how this may be so, it is best to begin with a look at Books 11–12, then return to 9–10.

[i] *Books 11–12: the spheres of communal life, brought to view together.* We must start by acknowledging a peculiar difficulty: interpreting the role of Books 11–12 in the Athenian's exegesis of the Magnesian constitution is complicated by the apparent fact that, at least up until the introduction of the Nocturnal

Council at 960c, these pages have not been subjected to a final drafting or even editing. The evidence for this state of unfinishedness is manifold: with the exception of a very few one-line utterances,[20] the text takes the form of straightforward expository prose, with no dialogue with Cleinias and Megillus and with none of the internal dramatization of the law-giver's address to the Magnesians that Plato has the Athenian make such frequent use of in Books 1–10; nor is there any connective tissue to make for natural conversational transitions from the consideration of one topic to the consideration of the next;[21] finally, at 953e–956b there is a veritable heap, seemingly random in sequence, of short declarative edicts on unrelated matters.[22] This is not to say that there is no discernible order and grouping in Books 11–12—on the contrary. But if it is true, as the state of the text up to 960c does suggest, that Plato never subjected them to a final drafting, then we have only that order and grouping, and none of the sort of rhetorical and dramatic cues that we do find everywhere else in the text (including, thankfully, in the final section at 960c through the end), to take our bearings from in trying to understand how Books 11–12 fit into the *Laws* as a whole.

What, then, can we make out? There are two basic features to note.

First, if we step back and survey the kinds and the sequence of the laws the Athenian proposes, we will see that he moves by family resemblance-style associations through four areas of communal life: (a) at 913a–922a he lays out various principles governing *movable property and commercial "transactions"* (συμβολαίων, 913a), ranging from the prohibition of taking what belongs to another through restrictions on exchange and retail trade and the obligations binding craftsmen;[23] (b) at 922a–932d, turning to the last important kind of "transaction," wills (922b), he moves into *family law,* establishing rules of inheritance that preserve through death each family line's allotment of land and various regulations for the associated matters of the treatment of orphans, the disowning of bad children and deranged parents, divorce, and the neglect and dishonoring of elderly parents; (c) at 932e–938c he proposes laws in the area of *personal injury,* prohibiting and punishing poisoning, theft and physical injury, letting mad relatives run loose in the city, verbal abuse and ridicule, beggary, and—as cases that make for a transition into the next category—giving false testimony and hiring a professional orator as one's advocate in court; and (d) at 941a–953e he takes up a host of obligations that citizens have to the state when they operate as *its agents in official capacities* ranging from ambassador, herald, and soldier through officer and/or auditor of officers, attendant and performer at religious festivals, and, finally, traveler abroad or receiver of visitors from abroad.[24]

Second, this movement through four categories of law not only supplements the Athenian's earlier treatments, respectively, of production and commerce in Book 8, of the family in Books 6–7, of bodily injury in Book 9, and of the duties of officers in Book 6, but in doing so, it turns our attention back to these, and now, accordingly, not as regions of communal life to be grasped for the first time but rather, since we are already aware of them, as aspects of this life to be considered in their interrelations.[25] Thus we pass from (a) the sphere of material goods, craft production, and commerce, a sphere from which the citizens proper, denied participation in trade and the crafts, are largely banned, to (b) the family, both the biological root of the citizenry and the legal bearer, in trust from the city, of the land as property, to (c) the individuals who are materially supported and raised and nourished in the first two spheres; and here we move from the individual as patient, as the body and soul that must be protected from injury and insult, to (d) the individual as agent of the community, exercising the duties of the various offices and so, in all the ways laid out in Book 6, taking responsibility for communal life itself.

Is it well-taken, then, to see in the grouping and sequence of topics in Books 11–12 the indication of Plato's plan to put "all [the] parts," πάντα μέρη, both of the Athenian's exegesis and, correspondingly, of the city itself, before the reflective reader? But we should proceed slowly here; as consideration of Books 9–10 and of the closing pages on the Nocturnal Council will bring to the fore, our picture is still incomplete in at least two crucial ways.

[ii] *Books 9–10: the god as measure of the city.* The first word of Book 9 is Δίκαι. Thus the Athenian signals that he will now keep his earlier commitment to return to a treatment of "suits and prosecutions" after having completed his exegesis of "offices" and the "laws" by which the various officers must govern. But this is not all. He begins Book 9 with a discussion of "temple robberies" or— to give ἱερῶν ... συλήσεων (853e5–6) its more general sense—"plunder of the sacred," and he then devotes most of the book to the kinds of homicide, which, as he makes clear in invoking the support of "mystery rites" and the traditional notions of pollution and purification at 870d–874d, is also a class of impiety. Thus he sets the stage for Book 10, the treatment of atheism in which he gives his extended proof for the existence of the gods. This proof is indeed, as Plato has Cleinias say, "a departure from the realm of law-giving" (νομοθεσίας ἐκτὸς ... βαίνειν, 891d7–8), but it is a departure that goes to the very heart of the Magnesian project; hence Plato also has Cleinias call the proof "just about the noblest and most excellent prelude our laws could have" (887b–c). The Athenian mounts a threefold argument to show, first, the existence of the gods—above all, of that "soul which, availing itself of mind (νοῦν), [is] rightly a god to gods and

guides all things to flourishing and what is right" (897b1–3);[26] second, that the gods "pay heed to" (φροντίζειν, 899d5) and "care for" (ἐπιμελοῦνται, 905d2) human affairs; and third, that they are "beyond being swayed" by special pleading in the form of sacrifices and prayers.[27] Thus he gives specific content to the notion of "the god" that he began with in his first prelude to the Magnesians. In its care for all things, in particular all human things, and in its impartiality, this mindful soul is that figure of supreme goodness and justice, respectively,[28] that is therefore rightly the "measure of all things" (716c) and that, by the rule of law we institute for our communal life, we must "do all in [our] power to become like."

[iii] *Book 12, 960b–969d: the Nocturnal Council as "mind" and "sight" and "hearing" of the communal "animal" as a whole as, in turn, the likeness of the god.* If we now turn back to Books 11–12, we can see the appropriateness of the Athenian's ending with the presentation of the Nocturnal Council. In making his way through the various regions of the life of the city, he has just reached the several ways in which its officers are the city's agents, taking responsibility for its communal life. In the Nocturnal Council he reaches the epitome of this agency. But, strikingly, he leaves indeterminate the particular actions the Nocturnal Council may take, specifying instead the purpose and basis of its actions.[29] The Council is charged to be the "safeguard" of the city, making the rule of its laws "irreversible" (960d). The basis for whatever it may do to fulfill this purpose is two-fold. Its younger members will monitor present life in the city, serving as the organs of "sight" and "hearing" (961d, also 964df) for the elder members, who will, in turn, provide "memories" (964e5) of its past. These elders, thus, will be the "mind" (νοῦς) of the city, taking the lead in "deliberation" (βουλεύεσθαι, 965a2) aimed at understanding, above all, the moral-ethical goal of the laws, the realization of virtue, and its religious basis, the gods (966c–d). To this end, the members of the Council will receive a "more precise education" (ἀκριβεστέραν παιδείαν, 965b1) than the rest of the citizenry, focusing especially on the unity and diversity of virtue (965d–e) and on the arguments that establish the seniority and divinity of soul and the responsibility of "mind" (νοῦς) for the orderly arrangement of the heavenly bodies (966e).

These synoptic notes put us in position, at last, to appreciate the visionary experience that the Athenian intends the exegesis, "spoken like a work of poetry," to occasion. With his turn to the Nocturnal Council, he completes the gathering of "all [the] parts" of his exegesis and, correlatively, of the city. That he intends us to envision these *as* parts, he makes clear by his recourse to the simile of the city as an "animal" with the Nocturnal Council as its "soul and head"— or, correlatively, its "mind" and its faculties of "sight and hearing" (961d)—atop its "torso" (964d, 969b). And that he intends us to understand this living whole as aspiring for divinity, he makes clear by his specification of the aim of the studies that will occupy its "mind," the understanding of virtue and of the cosmic soul and mind; accordingly, he calls the Nocturnal Council itself ὁ θεῖος ... σύλλογος, "the divine council" (969b2). Thus, first recalling us to the figure of the god in Book 10 and then gathering up the "parts" of the city in 11–12, he invites us to experience "the almost completed waking vision" (σχεδὸν ὕπαρ ἀποτετελεσμένον, 969b5)[30] of Magnesia as a living whole that—in taking upon itself the work of caring for itself by the rule of law, hence with what is for human beings the fullest possible "mind," goodness, and justice—strives to internalize the care and impartiality of the god. This pairing of the god and the law-governed agency of the community as, respectively, measure and measured is the crux of the vision of "the whole in its precise structure" that the poetry of the *Laws* aims to let "become clear."

Notes

1. For the lover's transformative sight of the beloved's face, see *Phaedrus* 254b. For Diotima's ladder, see *Symposium* 210a–212a.

2. For the "study" of the Good, see *Republic* 505a and *ff*.; for the motif of the "longer way," see 435d and 504b–e. (I have tried to lay out the trajectory of this "way" as it leads from the *Republic* through the later dialogues in Miller 2003, 2007, and 2010.)

3. See Aristotle's controversial introduction of these notions and his claim that Plato introduced them to explain "good and ill" in *Metaphysics* A6. For a sense of the variety of recent interpretations that take Aristotle's report seriously, see Krämer 1990; Nikulin forthcoming; Sayre 2005; and Miller 1995, 2003. Note also the intriguing, if gestural, remarks of Kahn 2001, 58–62.

4. See Robins 1995, Miller 1999.

5. I say "it seems" advisedly. There is an intriguing exchange at the very close of the dialogue in which the Athenian, punning on ἀπόρρητα and ἀπρόρρητα ("indescribable" and "imprescribable" in Bury's deft retrieval in Bury 1926), points to the further studies that the Nocturnal Council members will need to undertake but declares it pointless to specify what they are until the Council members have studied deeply enough to understand the specification and take them up. Thus he places these unidentified studies beyond the horizon of his conversation with the quite non-mathematical Cleinias and Megillus.

6. The translations in this essay are my own. But I have consulted the translations of Bury 1926, Saunders 1975, and Pangle 1980, and I have learned a great deal, as always, from conversation with my Vassar colleague in Greek and Roman Studies, Rachel Kitzinger.

7. For discussion of these convergences and divergences, see especially Schofield 1999.

8. See *Statesman* 268d–274e, noting its references to the rule of Cronus at 269a, 271c, and 272b. For discussion, see Miller 2004, ch. 3.A.

9. I follow both Saunders 1975 and Pangle 1980 in translating εὐνομίαν as "good laws." Bury 1926 has the less determinate "orderliness" and, so, fails to convey the strong suggestion—reinforced by the following δίκης—of νόμος, "law," in εὐνομίαν.

10. I leave for another occasion the complex and controversial question of what irony there may or may not be in Socrates' projection of this "community" and, indeed, in his denials of private property and family to the guardians.

11. Laks 2001, reaffirmed by Bobonich 2002 (482n7), while stressing these resonances of the *Republic* in the *Laws*, argues that the "first" and "best city" posited in the *Laws* is not Socrates' just city, for in the latter private property and the private family are abolished only among the guardians, not throughout the whole city. I don't see this as a distinguishing point, for in both Socrates' and the Athenian's formulations the principle of κοινὰ τὰ φίλων is to be realized only ὅτι μάλιστα, "as far as possible." Thus Plato has the Athenian make the very same general concession, and in the same words, that Socrates did; accordingly, there is no reason to presume that the Athenian thinks that in the "first" and "best city" "friendship" will extend to all the citizens nor, therefore, that the sharing of everything can be realized among all the citizenry. The restriction of the sharing to the guardians in the *Republic*, then, should not be taken as a point of distinction of Socrates' just city from the Athenian's first and best city. Laks acknowledges the possibility of this reading but argues for a distinction between the grounds for the restriction of the principle of sharing in the just city of the *Republic* and in the "first" city in the *Laws*—see especially 109.

12. This is Bury's translation of τάξιν. The more general "order" would be misleading, for "order" belongs to the rule of knowledge as well as to that of law.

13. Plato has the Athenian say, "no law or any ordinance is κρείττων than knowledge." Κρείττων, the comparative form of ἀγαθός, means both "stronger" and "better." My translation follows Saunders 1975 in trying to avoid choosing between these.

14. For different approaches to the structure of the *Laws*, see Laks 2000, esp. section 2, and Voegelin 1957.

15. This passage provides a rich exhibition of the adage that translation is interpretation. Compare Saunders's alternative renderings of παντάπασι ποιήσει τινὶ προσομοίως as "just like a literary composition" and of οἷον ἀθρόους as "my 'collected works,' so to speak." Saunders's evocations of the literary and the editorial rather than the poetic at least open the way for the reading of the passage as Plato's ironic undercutting of the Athenian's authorial pride that David Roochnik advances with such wit at the close of his essay in this volume.

16. Though taking this up here would lead us away from the focus that the Athenian's description of his retrospective experience suggests, the syntax and phrasing of the *Laws* are interesting topics. See Nails and Thesleff 2003 and, on the heavily periodic style of many of the "later" dialogues, including the *Laws*, that he calls ὄγκος, see Thesleff 1967.

17. In the remaining reflections in this essay, I hope to contribute an idea that complements the arresting analysis of Nightingale 1993. She brings to focus the analogously un-Socratic posture that—to go level by level—the Athenian takes in addressing Cleinias and Megillus, that the legislator (as the Athenian portrays him) takes in addressing the Magnesians, and that Plato takes as he relates to the readers of the *Laws*: at each level the effort is not to liberate the one addressed for independent inquiry but

rather to win his acceptance of the *quasi*-scriptural authority of the proposed laws. Though she recognizes the extensive stretches of argument in the *Laws*, she argues that they are meant to persuade, not to elicit the sort of destabilizing questioning so often at the core of the dialogues. I suggest that this discursive work is consummated in, and the receptive reader's grasp of it is oriented by, the visionary experience that, I will try to show, the *Laws* is structured to occasion.

18. Τὸ δὲ ὅλον καὶ ἀκριβὲς περὶ ἑνός τε καὶ πάντων τῶν κατὰ πόλιν καὶ πολιτικὴν πᾶσαν διοίκησιν οὐκ ἔστι γενέσθαι σαφές, πρὶν ἂν ἡ διέξοδος ἀπ᾽ ἀρχῆς τά τε δεύτερα καὶ τὰ μέσα καὶ πάντα μέρη τὰ ἑαυτῆς ἀπολαβοῦσα πρὸς τέλος ἀφίκηται (768d6–8). I follow Bury 1926 in preferring διοίκησιν, proposed by Ast and Schanz, to διοικήσεων.

19. Cf. Laks 2000, esp. section 6.

20. In *Laws* 11–12 up to the discussion of the Nocturnal Council at 960c, Cleinias is given stand-alone one-line utterances at 918c8 and 951c5; a cluster of three one-line utterances at 931b1, b4, and d3; and a cluster of five one-line utterances at 922c6, c10, d3, d9, and e5. Megillus has no lines.

21. Detailing this would take the space of a full essay. But note the twenty-eight two-line breaks that Pangle 1980 inserts throughout *Laws* 11–12 in his translation.

22. The Athenian suggests codes addressing, in this order, pledging security, searches, statutes of limitations on claims, preventing a fellow citizen's appearing at trials and contests, receiving stolen goods, harboring exiles, making private war or peace, bribing officials, taxation, and votive offerings.

23. His final topic is, strangely, the "wages" due to military experts as the "craftsmen [δημιουργῶν] of our security" (921d4)—namely, "honors" (921d–922a).

24. I deliberately forego further comment on 953e–956b and on the pages following this section and preceding the resumption of dialogue and the introduction of the Nocturnal Council at 960c. The former reads as a mere aggregate of items that are undeveloped in content and, so far as I can tell, not put in any significant order; I am tempted to think of this as, to resort to anachronism, a folder of items held in reserve for future consideration. The immediately following pages divide into short treatments of judicial procedure (including paragraphs on the three levels of courts, appeal processes, and jury selection) and funerals (958c–960b). The latter may be placed here in a playful mirroring of the life of the citizen by the trajectory of the dialogue itself; both are nearing their "ends," their τελευτή (958d2) and their τέλος (960b5), respectively. But I wonder whether these sections shouldn't be counted as two more items in the "folder" of 953e–956b, which would then extend to 960b. Both passages lack both dialogue form and any connective rhetoric that would link them and indicate a deliberate place in the flow of the text.

25. There is a further sense in which *Laws* 11–12 may be seen as a kind of "return." As Eric Sanday shows in his illuminating discussion in this volume, the property-related crimes picked out by the laws in *Laws* 11 reflect a lapse or breakdown of the subordination of the private to the common, and the suits and prosecutions authorized on the basis of these laws aim to restore it. Analogous rhythms of lapse and restoration may be seen, I think, in the Athenian's treatments of family and of the person in *Laws* 11 and of communal agency in *Laws* 12.

26. In fact, there is a dispute among editors about whether the phrase θεὸν . . . θεοῖς, "a god to gods," belongs to the original text or is a later revision; see the apparatus to

the Oxford text, ad loc., also Pangle 1980, 534n22. I quote it here in order to provide occasion to acknowledge that there are a host of questions to be raised about the Athenian's argument in *Laws* 10, with the relation of the soul that "avails itself of νοῦς" to "the gods" only one among them. Equally question-worthy are the sense of "virtue" as it applies to that soul; the distinction and relation of the astral gods and the Olympians who are the dominant figures in the ritual activities of the city and its twelve tribes; and the very senses in which, first, that soul may be understood to "care for" human affairs and, second, is available to respond to prayers and sacrifices in the first place, since it is expected not to be swayed by partisan ones. Even while Plato has the Athenian formulate his arguments in ways that invite these and many other questions, he also has the Athenian ignore these questions, leaving them, as I put it in part 1, "beyond the horizon" of the conversation. Are they, however, beyond the horizon to which their "more precise education" will lead the members of the Nocturnal Council? This is a question Plato seems to have the Athenian leave intriguingly open with his distinction between what "most of those in the city" and the members of the Nocturnal Council understand of the gods, at 966c, and with his closing deferral of a specification of the studies the Council members will pursue, made via his pun on ἀπόρρητα and ἀπρόρρητα, "indescribable" and "imprescribable"—see note 5 above.

27. See, for these three theses, 893b–899d, 899d–905d, 905d–907b, respectively.

28. This is the significance of the second and third claims that Plato has Cleinias recognize and point out at 887b.

29. This indeterminateness, combined with the Athenian's failure to specify the institutional relationship of the Nocturnal Council to the "offices" laid out in *Laws* 6, has allowed interpretation of the Council's role in the city to vary widely. Bobonich 2002, 390–408, argues persuasively against seeing in the Council Plato's last-minute reinstatement of anything like (to put this into my terms in part 2 above) an autocracy of the philosopher-kings of the *Republic* or the knowing statesman of the *Statesman*. This is too big a question to do justice to here, but a cautionary observation does seem timely: if one continues (as I do) to regard the *Laws* as setting these figures beyond the horizon of what is possible for its "second-best" city, then one must regard the Athenian's recourse to the metaphor of the Nocturnal Council as "mind" and "sight" and "hearing" as part of his larger recourse to the simile of the city as an animal and, so, as part of his attempt to envision its living unity, and not as an indication that the Council has absolute superiority over the city's other organs and functions.

30. Why does the Athenian say only σχεδὸν . . . ἀποτετελεσμένον, "*almost* completed"? Because, presumably, he has not yet specified the studies that will constitute the "more precise education" of the members of the Nocturnal Council. Note that Socrates in the *Republic* cites this notion of "precision" (ἀκρίβεια) numerous times as what distinguishes the "longer way," the educational path of the philosopher-to-be—see 435d1 and 504b5, e1, and e3. The Athenian invokes the same notion seven times in distinguishing the understanding the members of the Nocturnal Council must, by their "more precise education," achieve—see 965a6, b1, c1, c10, 967b2, and b3. Does Plato thereby point to the "longer way"?

2 Ἔρως and the *Laws* in Historical Context

Mark Munn

The *Laws* holds a special interest for historians, though not without the interpretive challenges that face anyone approaching a Platonic text with historical interests in mind. As opposed to Plato's early dialogues, which represent themselves as, and in some cases may well reflect actual gatherings from the life of Socrates, the *Laws* does not generate historical interest by virtue of its narrative setting or of the personalities presented in the dialogue. Rather, historical interest arises from the *Laws* because it is the most socially descriptive, detailed, and, in a broad, cultural and historical sense, the most highly contextualized of Plato's works. Although Plato envisions the formation of an ideal society in this work, historians of fourth-century Athens detect in it reflections of actual institutional developments, showing this work, theoretical as it is, to be remarkably specific to its historical context, the mid-fourth century.[1]

My observations here will begin by focusing on aspects of the *Laws* that I find particularly salient to students of Athenian institutions of the mid-fourth century. I will follow these historical observations with an appreciation of a more broadly cultural aspect of the *Laws* that leads to the same conclusion, namely, that the *Laws* reflects mores and attitudes that have shifted appreciably from those associated, in Plato's earlier dialogues, with the lifetime of Socrates in the late fifth century. The aspect in question is the perspective on ἔρως that is presented in the *Laws*. Plato's works as a whole naturally have a significant place in the study of ἔρως in classical Greek thought. Given the complex layering of voices and viewpoints presented to us in the works of Plato, we cannot simply take what we find in Plato's writings to be the expressions of his own attitudes. But assuming, as I do, that in his Socratic dialogues Plato presents voices that are representative of salient attitudes and viewpoints current in his life and times, I find it instructive to compare the circumscribed role that ἔρως plays in the *Laws* to its comparative prominence in earlier dialogues. It is no accident that the *Laws* is seldom mentioned in books like Waller Newell's *Ruling Passion: The Erotics of Statecraft in Platonic Political Philosophy* and Laurence Cooper's *Eros in Plato, Rousseau, and Nietzsche*.[2] Ἔρως, and the erotics of politics as depicted especially in the *Symposium* (or in the *Symposia* of both Plato and Xenophon), and as a theme reflected in the comedies of Aristophanes among other literary works, is a distinctive phenomenon of the later fifth century. The restricted play given to ἔρως in the *Laws* is symptomatic, I would argue, of a shift in attitudes since the lifetime of Socrates. A crude measure of this shift can be found in the fact that references to ἔρως and its cognates are about half as numerous in the *Laws* as they are in the *Republic*, leaving aside the dialogues, *Symposium* and *Phaedrus*, where ἔρως is announced as the topic of discussion.[3] The *Laws* stands at the far end of Plato's biographical relationship with fifth-century discourse. It is probably significant that references to the *Laws* figure more prominently in Kathy Gaca's book, *The Making of Fornication: Eros, Ethics, and Political Reform in Greek Philosophy and Early Christianity*, than do references to any other selections from the Platonic corpus. Gaca examines the subject of desire and its sublimation primarily from the perspective of Hellenistic philosophy and its aftermath, and the *Laws* is a major element in her point of departure (Gaca 2003, 23–58). As opposed to Plato's other works, populated as they are with personalities from the lifetime of Socrates, in the *Laws* Plato has almost turned his back on the fifth century.

The *Laws* in historical context

We may begin by considering the *Laws* as a work that reflects its historical place late in Plato's lifetime, not far from his death in 347. At first glance, the setting of this conversation among three men is virtually timeless. The speakers themselves, Kleinias of Knossos, Megillus of Sparta, and an unnamed Athenian, are unknowns, and give us no historical anchor. The theme of lawgiving at the foundation of a new state aims at eternal truths and enduring institutions, and the scene is invested with an aura of venerable tradition. The cave of Zeus, which is the professed destination of this ambulating trio, is the place of origin of the most ancient laws known to the Greeks, the laws that Minos, first king of Knossos, received from Zeus, his father. The laws of Sparta represented by Megillus are another respected tradition, not so ancient as Cretan laws, but also expounded by a god, Apollo, to the revered Spartan lawgiver, Lycurgus. The Athenian speaks for no epichoric tradition, since Athenian laws were notoriously changeable (from Plato's perspective[4]), but his relentless intonations represent the voice of philosophy stripping away the contingencies of local custom and tradition to lay bare what he sees as the essential framework of the relationship between a community of free citizens and immortal truth. The city whose re-foundation they envision, Magnesia, is represented as abandoned, or nearly so (919d, cf. 848d, 946b), and in any event is practically unknown to history.[5] It is the perfect tabula rasa on which to inscribe an ideal constitution.

So much for the explicit setting of the dialogue. But what are the clues that reveal its place in time and in Greek, and even specifically Athenian cultural history? To start with, there are very few explicit chronological markers in the *Laws*, and these generally appear as remote background to the situation in the unspecified present time of the dialogue. In Book 3, broad sketches of Dorian and Spartan history (692c–693a), of Persian history (694a–695e), and of Athenian history (698a–699e) mention events no later than the outcome of the Persian Wars (see also 707b–d). Two incidental references to historical events in Book 1, however, indicate that the conversation is envisioned as taking place in the midfourth century. When the Athenian observes that victory in war often has more to do with superior numbers than with any other quality, he cites the Syracusan defeat and subjugation of Locri and the Athenian conquest of the island of Ceos (638b). The first of these events, the subjugation of Locri in southern Italy, cannot be identified with a known event, but certainly belongs to the age of Syracusan imperial expansion in the 380s–350s, under either Dionysius I or II.[6] The Athenian conquest of Ceos is better attested. It took place in 363 or 362, following a brief uprising against Athens.[7] So much would allow us to conclude, if it were not otherwise known, that the *Laws* was a work of the mid-fourth century, and that the conversation among Kleinias, Megillus, and the Athenian was likewise envisioned in this time frame.

Beyond such chronological markers, however, there are themes in the *Laws* that resonate with concerns known to be at the forefront of Athenian politics in the mid-fourth century, and with institutional developments that relate specifically to the education of citizens in ways that are echoed in the *Laws*. Some of these connections exist only at a very general level, and it would be hard to make from them alone the case that Plato was responding to contemporary events more than perennial concerns. But in a few instances the connections are so remarkably close that it would be hard to deny that Plato was attuned to debates going on at Athens. There is even enough circumstantial evidence to suggest that Plato's ideas were having an impact on those debates, through the agency of men who were partners in his circle of followers at the Academy.

These connections surround the preparations for war, which at the beginning of the *Laws* both Kleinias and Megillus identify as the chief object of lawgiving, and which make up significant aspects of the institutions that the Athenian speaker would see established in the new Cretan city. Before he frames the institutions of military training and preparedness for war, in Books 6 and 8, the Athenian confronts the view, articulated by Kleinias, that "the peace of which most men talk . . . is no more than a name; in real fact, the normal attitude of a city to all other cities is one of undeclared warfare" (626a).[8] The Athenian does not directly refute this ancient truism, which was the cornerstone of Cretan and Spartan law, but he subordinates the priorities of war to the goals of peace, and in so doing identifies the higher goal of lawgiving with conditions that can only be realized in peace. So he states, "If a man takes such a view of the happiness of the city, or indeed of the individual man—I mean, if external wars are the first and only object of his regard—he will never be a true statesman, nor will any man be a complete lawgiver, unless he legislates for war as a means to peace rather than for peace as a means to war" (628d). The embrace of peace as the measure of happiness and as the condition under which the true goals of lawgiving can be achieved is a development reflected with increasing frequency in Greek and particularly Athenian political discourse as one approaches the middle of the fourth century. The Athenians, for example, established an altar of Peace in 375, and dedicated a celebrated statue of Peace holding the infant Wealth in front of their council house in 361. But it is particularly in 355, at the end of the brief but exhausting war between Athens and the most powerful of her Ionian allies, known as the Social War, that we find the argument that peace should not only be the outcome but even the instrument of policy. This is the argument of Isocrates, in his *On the Peace*, in which he asserts that Athens' own best interests demand the renunciation of imperial ambitions. Only then can the Athenians achieve secure happiness won by "virtue and all its parts" (Isocrates 8.32). Isocrates here gives a very close précis of the argument in Book 1 of the *Laws*, recapitulated in Book 12, where the Athenian speaker identifies ἀρετή as the true object of the lawgiver. Isocrates even goes so far as to suggest that Athens, if it allowed her true virtue to show, could hope to achieve in peace what she had failed to achieve in war—the voluntary adherence of other Greek states to her leadership. This is very close to the sentiment expressed in Book 3 of the *Laws*, where the Athenian imagines that if the founders of the Dorian constitution of Sparta had understood their task properly (in other words, if ἀρετή had been their highest aim), then they would have secured their state forever in freedom and as the leader over all mankind, Greek and barbarian (687a).[9]

Sparta had had her turn at leadership and had failed, however, and the mood at Athens in the 350s was for the Athenians to consider if they themselves might again rise to leadership. If the Athenians did not formally renounce aggression and all ambitions to overseas possessions in 355, their priorities did shift appreciably in that direction, as we find Demosthenes, within a few years, railing at the Athenians for their unwillingness to fund expeditionary military forces to oppose the aggressive expansion of Philip of Macedon, and taunting the Athenians for electing their military officers "more for display in the Agora than for action in the field" (paraphrasing Demosthenes *First Philippic* 26). Moreover, this is the decade, the 350s, when we first hear of a new institution in the Athenian στρατηγία, when one of the ten annually elected generals of Athens was assigned specifically to see to the protection of the countryside, as the στρατηγὸς ἐπὶ τῆς χώρας and when the defense of the countryside, φυλακὴ τῆς χώρας, became an item for required discussion on the agenda of each of ten annual mandatory meetings of the Athenian assembly.[10] The Athenian polis had now become identical, in spatial terms, with its χώρα, its territory, in a way that it never had been in the fifth century.[11] Athenians collectively were increasingly looking inward for what it meant to be Athenians, and were less and less inclined to identify their state with its aspirational goals across the Aegean and beyond. Athenian self-awareness had moved far from the expansionist visions of Alcibiades on the eve of the Sicilian expedition, and even from Pericles in his funeral oration, as reported by Thucydides.

In the *Laws*, Plato has envisioned a city in which this self-containment could be perfected in a way that it never could be at Athens. Although the sea is not far away, the new Magnesia has as little to do with the sea as any city might. Magnesia has no navy. The deleterious effects of the sea and seaborne commerce are spelled out at the beginning of Book 4, and the theme of restricting foreign contact and commerce is reiterated several times later (*Laws* 8, 11, and 12). All of this resonates with Spartan ideals and custom, which had a significant influence on the more elitist ideals of the Athenian aristocratic tradition, as it is sometimes reflected in Platonic writing.[12] But Sparta and its laws had proven themselves vulnerable and inadequate, as the Athenian speaker hints at the opening of Book 1 and makes more explicit in his critique of the Dorian legacy in Book 3. There is no mention of the disastrous defeat of Sparta at the hands of Thebes in 371, though this revolution in the Greek world lies implicitly behind the willingness of the Spartan, Megillus, to take instruction in the framing of laws from his Athenian friend. Spartan ideals guide the stipulations that citizens of Magnesia, male and female, subject themselves to the disciplines of ἀρετή which will not admit the practice of any banausic arts, and likewise submit themselves to training for war. But the goals of this training reflect an emergent Athenian idealism more closely than they conform to Spartan practice.

The military forces of the new Cretan city are to be prepared and trained for territorial defense only. There is no hint that military forces might cross the borders and march on neighboring states, or even join allies abroad in any action against mutual enemies. The rugged territory of Magnesia suits its isolationist disposition, and its citizens are to be trained to make the most effective use of this rugged terrain in defense of their homeland. Here is where we find a clear departure from Spartan practice. Magnesian warriors are to be trained in missile weapons—archery and javelins—and light-armed fighting in general—πελταστική. Such tactics were traditional on Crete but were inimical to Spartan citizen identity as heavily armed hoplites. The Spartans famously jeered at light-armed troops, whose method of hit-and-run fighting was a species of cowardice in Spartan eyes. However, light-armed peltasts under an Athenian leadership had twice dealt crushing blows to Spartan self-esteem, first under the command of Cleon at Sphacteria in 425,[13] and later under the command of Iphicrates at Corinth in 390.[14] These had been mercenary troops, but since then Athenian commanders had recruited and trained Athenians to fight as light-armed peltasts, because in certain conditions they were clearly superior to heavily armed hoplites.

These developments were noticed in Socratic circles. In the third book of his *Memorabilia*, Xenophon depicts Socrates quizzing the younger Pericles about various skills that would make him a better statesman: "Have you considered this, Pericles, that great mountains reaching Boeotia protect our country, through which the passes are narrow and steep, and that that interior of our country is divided by sheer mountains?" The point is conceded by Pericles, and Socrates goes on: "Don't you think, then, that young Athenians armed with light weapons and occupying the mountains that protect our country could do injury to our enemies while providing a strong bulwark of defense to our citizens in the countryside?" (*Memorabilia* 3.5.25–27). Xenophon here reflects thinking about the φυλακὴ τῆς χώρας which would have been out of place in the putative setting of this conversation, in the last decade of the fifth century, but which exactly answers to thought and practice of the 360s, when Athenians and Boeotians were again at war and when this passage was probably composed.

In the 370s and 360s, Athenian commanders were innovating with the armament of Athenian citizens, training a corps of peltast troops, and developing the standards according to which they were to carry out the φυλακὴ τῆς χώρας. Foremost among these commanders, along with Iphicrates, was the general, Chabrias, who had commanded peltasts and citizen troops in the Boeotian War of the 370s. In that war Chabrias was also involved in developing a novel device for territorial defense, a cross-country field wall constructed as a ditch and palisade with periodic sally-ports, which would enable a smaller but highly mobile defending force to hold off a much larger attacking army. This earthwork and palisade no longer exists (it is known from Xenophon's account of the Boeotian War in the *Hellenica*[15]), but a closely similar cross-country field wall built of rough stonework still stands outside of Athens, blocking the pass between Mount Aegaleos and Mount Parnes, which is the widest pass into the plain of Athens from the west, and which was the route of invasion used by Spartan armies during the Peloponnesian War. This wall, known by its modern name as the Dema wall, was almost certainly a construction of the Boeotian War also carried out by Chabrias, who had now developed the art of fortification so that it could protect the greater χώρα of Athens, and not just the city and the Piraeus harbor.[16]

The strategic thinking represented by the Dema wall and the generalship of Chabrias is embodied in the precepts for the defense of the χώρα of Magnesia as they are laid out in Book 6. After describing the posting around the twelve districts of the countryside of twelve tribal brigades of young warriors under their respective "watch commanders," the φρούραρχοι, our Athenian specifies that their first duty is to "provide for the most effectual blocking of the territory against an enemy by the construction of all necessary dikes and trenches and other built works to check any would-be plunderers of territory or cattle" (760e). Later, continuing on the subject of defensive preparations, the Athenian observes:

> Concerning [city] walls, Megillus, I am of the same mind as Sparta. I
> would let walls sleep in the ground and not wake them, for these reasons.
> First of all, as the poet's verse so aptly puts it, walls ought to be of bronze
> and iron, and not of stone. Secondly, our practice would be justly ridiculed
> when each year we sent out our young men into the countryside to block
> an enemy's path by ditches, entrenchments, and various constructions, all
> in order to keep the foe from crossing our borders, while at the same time
> we surrounded ourselves with a wall, which . . . invites the inhabitants to
> seek refuge within it, and not to ward off the enemy. (778d–e)

Although the Athenians of Plato's day did not do without their city walls, as the Spartans did, they were innovating in the area of territorial defense in ways that the Spartans never were. It must be significant that Chabrias, who is most closely connected with the development of such defensive strategies, is said by both Plutarch and Diogenes Laertius to have been an associate of Plato's and to have attended the Academy.[17]

Also of note is the fact that over the middle decades of the fourth century, Athenians were debating how best to utilize the military training of their young men, in formal institutions of the Attic ἐφηβεία, for the purposes both of defending their territory and of molding them into patriotic, upright citizens. The Attic ἐφηβεία took in young men in their eighteenth and nineteenth years, as opposed to the young Magnesians selected when they were between the ages of twenty-five and thirty; but in many respects the institutions were comparable. Aristotle, in the Ἀθηναίων πολιτεία (42.1–5), describes the ἐφηβεία as it existed in his day, certainly by the 330s, as a two-year curriculum of ceremonial duties, training in diverse weaponry, and garrison service, first in the fortresses of the Piraeus and then in the garrison forts in the Attic countryside. In addition to regular military commanders, these young ephebes had special disciplinary officers, σωφρονισταί and κοσμῆται, selected by their tribes and by the state to supervise them. Besides Aristotle's account, this institution is best known from the surviving decrees on stone, spanning the 330s and 320s, awarding public honors to the commanders, to their σωφρονισταί and κοσμῆται, and to the ephebes themselves for their φιλοτιμία, their εὐταξία, and their σωφροσύνη displayed while on duty.[18] In the Laws, the term κοσμητής is a descriptive term applied both to military officers and to supervisors of choruses; σωφρονιστής does not occur as an official agent, although the concept of σωφροσύνη certainly plays an important role as an essential accompaniment to virtue (696b–e). It is not clear if the Attic ἐφηβεία was ever compulsory for all young Athenians (it probably was not), but the institution certainly became the conventional avenue into participatory citizenship. It represents the closest that Athens ever came to adopting the principles of service, of discipline, of devotion to military and athletic training, and above all, of public honors for excellence that Plato advocates for the training of young citizens in the Laws as he also does in the Republic.

Once again, there is a personal link between Plato and this institution. Phocion, a military man and an Academic, who happens also to have been the protégé of Chabrias, was both an influential speaker in the Athenian assembly and a popular general.[19] Phocion was elected to that office a remarkable forty-five times, according to Plutarch (Phocion 8.1–2). This might appear to be the record of a populist politician and orator, but Phocion was famous for never campaigning for office, for delivering concise speeches, and for generally opposing popular sentiment whenever the crowd called for military action (he was famous for his opposition to Demosthenes' interventionist policies). His moderate stance placed him well to serve as a mediating figure when Athens fell under the power of Macedon after the death of Alexander, and for that role he was condemned and made to drink hemlock during the brief revival of a radical democracy at Athens in 318, shortly before the city fell back under Macedonian influence during the contests of the successors to Alexander. Some scholars have suspected that aspects of Phocion's biography were exaggerated by Academics who wished to compare him to Socrates, the man who always reminded the Athenians that they did not fully understand what they were doing, and who, in the end, was put to death by them for his troubles.[20] But the suspect details of his biography ring true if we suppose that most of his generalships were ἐπὶ τῆς χώρας (as we know that some were). This relatively unglamorous post would both require Phocion to address the assembly at least ten times a year on the subject of the defense of the countryside, and would, by the nature of his responsibilities, encourage him to follow a conservative path in the policies of war and peace. Overseeing the defense of Attica, Phocion would also have had overall responsibility for the conduct of the ἐφηβεία, and may well, therefore, have had a decisive hand in bringing this institution to the prominence that it achieved in public record in the decades immediately following the death of Plato.[21]

Such, then, is the evidence by which we can recognize the *Laws* as a product of its times, in the mid-fourth century. It *is* a work of Plato's art, and by that it connects with his larger body of thought and achieves a certain timelessness, but it is also a work aimed at the minds of his contemporaries, and in that it is a reflection of concerns of the day, and of new ideas of the time.[22]

Ἔρως and the *Laws*

The place of ἔρως in Plato's thought provides another indicator, albeit more subjective in nature, of the relationship between the concerns of the *Laws* and contemporary attitudes. Support for this claim requires an appreciation of the shift in attitudes toward ἔρως that are perceptible through various expressions of Athenian values, some literary and some material. The topic is a large one, and the present essay's scope allows only for an outline of the evidence for this shift.[23] In this connection, again, I believe that the evidence is sufficient to show that Plato, in the *Laws,* has articulated his distinctive vision of order in society in a manner that is consonant with attitudes that have changed since the heady days of Alcibiades and imperial Athens, in his youth.

Why there should be such a change has to do with the difference between an Athens that was asserting its primacy around the Greek Mediterranean in the fifth century and an Athens that was preoccupied with defending its territorial integrity in Attica in the fourth. Within twenty years of the fall of the Athenian empire at the end of the Peloponnesian War, the Athenians, chastened by the outcome of another war against Sparta (the so-called Corinthian War of 395–386), were finally ready to renounce the ambition of turning the Aegean into the inland sea of Athens. Here is where the vision of greatness born of restraint, a vision articulated in Isocrates' *On the Peace*, began to supplant the vision of greatness born of unrestrained ambition, a vision articulated in the funeral oration of Pericles and pursued most singularly in the life of Alcibiades. A shift in the rhetorical and artistic prominence of ἔρως is the most potent sign of this transition.

In the world of Periclean Athens, ἔρως, the manifestation of desire, was the principle that justified the investment of sovereignty in the majority will of the Athenian demos, and that propelled the Athenian demos to cleave to the path of sovereign hegemony. By the simple logic that ἔρως is what draws every person toward the beautiful, and the beautiful (in Greek τὸ καλόν, or κάλλος) is logically and semantically what is noble or good, then ἔρως should be the agency by which every person is inspired to embrace what is good. If a city, such as Athens, embraces what is truly beautiful, noble, and good and invites its entire populace, even in a sense, the entire world, to join its pursuit of the beautiful, the noble, and the good, then it is in alignment with ἔρως, which becomes the active agent of democracy.

This principle underlay the beautification of the city in the Periclean building program. That program got underway in the later 450s, at about the time that Plato, in the *Parmenides,* depicts the young Socrates becoming interested in philosophy. As the son of a sculptor, a creator of facsimiles of being and beauty, whose craft must have been sustained by the Periclean program, it would not be implausible to suspect that the young Socrates became absorbed by the inquiry into the nature of being, the essence of virtue, and the truth of beauty, which in some sense underlay the project to embellish the city with temples, and with sculptures of unparalleled beauty. It is significant that, in the most famous monument of the Periclean program, the Parthenon, the figure of ἔρως personified is represented in heretofore unprecedented ways. Ἔρως occurs, for the first time in monumental sculpture, as a regular companion of the twelve Olympian gods three times on the east face of the Parthenon. He is depicted in the assembly of gods witnessing the birth of Athena on the east pediment; he is depicted in the east metopes, as one of the gods defending the rule of Zeus against the onslaught of the Giants; and he is depicted in the east frieze, leaning on the lap of Aphrodite, among the gods who observe the Panathenaic procession. Ἔρως also occurs at least once more on the metopes of the Parthenon, intervening between Menelaus and Helen in the north metopes that depict the sack of Troy. And he is present among the gods assembled on the east frieze of the temple of Athena Nike in front of the Acropolis.[24]

Then there is the rhetorical presence of ἔρως, the agent of passionate desire. He appears most famously in that figure of speech from the funeral oration of Pericles, where Pericles calls upon the Athenians, and indeed even the non-Athenians present on the occasion, "fix your eyes every day on the power of Athens and fall in love with her [or, become her lovers, ἐρασταί]" (*Thucydides* 2.43.1). Aristophanes shows that such phraseology in Pericles' speech is not just the invention of Thucydides writing years later. His plays several times make fun of demagogues who declare themselves lovers of Athens, as in the *Acharnians* (141–144), or lovers of the Demos, as in the *Knights* (732–733, 1163, 1342, e.g.). In the *Birds*, Aristophanes composes a hymn to ἔρως, and represents his cosmic hero, Peisetairos, consummating his cosmic rule over heaven and earth in a sacred marriage attended by ἔρως (693–704, 1737). I have argued elsewhere that this cosmic fantasy is a direct and not unflattering reference to the ambitions of Alcibiades.[25] About this same time, just before and just after the launching of the Sicilian expedition, are the dramatic dates of the two Socratic *Symposia,* that of Plato and that of Xenophon, both of them depicting paeans for the glorification of ἔρως.

What is most conspicuous in the rhetoric of ἔρως, however, is the problematic nature of ἔρως. Aristophanes' lampoonery, especially in the *Knights,* already reveals how ridiculous ἔρως can make his devotees appear. Socially textured criticism appears in the speeches in Plato's *Symposium,* particularly the speech of Pausanias, where Heavenly and Common ἔρως are deduced from the cults of Aphrodite Ourania and Aphrodite Pandemos. The *Phaedrus* and the *Republic,* too, show a double nature to ἔρως, and many of the same themes appear in Xenophon's work, most notably in his *Symposium, Memorabilia, Hieron,* and *Cyropaedia.* Thucydides, who preserves the reference to the worthiness of erotic passion in the rhetoric of Pericles, also signals its dangerous side in his own words when he refers to ἔρως as the impassioned desire that clouded the judgment of all Athenians, young and old, when they contemplated the prospects of their expedition to Sicily (*Thucydides* 6.24.3). The failure of empire, and I would argue the failure of democracy, in the view of intellectual circles that included Socrates and his followers, could be assigned to the indiscriminate arousal of erotic passions among the demos by Pericles, Alcibiades, and their ilk.

In the century after the fall of the Athenian empire, there are no new manifestations of an admirable ἔρως in public monuments at Athens, and few in rhetoric. Ἔρως is still invoked in private or personal contexts, as in Aeschines' praise of freely given love as opposed to sex for hire, or in the depictions of marriage on late red figure vases. Praxiteles created a famous statue of ἔρως, we are told, but it was not a public commission; rather, it was a gift to the source of his inspiration, the courtesan, Phryne. Impassioned desire is not openly invoked as a collective attribute of the demos. Where something of this nature does appear in literature, as in Plato's depiction of the luxurious city in the second book of the *Republic*, the indulgence in desirable things is shown to invite indiscriminate expansion and to be the source of war (372d–373e). In Plato generally, as in Xenophon, ἔρως most often appears as a force to overcome or to guide from base to proper ends, through the exercise of σωφροσύνη, temperance or soundmindedness, and above all, ἐγκράτεια, self-restraint (cf. Xenophon *Memorabilia* 1.5.4, 2.1.7, 4.5.8–9).

This is certainly its principal role in the *Laws*. In Book 1 we find the Athenian recommending the exercise, for those who are sufficiently mature to handle it, of controlled imbibing of wine as a way of testing their abilities to comport themselves without shame in the presence of inducements to the passions and pleasures of, among other things, ἔρως (649c–650b). Ἔρως thus has a rightful place in the soul of the lawgiver who can temper desire appropriately. We find it enumerated as an accompaniment of the aspects of virtue that should be at the forefront of his intellect: "judgment (φρόνησις), the leader (ἡγεμών) of all ἀρετή, and intellect (νοῦς) and sound opinion (δόξα) along with ἔρως and ἐπιθυμία following these" (688b). The nature of ἔρως here is somewhat ambiguous: is it desire for sex, or more abstractly the capacity to desire deeply? As further context is added, the latter appears to be the case.

When the new foundation begins to be envisioned, in Book 4, the discussion turns to the ideal nature of the lawgiver who could most effectively institute this new foundation. He turns out to be a young tyrant (τύραννος νέος), who is quick to learn (εὐμαθής), of retentive memory (μνήμων), bold and high-spirited by nature (μεγαλοπρεπὴς φύσει) who also possesses σωφροσύνη (709e–710a). What will motivate such a tyrant to sound legislation, we are told, is a "divine passion" (ἔρως θεῖος) for temperance and justice (711d). This is the more abstract aspect of ἔρως, an intensity of the emotions that activates the soul.[26]

Ἔρως thus has an essential role to play in the soul of the lawgiver, and so too does it play a part in inspiring all of the young citizens of the new city. In Book 1, where the Athenian extols the importance of true education, Plato expresses the power of erotic passion as a desirable quality in a way that echoes the summons of Pericles for Athenians to devote themselves passionately to Athens. The speaker says that true education draws a child toward virtue "by inspiring a desire and ardent passion to become a perfect citizen (ποιοῦσαν ἐπιθυμητήν τε καὶ ἐραστὴν τοῦ πολίτην γενέσθαι τέλεον), understanding both how to rule and be ruled with justice" (643e).

Here we find Plato transforming the ideals of the eroticized political rhetoric of a past generation to the goals of his own vision of political perfection. To do so, he must insist on starting with a clean slate, both in terms of the physical space that the new city is to occupy, and in terms of its human capital. When he appeals to the tyrant as the ideal person of the lawgiver, he is reckoning with the difficulty of creating any new state without being overwhelmed by the inherited habits and customs of the people who must come together to found a new city. Ἔρως among them is ungoverned, possibly ungovernable except through the decisive dictates of an impassioned tyrant. But once a new civic order is in place, and its own generation and regeneration is underway, it is possible, by starting with the young and carefully schooling their passions, to direct them constructively toward the greater good. This is the fantasy Plato entertains in the Laws. The subject of youthful erotic passions, the simple lust for sex as a natural feature of the human condition, among the citizens of the new city are addressed in detail in the routines of training laid out in detail in Book 8.

The general thrust of Plato's assertions about carnal ἔρως in his young citizens also applies the erotic nature of his city as a whole: restraint is necessary, and self-restraint is best. Plato's new city is the ultimate city of ἐγκράτεια—a city of self-restraint. Its passions are disciplined and not allowed to fix their gaze on things beyond its borders, which may signify that its passions are not to be for the things of this world. It is the opposite of an imperial city. It is the philosophical counterpart of the appeal of Isocrates for Athenians to cultivate virtue above all, from which choice εὐδαιμονία will come to them.[27]

Conclusions

Plato, in the Laws, envisions a state that could never exist in fact, but one that equally could never be imagined outside of a particular milieu. The foreground of that milieu is Athens of roughly 360 to 347; in the middle ground is Sparta of the same era. Both were great states that had shared the lead in shaping the political values of Greece in the fifth century, but which, by this time, were both struggling to identify and recover that which had formerly made them great. In the background is Crete, seen not so much in a contemporary perspective as in the guise of the primeval home of law and divinely ordained order, the original source of Lycurgus's legislative inspiration and now, in the fourth century, reduced to tabula rasa on which law and inspiration could be re-inscribed. But it is from Athens that the elements of that new order are chiefly drawn.

It is not possible to weigh the extent to which Plato was shaping versus responding to current concerns; there is reasonable likelihood that both were the case. If we can trust the tradition that makes men like Chabrias occasional visitors to the Academy (and I see no good reason to be skeptical), then we can imagine a setting in which men, well connected among the political movers at Athens, debated the appropriate manner in which the youth of the state should be educated for citizenship and trained to see to the defense of its territory. These discussions bore fruit in the decades immediately following the death of Plato, in the institutions of the Attic ἐφηβεία, and in the rise to prominence of political leaders with ties to the Academy. In the ἐφηβεία, the youth of Athens were placed under the authority of elected instructors called σωφρονισταί and κοσμῆται. We know nothing specific about the forms of discipline imposed by these tutors of continence and order (aside from military drill and arms training), but we can suppose that their charges were placed under regimes designed to encourage ἐγκράτεια in all manner of appetites. In other words, ἔρως in at least some of its manifestation came under disciplinary restraint. The era of the fully developed Attic ἐφηβεία was also the era of the political prominence of Phocion, follower of Chabrias and nemesis of Demosthenes, known for his conservative anti-democratic leanings. A still more conservative opponent of democracy with his roots in the Academy just after the death of Plato was Demetrius son of Phanostratus, known as Demetrius of Phaleron. Drastic restrictions on the public display of wealth were among the more famous of Demetrius's legislative measures, imposed during the decade 317–307, when he exercised authority over the administration of government and law at Athens.

Plato and his Academic circle were a strong influence on the currents of intellect and sentiment that shaped the institutions of Athens in this way. I do not want to overstate these influences, however, so it must be noted that they were in constant tension with populist sentiments and policies, and ultimately were overwhelmed by the power politics of the warlords of Macedonia and Rome. But from the generation educated in the lifetime of Plato on, at least down to the time of Sulla three centuries later, many of the leading statesmen and spokesmen of Athens were educated in the schools of the Academy or its first offshoot, the Lyceum of Aristotle. And whether it was under the influence of these schools or through the popular sentiments that ebbed and flowed with the tides of politics, Athens saw the rise and fall of several men who might have been taken for, or might have presented themselves as a τύραννος νέος guided by an ἔρως θεῖος. Plato in the *Laws* offered an idealized framework within which such a leader might perfect his authority; Athens was the stage on which some attempted to act out this role.

Notes

1. Others who have recently drawn attention to the manner in which the *Laws* is a work that reflects Athens in the fourth century include Nightingale 1999 and Dusanic 2002.

2. Newell 2000; Cooper 2008.

3. Cognates of ἔρως, including ἐραστής and ἐρόμενος, occur twenty-two times in the *Laws*, as against forty-one in the *Republic*. For comparison's sake, they occur 140 times in the *Symposium*, 136 in the *Phaedrus*, 128 times in the entire Xenophontic corpus, and ninety-five times in the entire Aristotelian corpus.

4. As reflected, e.g., in the *Seventh Letter* 324b–325b, and in the Aristotelian Ἀθηναίων πολιτεία 1–41 (esp. 41).

5. The sparse evidence for the existence of a Cretan Magnesia is cited by Morrow 1960, 31. For a more comprehensive review of this issue, see Clay 1993.

6. The impossibility of deriving a specific date from the reference to the subjugation of Locri is discussed by L. A. Post (Post 1929, 8–10), summarized by Thomas L. Pangle, 1980, 517n45. There is no doubt, however, that this reference describes conditions at some point in the reign of either Dionysius I (who died in 367) or Dionysius II (who was in power 367–357).

7. Capture of Ceos is a reference to events of 363 or 362, attested in an inscription of 362 (*Inscriptiones Graecae* II^2 111) describing terms of a settlement imposed on the Ceans after a military intervention by the Athenians. For a translation of the inscription, see P. Harding, 1985, 74–76; for discussion of these events, see M. N. Tod, 1948, 130–132 (text no. 142); J. Cargill, 1981, 169; P. Brun, 1989, 121–138. It is incorrect to state, as Pangle does (following Post), that "the Athenian stranger is not referring to any particular event in the case of either Locri or Ceos, but only to their general condition of figurative 'enslavement,' Locri to Syracusan hegemony and Ceos to the Athenian empire." *Laws* 328b1 explicitly describes "enslavement" after defeat in battle against overwhelming forces, which is the point of the reference.

8. Here and in most of the following quotations from the *Laws*, I am using the translation of A. E. Taylor.

9. L. A. Post has drawn attention to passages from another work of Isocrates, the *Antidosis* written in 353, where, in his view, Isocrates is responding directly to Plato's *Laws* (Post 1929, 9–11). This is a reasonable possibility, but not nearly as certain as Post asserts.

10. Τὸν στρατηγὸν τὸν ἐπὶ τὴ[ν φυλ]ακὴ[ν τῆς χ]ώρας is first attested in an inscription of 352/1, *Inscriptiones Graecae* II^2 204, lines 19–20. The office is mentioned by Aristotle, *AthPol* 61.1. The subject of the φυλακὴ τῆς χώρας on the agenda of the ἐκκλησίαι κύριαι is noted at *AthPol* 43.4. For a discussion of the emergence of this concern with the φυλακὴ τῆς χώρας in fourth-century Athens, see Munn 1993, 3–15, 25–33, 186–195.

11. Athenian concern for the integrity and defense of the Attic χώρα as a development of the fourth century is discussed by (in addition to Munn 1993, previous note), Garlan 1973, 1974, and Ober 1985.

12. Sparta and its laws are regarded approvingly, e.g., at *Crito* 52e, *Protagoras* 342a–e, *Gorgias* 515e; for evidence that this view was commonly attributed to Socrates and his circle, see Aristophanes *Birds* 1280–1283.

13. *Thucydides* 4.32–38. The Spartan disdain for missile weapons is captured in the retort of a Spartan captive, as reported by Thucydides (4.40.2), to the sarcastic question, were the good and noble Spartans the dead ones, that arrows would be worth a great deal if they could pick out good and noble men from the rest.

14. Xenophon *Hellenica* 4.5.11–17.

15. Xenophon *Hellenica* 5.4.38–39, 49, discussed in detail in Munn 1987.

16. On the Dema wall, the career of Chabrias, and the defensive strategy developed at this time, see Munn 1993 (above, note 11).

17. Chabrias and Plato: Plutarch *Moralia* 1126c, *Phocion* 4.2; *Diogenes Laertius* 3.23–24. Chabrias was related by marriage to Eryximachus (Chabrias was probably his son-in-law), who was either identical with or a kinsman of the Eryximachus mentioned in *Phaedrus* 268a and appearing in the *Symposium* 175a–177d, 185d–189c; see Davies 1971, 462, 560–561. Chabrias was also the Athenian commander who captured Ceos in the event alluded to in Book 1 of the *Laws;* see the inscription cited in note 7, above. Chabrias was killed in battle in 356, at the outset of the Social War.

18. For a review of the history of the Attic ἐφηβεία and an edition of the earliest ephebic inscriptions, see Reinmuth 1971.

19. For an assessment of the career of Phocion, see Tritle 1988.

20. This is the view of Bearzot 1985.

21. The role of Phocion as στρατηγὸς ἐπὶ τὴν χώραν is examined in Munn 1993, 189–195.

22. Compare Post 1929, who argues that Plato makes reference to his work on the *Laws* in connection with his visits to Sicily, in his letters 3 and 7, and that the work of Isocrates reflects contemporary awareness of this work of idealized lawgiving. Note also that Louis Gernet, in the introduction to the Budé edition of Plato's *Laws* edited by É. des Places, observes that "his laws follow actual developments at Athens and envision conditions as they existed there, with some influence from other states," in the words of Post in his review of des Places in Post 1954, 202.

23. The relationship between ἔρως and Periclean democracy is the topic of a larger project that I am presently engaged in (note 24 below cites one of the first published elements of this project). A recent work that takes account of the remarkable nature of political ἔρως in fifth-century Athens is Wohl 2002.

24. Although these appearances of Ἔρως in the sculptures of the Parthenon are well known (see, e.g., Boardman 1985; Palagia 1998), the innovation and novelty of his appearance has not been generally noted. I have observed these circumstances in a recent paper, "The Nike Balustrade and the Erotic Attraction of Victory," presented at the Archaeological Institute of America Annual Meeting, Philadelphia, January 8–11, 2009.

25. Munn 2000, 124–126.

26. This ἔρως of the young tyrant sounds dangerously close to the ἔρως of the tyrannical man in *Republic* 9. In the *Laws*, however, tyrannical ἔρως sounds more like the

beneficial passion experienced by the legitimate king (see *Republic* 9.587a–c). It can be compared also to the mastery of erotic passions depicted by Xenophon in his portrait of Cyrus (*Cyropaedia* 4.6.11, 5.1.2–18, 6.1.31–36, 41–47, 6.4.2–11, 7.3).

27. Note the manner in which the Athenians should achieve εὐδαιμονία, according to *Isocrates* 8, *On the Peace* 18, 26, 32, 63–64, 136, e.g.

3 The Long and Winding Road: Impediments to Inquiry in Book 1 of the *Laws*

Eric Salem

It is dawn or perhaps just before dawn—a good time, we later learn, for discussing regime change, nation building, and legal reform (722c; 951d; 961b). The day promises to be hot and sunny, and since it is, as we also later learn, just around the summer solstice, the day will certainly be very long—long enough, say, for a very long conversation (625b; 683b). Three old men, a Cretan, a Spartan and an Athenian, stand outside the walls of Knossos and ponder the day ahead of them. They will hike together to the cave of Zeus—the well-spring of Cretan laws—and as they hike (and rest, as needed) they will pass the time talking and listening to talk about "regime and laws" (625a–b). Three grand old men, representatives of three great Greek powers, have already taken their stand together outside the walls of the city. And they will now make their way, in speech as well as deed, into the dawning light. They will ascend together from Knossos to the source of Knossos, from effect to cause, from convention to nature.

Or that, at least, is what we might expect them to do. This long hot summer day turns out differently than the day just sketched out. There is no indication that the trio of elders ever makes it to the cave of Zeus. In fact there is no indication that they ever make it past the first rest stop: there is more talk at the beginning of the dialogue about resting than staying in motion, about taking it easy (μετὰ ῥᾳστώνης) than toughing it out, about staying out of the summer's heat than moving forward into its light (625b–c; 722c).[1] And what holds true of the action, the *ergon*, of the *Laws* holds true of its argument, its *logos*, as well. There is something shady, something murky, something irresolute and disorienting about the whole enterprise. Put in another way: it becomes clear over the course of Book 1 that the Athenian Stranger is full of interesting questions about "regime and laws." But it is also true that those questions emerge only in fits and starts and it is *not* clear what purchase they will have within the ensuing conversation: Are those questions going to anchor and direct the conversation or just bubble to the surface now and then? "Where are we and how did we get here?" "What exactly is the question on the table?" "Was that an argument for something?" These are questions that every reader of other Platonic dialogues must ask now and then. They are one's constant companions when reading the *Laws*.[2]

Why is that? What accounts for the murkiness of the conversation in the *Laws?* What stands in the way of an intense focused inquiry into the root sources of "regime and laws"? Three possibilities come to mind.

(1) The *setting* of the *Laws* may have something to do with its peculiar character; this is the only Platonic dialogue to take place in a foreign land; it may be one thing to have a conversation outside the walls of Athens, another altogether to talk outside the walls of Knossos.[3] Perhaps, to borrow Cleinias's phrase, "the nature of the χώρα, the landscape" has some effect on the nature of the conversations possible within that landscape (625c).

(2) The *subject matter* of the dialogue may also shape it in fundamental ways. Some things are harder to talk about than others; mud, hair, and dirt may be harder to talk about than virtue.[4] Now, regime seems to be something one can talk about in a relatively straightforward way; consider the *Republic*. But the subject matter of the conversation in the *Laws* is not regime but regime and laws. Perhaps νόμοι are the sticking point here—perhaps laws or the pair "regime and laws" are *in themselves* more difficult to get hold of and to discuss than regime by itself.

(3) Of course the conversation in the *Republic* can only take off once Cephalus is out of the way: imagine having a ten-hour conversation with Cephalus about regime or laws or anything at all. *Interlocutors* matter, and that brings us to a third possibility and the one that will be the focus in what follows. The *Laws* is not a monologue or near-monologue. As their responses indicate, Cleinias and Megillus are full participants in the conversation even when they stand there—for whole books at a time—silent, listening. This conversation matters to them and they matter to the conversation. What effect do their characters and their ways of looking at the world have on the conversation in the *Laws*—or at least on the conversation in Book 1? How do they impede, alter or otherwise shape it?

I propose to examine this question by focusing in on two moments of high drama—or what passes for high drama—in the *Laws*.[5] The first comes early on in Book 1; it involves Cleinias and is a moment of high praise for the Athenian. The second comes at the precise center of Book 1; it involves Megillus, and is a moment of intense but indirect blame. I focus on these moments because in Platonic dialogues, as in life, basic characters and ways of looking at the world tend to come to the fore in moments of passionate engagement. Human beings show what they are made of when they are put to the test.

Let us begin with Cleinias. The scene in question unfolds thus. The Stranger asks why "the law has ordained the common meals for you all (ὑμῖν) and also the gymnastic training and the weapons you employ" (625c).[6] Cleinias is ready with an answer. He explains at some length that Cretan military (and presumably gymnastic) practices have their origin in the Cretan landscape and that those practices, as well as the practice of common meals, stem from the insight of the lawgiver that peace is just a name—that in fact by nature there exists an "undeclared war among all cities" (625c–626b). The Stranger fixes on this last point and pushes Cleinias to agree that the undeclared war of all against all that characterizes political life not only exists between village and village, household and household, man and man; it is also at work in the very souls of human beings (626b–626c). Cleinias bursts into extravagant praise:

> O Athenian Stranger—I would rather not address you as merely Attic, for you seem to me worthy of being rather called by the name of the goddess— you have correctly followed the argument up to its source and have thus made it clearer, so that you will more easily discover (aneurēseis) that we were correct just now in saying that all are enemies of all and in public and in private each is an enemy of himself. (626d)[7]

What can we learn from this scene? Notice first that although the Athenian Stranger directs his opening question at Cleinias (λέγε), he is in fact asking about practices *common* to Sparta and Crete (ὑμῖν) (625c). The Stranger had no doubt wanted, quite reasonably, to begin their common inquiry into "regime and laws" by starting with what his two Dorian companions have in common. It is *Cleinias* who leaps in and focuses exclusively on Crete. He commits an act of what might be called urbane aggression. Like a Cretan warrior he moves very fast over a lot of ground, leaving the heavy-armored, slow-moving Spartan in the dust (625d). Like a man who believes in the war of every man against every man, he moves quickly to take what he considers to be a very strong, perhaps impregnable position in the argument. In short, his manner of speaking reflects the content of his speech: he enacts his beliefs, turns his Cretan self-understanding into deed. The Athenian sees the situation clearly: right after Cleinias's speech the Stranger notes that he is well-practiced and well-gymnasticized (*kalōs gegymnasthai*), in his understanding of Cretan customs (626b).

Notice also the breezy confidence with which Cleinias introduces his account of Cretan practices. "Our things," he says to the Stranger "are in every way easy (ῥᾴδιον) to understand"—this is his opening line, and he repeats the word "easy" again near the end of his exchange with the Athenian (625c; 626d). Like so many men who think they have seen the darkness at the very heart of things, Cleinias thinks that truth can be found right there on the surface, readily available to the truly intelligent man. Nature—he uses the word twice in the space of twenty lines—may love to hide, but not from Minos and not from Cleinias either. Cleinias is absolutely sure that Minos got to the bottom of things and that he has grasped Minos's meaning in full. (A side note: In the *Minos* Socrates also speaks of discovery. He repeatedly says that law *wishes* to be the discovery of what is.[8] Cleinias, on the other hand, clearly thinks that the laws of Minos *are* the discovery of what is; they embody or encode the whole truth about human beings.) In short, Cleinias is a man in the grip of a theory, and one of the reasons he is so delighted by the Stranger's conclusion that "in private each is an enemy to himself" is that by "following the argument up to the source" the Stranger has provided him with a capstone for his all-encompassing vision of the world (626d).

But this is not the only reason for Cleinias's excitement. Cleinias is in the grip of something more than a theory. The Stranger no doubt meant, in the lines leading up to Cleinias's outburst, to bring Cleinias to recognize the absurd or at least shocking consequences of his dark vision of the world. But Cleinias embraces those consequences with a passion, and his excitement suggests that he *sees himself* in them. The Stranger has helped the old man to make sense of his life, and he is grateful. Through the Stranger's words he has seen, perhaps for the first time, the deep connection between his own inner turmoil and the outer life of his city. Cleinias is conflicted, torn, divided against himself; he is a man at war with himself, a man who thinks that "being defeated by oneself is the most shameful and at the same time the worst of all defeats" (626e). He is a man, in other words, for whom self-control requires the most ruthless self-suppression. What must Cleinias suppress? Who is the enemy within? He does not say. It could be fear, but passages later in Book 1 suggest that desire is the enemy, and still other passages suggest that the desire he must master is a form of ἔρως he would rather not admit to or discuss (636b–d; 841d–e). This makes a certain sense. For Crete is not only the land of Minos the lawgiver. It is also the land of lawless love, the land of Pasiphae and the bull—it is the land of the Minotaur.

If Cleinias is, as has just been suggested, a man ready to do battle in speech on behalf of Crete and the Cretan understanding of the world—an understanding that implies that every man is the enemy of every other—and if, moreover, he is a man divided against himself and haunted by powerful desires, it seems unlikely that he could engage or engage right away in the kind of frank, direct inquiry into political and human affairs sketched out earlier. For that sort of inquiry presupposes a certain kind of openness—not the vapid toleration of all possibilities that amounts to a form of self-closure, but an openness to the possibility that one's own ways may not be the best ways, that other human beings, even foreigners, may have something to teach one, that thought and sometimes feeling, too, can be better guides in life than mere custom or law. The Cleinias we see at the beginning of the dialogue is closed off from all these possibilities and if he is to be readied for inquiry he must be retrofitted, re-educated, turned around. We do not *see* this turning around in Book 1—there is no dramatic moment of conversion here—but everything the Athenian Stranger says and does in Book 1 is delicately calibrated to bring it about.

For example, the Stranger's defense of peace and harmony in the city and the soul is meant to show or remind Cleinias that there are political and moral possibilities that his radical interpretation of Minos has blocked from view (627e–628d). But it is also meant to shed light on *his own* situation, on the drama he is currently involved in; it is meant to convince Cleinias that, whatever the focus of the Laconian and Cretan regimes, *they,* the participants in the dialogue, need not and "should not fight harshly with one another, but should rather make calm inquiry" (629a). The Stranger's subsequent elevation of Theognis over Tyrtaios and the whole of virtue over courage, which elicits the angry response, "Stranger, we are consigning our lawgiver to a pretty low rank among lawgivers," is *meant* to elicit that response—for Cleinias must begin at some point to confront his own passionate attachment to the ways of Crete (628a–630d). And the Stranger's brilliant follow-up, his (probably false) claim that Minos as lawgiver was indeed looking to the whole of virtue and not just courage is both meant to calm Cleinias down and also to give him, at least temporarily, a new way of approaching his own regime: in order to hold on to his patriotism he must abandon his pet theory and look at Crete with fresh eyes (630e; 632d–e).

Another example of Cleinias's turning is the Athenian's strange broadening of the meaning of courage. By including in his definition of courage the enduring of pleasures the Athenian intends to take Cleinias's education one step further, up to the point where he can begin to see that his own inner conflict and pain is in fact a direct consequence of the defects in his Cretan education (633d–634b; 635c–d).[9] Even the Stranger's defense of drinking parties as a legitimate form of political education is meant to be part of Cleinias's own education in the art of inquiry, his own re-ordering of soul.

Is the education successful? Does it "take"? As was mentioned above, there is no moment in Book 1 where we see Cleinias cross a threshold, that is, no single moment where we see him pass from one state of soul to another. Still, there are signs that something has happened to him, even in the course of Book 1. The wary politeness toward the Stranger that we see early on begins to give way to friendly feeling, a friendly feeling that Cleinias himself announces publicly just before the Stranger begins his defense of drinking parties (642e–643a). Moreover, at just about the same time, Cleinias begins to display a genuine interest in matters far beyond his ken. When the Stranger offers to break off his defense of drinking as a form of education, Cleinias begs him to go on. He *wants* to hear about drinking parties and about education in general; he *wonders* about them, although he knows nothing about drinking and used to think he was very well educated. Perhaps it would be going too far to say that Cleinias's ἔρως has been redirected over the course of Book 1—but he certainly seems to have left behind his placid confidence in himself and his city.[10] Finally, we see Cleinias begin to *trust* in the Stranger's ability to navigate them through these strange waters. This is an important step since "trustworthiness in the midst of dangers is," within the terms of Book 1, a sign of the presence of whole virtue and above all prudence (630b–d). When Cleinias associated the Stranger with Athena and wisdom at the beginning of the dialogue, it was a back-handed way of asserting the superiority of his own vision of the world. Now he seems willing to attribute intelligence and prudence—the most divine of divine goods—to the Athenian Stranger (631c). In short, something approximating a genuine community of inquiry has begun to form by the end of Book 1 and Cleinias is ready to acknowledge the Stranger as its proper leader. This is progress.

What about Megillus? We left him in the dust some time ago. It is now time to bring him back into the picture. Does he, too, receive an education from the Stranger, and if he does, is it successful? All the steps of his education cannot be traced here, but the answer to both of these questions is "yes." In fact Megillus exhibits the same signs of transformation as Cleinias does: as Book 1 comes to an end, he, too, displays confidence in the Athenian Stranger's ability to lead, a willingness to be led into new territory by him, and a friendly feeling toward him. We might be tempted at first to think that Megillus is just following Cleinias's lead here—it is easy to imagine the Laconian nodding his head a lot while Cleinias speaks—but it is in fact *Megillus* who takes the lead in expressing friendly feeling toward the Stranger and in asking him to continue his account of drinking and education (642b–d). Apparently by the end of Book 1 Megillus is at least as caught up as Cleinias in the enterprise of inquiry.

How and when did this happen? It is difficult to say. Throughout much of the first half of Book 1, Megillus seems passive, unwilling to risk a thought or venture an opinion. For instance, at the point when the Stranger proposes to start over again by asking in what way Sparta and Crete promote virtue as a whole, Megillus proposes that the Stranger test Cleinias rather than himself. He evades responsibility, in spite of the efforts of the Stranger to draw him into the inquiry, forcing the Stranger to remind him that "the discussion is common to us all" (633a). If there is a turning point it seems to come at the moment alluded to earlier. Here, at the very center of Book 1, Megillus steps forward to rebuke the Stranger; only a few pages later he steps forward again to urge him to go on. Something important must have happened in the meantime.

Here is a rough outline of the scene in question. The Stranger asks what features of the Spartan and Cretan regimes promote moderation. He then uses Megillus's answer to provoke an unrestrained free-for-all in which all parties get smeared for tolerating or even promoting lack of self control: Spartans are cuckolds, Cretans are hypocritical homosexuals who use piety to disguise the unnaturalness of their activities; and the rest—including, though they are not mentioned by name, the Athenians—are drunken louts (636a–637b). Two things about this melee are especially worth noting. First, Cleinias does *not* take part in it. Although Crete and Cretan erotic practices (and hypocrisy) are the prime target of the Stranger's attack, Cleinias does not rise up—as he surely would have earlier—in defense of his regime. The Stranger deliberately confronts him with the reality of the Cretan situation, and Cleinias gets the point. His very silence reveals his movement away from Crete and toward the Athenian. Second, Megillus *does* rise up. He admits right away that words do not come easily to him and then proceeds to make his longest speech to date. He displays courage. He steps up when it matters. Megillus is a stand-up guy. If the Stranger embodies divine intelligence and Cleinias embodies desire, then Megillus is spirit or spiritedness itself: *Cleinias* may have fallen silent, but *Megillus* is still loyal to the Spartan (and Cretan) view that fleeing from pleasure is the only true source of moderation, and he is still willing to argue against the view that loss of self-control could ever be a good thing (636e–637a).

What makes him begin to change his mind? It could be the series of sober arguments that the Stranger begins to make right after this scene—for instance, the argument that customs, even the custom of drinking parties, need to be evaluated within their proper context, or the argument that communities, even drinking communities, can only be properly judged when they are correctly ruled (638e–640e). But it seems unlikely that arguments, sober or otherwise, could have much weight for Megillus in his current state. It is more likely that two other things begin to move him in the Stranger's direction.

First, the Stranger does not flinch in the face of Megillus's attack on drunks and drunkenness. On the contrary, instead of backing down he proposes something totally outrageous: to examine the whole issue of drunkenness under the rubric of education (641b–d). This takes courage. The Athenian Stranger displays an audacity and daring at least equal to Megillus's own; surely the Spartan must admire and respect this quality in him. In fact we see evidence of this admiration and respect a bit later in his display of friendly feeling toward the Athenian, when he notes that Athenian excellence is natural excellence—some Athenians can manage to be courageous even without a steady diet of black-bean soup and strenuous exercise (633b–c; 642c–d).[11]

The second enticement that draws Megillus—and Cleinias, too—in the direction of the Stranger (that is, in the direction of full-fledged inquiry) is a little harder to articulate. In a certain sense this lure has been at work since the beginning of Book 1. From the outset Cleinias and Megillus have been hearing things they have never heard before; the horizons within which they have lived for many years have expanded immeasurably.[12] The Stranger's proposed inquiry into drinking parties takes this expansion to a new level. As Cleinias himself admits, neither he nor Megillus have had experience of such communities— and we know that Megillus finds the very thought of Dionysian excess repulsive (637b; 639e–640a). To follow the Stranger's words they must stretch themselves; they must leave behind the familiar and enter a world where what was previously unthinkable—drinking and getting drunk, for example—becomes possible, where what stood still, νόμος, starts to move and change its shape, where what was self-same and stable starts to seem strange and different. If to get drunk is to endure the dissolution of differences, then as they drink in the Stranger's words at the close of Book 1, as they gradually get drawn into and become part of the Stranger's inquiry, Megillus and Cleinias get drunk. If the Stranger is to succeed, intoxication must become not only the subject of conversation but the manner of it. For truth, as we know, is a bacchanalian whirl in which no member is not drunken.

I want to conclude by returning very briefly to the other inquiry-shaping possibilities mentioned earlier: setting and subject matter. Does the *setting* of the *Laws* make a difference? Surely it must. The proper home of philosophy is Athens: in Athens everybody is a philosopher, or at least everybody's *hobby* is philosophy. The borders of Athens are porous, and life there, including intellectual life, is influenced by this very shapelessness. That is why foreigners can come to

Athens and say pretty much whatever they want to. That is why Socrates has to work so hard to get Athens to kill him: it is hard to get taken seriously in a city where everyone—or at least every man—sits around all day talking. In Athens ἔρως is free-floating; anything—almost anything—goes; ἔρως can take on almost any shape, including, sometimes, the shape of philosophy.[13]

Things are very different in Crete. In Crete ἔρως is a monster pent up in a labyrinth and it takes a stranger from Athens—a new Theseus—to thread the maze. Here talk is not cheap, strangers look strange, and all men, especially strangers, must be careful what they ask and when.[14] It *means* something to ask a question in Crete, and to get an inquiry, any kind of inquiry, going about fundamental matters is a great achievement. From the point of view of Athens—consider the *Minos*—Zeus's cave looks like a seminar room where Minos goes every ninth year for laws-workshops led by the great sophist Zeus; from the point of view of the *Laws,* the cave of Zeus is a temple where Minos goes to receive φῆμαι, oracles or revelations, concerning the laws.[15] In short, philosophy is an alien presence on Cretan soil, and the philosopher must act accordingly: in Crete the Stranger and his activity remain and must remain not only low-key, but nameless.[16]

The peculiar character of the *Laws* thus owes something to the people involved in the inquiry and something to the setting within which that inquiry takes place. But what was earlier called the murkiness or shadiness of the dialogue also owes something to its subject matter. The distinctive character of that subject matter turns up everywhere in Book 1. "Regime and laws"—from the very beginning we get a pair, one term of which is already many. The first law the Stranger asks about is already threefold, and each of the three practices he asks about—gymnastics, common meals, and weaponry—involves body and motion.[17] Some laws and practices—the ones just mentioned, for instance—turn out to serve multiple ends while others, for instance, drinking parties, change their meaning from context to context (636a). Even the apparently straightforward distinction with which the dialogue begins—god or man—is quickly transmuted into something rich and strange. The man in question—Minos—turns out to be the son of a god, while the distinction between divine and human soon becomes a distinction *within* the human, that is, a distinction between multiple divine goods, led by stable intelligence, and multiple human goods, all of which again involve motion and body (631b–d). All the other Platonic dialogues that focus explicitly on politics in some sense look away from the here and now, toward something that is single and stable. The *Republic* is or becomes a search for the *one* best regime; the *Minos* is emphatically a search for law in the singular, and the *Statesman* attempts to peel away imposters and subordinate arts to discover the *one* art and *one* activity that characterizes the statesman as states-man (313a).[18] The *Laws* is an-other kettle of fish. Here multiplicity, materiality, and mobility are the order of the day. Here we are immersed—whether we like it or not—in the tangle and flow of political life. Perhaps, then, Cleinias is say-ing more than he knows when he invites Megillus and the Stranger to "see the nature of the χώρα" in all its irregularity. For here, in Crete, we can see, we are forced to see, the ever-shifting, ever-wandering source of what's both hard to take and hard to take in, about political life.[19]

Notes

1. Rest-words appear three times in the first passage, and in the second we learn (to our surprise) that the dialogue's participants have already been relaxing in an "al-together beautiful resting place" for some time. They are at rest and in the shade while the sun is at its peak. Of course, since their destination is a cave, as Mitchell Miller and Mark Munn point out, even if they complete their journey, the old men will merely have exchanged one shady spot for another.

2. Consider, for instance, the shift from *Laws* 2 to *Laws* 3. Comments made at the end of *Laws* 2 lead us to expect a discussion of gymnastic in *Laws* 3, to complement the discussion of musical education in *Laws* 2. Instead, we get a comprehensive account of Greek history—without any explanation for the abrupt transition. Or consider the tangle of topics concerning legal matters that occupies so much of *Laws* 11 and 12. Now to be sure, Eric Sanday and Mitchell Miller do much to untangle that tangle. And in very different ways Michael Zuckert and John Sallis make sense of the place of *Laws* 3 within the *logos* of the *Laws*. In other words, it is certainly possible to gain clarity about what seems incoherent and confusing in the *Laws*. But the dialogue lacks surface clarity at al-most every stage of the inquiry.

3. Mitchell Miller notes this parallel between the *Laws* and the *Phaedrus* but also observes that what we have in the *Laws* "over and over again" is a "lack of resonance" with other Platonic texts, a deliberate disconnect. I agree. The *Phaedrus* takes place out-side the walls of a city; much of the conversation takes place in the shade of tall trees and it is at least in part about the subject of writing laws. But here the connections between the two dialogues end. In particular, ἔρως, the great theme of the first half of the *Phae-drus*, is missing from the *Laws*. Or rather ἔρως is present in the *Laws*, but not as our pos-sible pathway to the trans-uranian realm. It is instead a pinched and narrow thing that causes nothing but problems. In fact, if Francisco Gonzalez is right, ἔρως is *the* insu-perable problem in the *Laws*. (But see Mark Munn's essay for a somewhat different view of the place of ἔρως in the *Laws*.)

4. See *Parmenides* 130b–e. Note in particular the response of old Parmenides to young Socrates at 130e.

5. In the Socratic dialogues Socrates' own sense of irony is often palpable, the thrust and parry of dialectic is everywhere evident, and outbursts and open threats are fairly regular occurrences. (Consider Socrates' encounters with Thrasymachus, Polus, Callicles, Anytus, and so on.) The atmosphere of the *Laws* is very different. Dialectical

passages are hard to find, outbursts are rare, the dialogue's tone is generally muted, and it is often hard to gauge how much praise or blame is concealed behind a given character's response. Archness and urbanity are the order of the day, as one might expect in a conversation between older men, two of whom are strangers in a strange land.

6. Here and in what follows quotations are generally taken from the translation of Pangle 1980.

7. Cleinias uses the same language of discovery a little earlier to characterize the first principle of Minoan legislation: "If you look at it this way, you are pretty sure to find (σχεδὸν ἀνευρήσεις) that the lawgiver of the Cretans established all our customs, public and private, with a view to (ἀποβλέπων) war. . . .)" (Pangle translation; 626a5–7). Incidentally ἀπο-βλέπειν is the verb Socrates often uses to invite his interlocutors to "look away" to some form. This is precisely *not* the looking that Minos engaged in, another sign that the orientation of this dialogue is different from most others—its gaze is horizontal rather than vertical. Hence, I suspect, the relentless sobriety of the dialogue, the dead-serious tone that David Roochnik highlights and accounts for in his playfully serious essay.

8. See especially *Minos* 315a7–2: "Now law (νόμος) wishes to be nothing less than a discovery (ἐξεύρεσις) of what is...but [human beings] are not always able to discover what the law wishes [to discover], namely, what is (τὸ ὄν)."

9. Strange, that is, until we see that the Athenian Stranger is still working with Cleinias's ingrained belief that courage is *the* virtue: if he can persuade Cleinias to see that what Aristotle calls continence is a part of virtue, it would aid in his understanding that real moderation is a genuine human possibility (628c–d).

10. I agree with Catherine Zuckert that the conversation in the *Laws* is at best "quasi-philosophical." Cleinias and Megillus are too ignorant of philosophy and perhaps too caught up in "mortal nature" to make their way very far along that path. On the other hand, they manage to remain involved in a very long conversation—think of Cephalus's hasty retreat—and, as Catherine Zuckert again points out, by the end of the dialogue the two old Dorians are trying to get their natural enemy to remain in Crete for the founding of the new city.

11. For more about the Spartan diet, gymnastic practices, and way of life generally, see Plutarch's *Life of Lycurgus*. Here we also get the suggestion that Spartan practices were borrowed, at least in part, from Crete.

12. Even the opening question of the dialogue—Are the laws of divine or human origin?—is one they have probably never asked themselves in a serious way before. At any rate, in the space of less than ten lines Cleinias, without blinking, concedes both alternatives.

13. I exaggerate, of course. But see Socrates' description of democracy and the democratic man in *Republic* 8 (especially 557b–d and 561b–d) and consider the free-wheeling conversations we see Socrates (and the Eleatic Stranger) engaged in everywhere in the dialogues, including the *Republic*. Note also the absence of any mention of philosophy in the Athenian Stranger's description of Athenian democracy in *Laws* 3 (693d; 700d–701c).

14. True, there is a Cretan law that apparently allows old men to discuss the laws (and forbids the young to do so) (634d–e). But the constraints on those discussions are severe—a magistrate must be present—and certainly no mention is made of permit-

ting foreigners to take part in them. No wonder the conversation in the *Laws* has to take place outside the walls of the city! The contrast with the *Republic* is instructive: here we have a conversation sharply critical of democracy and well-attended by foreigners that not only allows the young to participate but can only get started once old man Cephalus is out of the way.

15. *Minos* 319c–320b; *Laws* 624b.

16. As Catherine Zuckert points out, philosophy is mentioned only twice in the *Laws* and in neither case is the reference to the Stranger or his activity explicit.

17. I see a connection between this issue and something Mitchell Miller observes, namely, that the mathematical education of even the few in this city stops with astronomy. In the *Republic* the study of music—ratios and proportions among numbers—completes the study of the guardians and prepares the way for dialectic and the study of the Good (530d–531e); even astronomy proves to be an exceedingly pure study (528e–530b). Here in the *Laws*, by contrast, astronomy is emphatically a study of actual bodies in motion, and if Michael Zuckert is right, the god sought is not the Good but its image, the sun. Notice also that the city the old men found in speech is organized astronomically—as is their own walk (745b–e; 771a–b). It is as if, from the perspective of the *Laws*, participation in the orderly motion of heavenly bodies were the highest object of human aspiration. On this last point see *Timaeus* 35a–37c and 43b–44b; also Ptolemy's *Almagest*, 1.1.

18. *Minos* 313a–b; *Statesman* 268c.

19. *Timaeus* 48e–53c. For more on the χώρα see Sallis 1999. Sallis observes that χώρα, which turns up with "incomparable frequency" in the *Laws*, generally means something like land, country, or place (116–117). (See also Mark Munn's discussion of χώρα.) I don't disagree. But I wonder if the very frequency with which the term is used and the presence of suggestive phrases like the one just cited are meant to signal, perhaps especially to readers of the *Timaeus*, that "the χώρα of philosophy" is present everywhere in the argument and action of the *Laws*, disturbing every attempt to achieve clarity about its subject matter and—as in the *Timaeus*—forcing the Stranger to make new beginning after new beginning.

4   Education in Plato's *Laws*

John Russon

The basic story of Book 2 of Plato's *Laws* is easy enough to tell. The Athenian Stranger, who is discussing the establishment of a good state with Cleinias the Knossian and Megillus the Spartan, argues for the primary importance of education and discusses the importance of song and dance in this context.[1] Specifically, he maintains that children will have their adult perspectives formed through their early experiences of pleasure and pain, and that good education primarily involves training children to align their experiences of pleasure and pain with what wise adults would in fact recognize to be noble and ignoble behaviors respectively. Since children are playful by nature, it is through controlling their play that this education will be accomplished. Games, songs, and dances in particular are the structured forms of play in which children will participate in order to become educated into good citizenship (2.659e).[2] The communal experience of song and dance, which is the focus of Book 2, will primarily be enacted through three choruses—a children's chorus, led by the muses, a young men's chorus led by Apollo, and a Dionysian chorus of adults, including especially old men (2.664c–d). It is the oldest men who, being wisest, will appreciate what the children should learn, and it is their insights—which should be the equivalent of the needs of virtue—that will determine the implicit content of the songs, dances, and games learned by the children (2.659d; 7.797a). The message being communicated will mostly express the importance of maintaining the existing social order, and its central message (its "noble lie," so to speak—2.663d–e) will be the unity of justice and happiness (2.664b; also, 660e).

This manifest story produces an account of education that is in fact quite repressive. The story, however, has a variety of conflicts and tensions within it, and by pursuing some of the threads of these conflicts we can find another story of education lurking within the dialogue, another story, that is, that would elude our grasp (a common theme in the text) if we did not in our reading of Plato follow the method of "attending to the small" that is identified by the

Athenian Stranger (10.902c–d) as the method of experts.[3] I will follow out three conflicts that emerge in and from Book 2. First, I will look at a way in which the norms of victory and play are both distinguished and conflated by the Athenian Stranger; this (in conjunction with the hierarchy of the ten kinds of motion from 10.893–894) will allow us to develop from the conception of play that the Athenian Stranger introduces a more liberating conception than he himself develops. Second (drawing on the account of childhood education in Book 7 that is coordinated with the account in Book 2, and also on the argument for the importance of drunkenness in Book 1), I will look at the problematic way opposition is removed from the child's education, and consider the implications of the educational embrace of opposition that the Athenian Stranger's account elsewhere implies. Third, I will consider two ways in which the Athenian Stranger's account of education seems to ignore the lesson of his own account of equality in Book 6 (775b). Specifically, his imposing of adult goals on children and his emphasis on the rigid mathematical uniformity of education ignore the proportional character of true equality. By highlighting these conflicts embedded in Book 2, we will see the potential for a more open conception of freedom and human development—a notion, I conclude, that is defined by openness to transformation through hospitality to the strange.

I. Education and Play

A. The Limits of Victory

Early in Book 1, the Athenian Stranger introduces a challenge to the Cretan and Spartan legal systems. Cleinias has acknowledged that the entirety of the Cretan system is based on the goal of victory in war: "it appears," he says, "that our lawgiver had this in mind in everything he did" (1.625e).[4] Further, he acknowledges that this goal does not just pertain to relations between states (which we typically imagine to be the domain of war), but also in relations between villages, between households, between men, and, indeed, between man and himself (1.626b–d). The Athenian Stranger challenges this conception of the goal of human relations.

To the Cretan view of the primacy of war expressed by Cleinias, the Athenian Stranger opposes a view of the primacy of peace [εἰρήνη] and reconciliation [διαλλαγή, 1.628ab].[5] He describes the Cretan view as oriented solely to the virtue of courage, and to this he opposes a view oriented to the whole of virtue (1.630b, 630e–631a). This challenge also amounts to a challenge to the norm of competitive victory that is implied in the Cretan presumption of the primacy of combat. This superseding of the norm of victory in battle can be seen most clearly in the discussion of the best judge: in a contest between brothers opposed to each other, the best judge by far [μακρῷ ἀμείνων γίγνοιτ' ἂν ὁ τοιοῦτος δικαστής τε καὶ νομοθέτης], Cleinias and the Athenian Stranger agree, would be neither the judge who destroys the wicked ones, nor the judge who makes the wicked submit to the better ones, but the one who "destroying no one, reconciles them . . . and secures their friendship for one another" (1.628a).[6] In discussion of this, friendship (φιλία) is explicitly opposed to victory (νίκη) (1.628b). Indeed, shortly after this discussion, the Athenian Stranger explicitly notes that "victory in battle is a controversial [ἀμφισβητήσιμον] criterion" for superiority, because victory can come for reasons other than nobility (such as superior force or luck) (1.638a). Indeed, though education can bring victory, "victory can sometimes bring loss of education—we become insolent [hubristic] through victory" (1.641c). For this reason the Athenian Stranger says, "let's leave aside talk of victory and defeat" (1.638b) and instead recommends showing how something is or is not noble.[7]

What are the Athenian Stranger's core reasons for rejecting the norm of victory for matters of nobility? First, victory aims at destruction or domination of one party rather than reconciliation. Second, victory does not itself reflect superiority in virtue or nobility, but can be a simple reflection of force or luck. Third, victory can itself induce hubris.[8] We can also recognize the insufficiency of this criterion if we consider that to which it is opposed. In place of the love of victory (often spoken of abusively in later parts of the dialogue—e.g., 7.796a), true virtue—which is "gentle" and "soft" (1.645a) rather than forceful—offers "trustworthiness (πιστότης) in the face of the awe-inspiring (δεινοῖς)" (1.630c). I will delay a bit before endeavoring to bring out the significance of this opposition.

Despite his own exhortation to eschew talk of victory, the Athenian Stranger regularly relies on it and its attendant (ant)agonistic model of combat and conquest is his analyses. This practice is evident already in Book 1, for example, when courage is described as a victory over cowardice and moderation as fighting with pleasures (1.647c-d). This problem is more pronounced in the text that is my central focus, the discussion of education in Book 2.

B. Play

Book 2 (653d–654a) begins with an account of children, an account with which the Stranger and his interlocutors seem to agree (654a–c), and which is reiterated later in the book (673c–d). "Each young thing," the Athenian Stranger says, is incapable of remaining calm in body or in voice, but always seeks to move and cry: young things leap and jump as if they were dancing with pleasure and playing together, and emit all sorts of cries. (653d–e)

Childhood here is associated with spontaneity of expression, a spontaneous bodily motion and vocalizing that is communal and pleasant. These behaviors are here called "playing" [προσπαίζοντα], and the language of play is used again when this account is re-invoked at the end of Book 2:

[T]he source of this play [παιδίας] is once again the fact that every living being is by nature accustomed to jumping, and that humankind . . . thus engendered and gave birth to dance. When song recalled and awakened rhythm, the two in common gave birth to the chorus and to play. (673cd; also reiterated at 664e–665a and 672a–d)

"Play" names the activity of spontaneous expression that is characteristic of children (and other young animals). The Stranger later refers to play as "something [that] doesn't do any harm or any benefit worthy of serious consideration" (667e), and the basic sense of this fits the description of childhood activity: the child's jumping or crying is not *work,* not an effort expended in service of accomplishing some independently defined objective, but is pointless with reference to anything outside itself, any "serious consideration."

Though this play is pointless in the sense that it does not answer to any alien standard, it is not, for that reason, meaningless or arbitrary.[9] In his initial discussion of childhood spontaneity, the Stranger says,

The other animals . . . lack perception of orders and disorders in motions (the orders which have received the names of "rhythm" and "harmony"); we, in contrast, have been given the aforementioned gods [i.e., the Muses, Apollo, and Dionysus] as fellow-dancers, and they have given us the pleasant perception [αἴσθησιν μεθ' ἡδονῆς] of rhythm and harmony. Using this they move us. (653e–654a; cf. 673d)

We have, in short, an innate perception of rhythm and harmony.[10] Even as children, then, we are naturally discriminating, and our movements have meaning and order. This "meaning and order" is not, however, an answering to a "serious consideration"; that is, it is not answering to some rule set up by others and imposed upon us. It is, rather, a meaningfulness and order that spontaneously emerges within our experience. Our cries, too, are not meaningless or random but are, we find out later in Book 7, expressions of our feelings; that is, they are communicative, and communicative of a meaning spontaneously emerging within the child:

[E]very newborn animal customarily gives forth cries from the moment it's born, and this applies not least to humankind. . . . Babies make manifest what they love and hate through their tears and cries. (791e–792a)

In both the movement and the vocalizing of the child, then—both in deed and in word, we might say—we can see an organization and meaning. This order, though, is not defined elsewhere and imposed upon the child; rather, these activities are self-organizing. Finally, this self-organizing is again explicitly remarked by the Athenian Stranger when he discusses childhood games. There is no need, he says, to design games for them, because "the games," he says, "for children of this age spring up naturally, mostly discovered by the children themselves when they get together [παιδιαὶ δ' εἰσὶν τοῖς τηλικούτοις αὐτοφυεῖς τινες, ἃς ἐπειδὰν συνέλθωσιν αὐτοὶ σχεδὸν ἀνευρίσκουσι]" (794a). In the game, that is, we see the spontaneous emergence of a social order—a self-organizing community—and this is itself exemplary of the more general situation, namely, that it is natural (αὐτοφυεῖς) to children to organize themselves spontaneously into ordered, meaningful, and communicative social relationships and, indeed, to take pleasure in doing so.[11]

The Athenian Stranger had initially objected to the norm of "victory" in talking about human development, and in the notion of play we have an alternative model, namely, the model of natural growth or spontaneous self-organization. At the very beginning of Book 1, we have a striking celebration of this exact notion, this time from Megillus, the Spartan, speaking on behalf of the unique virtue of the Athenians:

I believe that . . . those Athenians who are good are good in a different way. They alone are good by their own nature without compulsion (ἄνευ ἀνάγκης αὐτοφυῶς), by a divine dispensation: they are truly, and not artificially, good. (642c–d)

Here very succinctly we have a statement of the opposition of nature and compulsion with the affirmation that the true good emerges naturally, as opposed to the merely artificial. This opposition resonates as well with the discussion of the ten kinds of motion in Book 10 (893b–895b), in which it is concluded that a reality moved by another is always dependent upon a more fundamental reality—soul (896a)—that moves itself, suggesting that the natural will always be prior and superior to the artificial. The quotation from Megillus also equates "doing something by one's own nature" with acting "by divine dispensation," a theme that again resonates with the story of the children, whose natural perception of rhythm is also called "being led by a god."[12] We will turn to this notion of divine inspiration shortly, but first, let us consider how the conversation between the Athenian Stranger and his interlocutors develops and, specifically, how they fail to follow the norm of "play," reverting constantly to the norm of "victory" in their educational proposals.

C. Education as Victory

Despite thus explicitly recognizing children's activity to be naturally self-organizing, the Athenian Stranger portrays the child as needing to be "reined in" and subjected to external force:

> [T]he child is the hardest to handle of all beasts, because insofar as it has within it, to a high degree, a not yet disciplined source of thought, it becomes treacherous, sharp, and the most insolent of beasts. That's why it's necessary to fetter it with many sorts of bridles, as it were. (7.808d–e)

Contrary to the celebration of natural self-development over compulsion and artificiality, and contrary to the thrice iterated emphasis on the spontaneous self-disciplining of children's behavior, (and, indeed, despite two suggestions in Book 2 that the child is easy to lead and teach [663e–664a, and cf. 671c]), the Stranger here seems to construe education more on a model of "breaking" horses than on the model of encouraging natural self-development. Indeed, after initially stressing powerfully in Book 2 that encouraging children to play freely will lead to their natural embrace of community and order, in Book 7 the Athenian Stranger is now arguing that the natural state of children—here called "undisciplined"—implies that the child *should be punished like a slave* (see 793e, 808a, e). Here, the natural is equated with the bad, and force is being used to win out over the bad—to suppress the natural—and impose a shape upon it. This is the prescription for dealing with the emotional life of children—what they spontaneously express in their cries—where "a motion brought from without [continuous rocking day and night (790c)] overpowers . . . a mad motion within, and, having overpowered it, makes a calm stillness appear in the soul" (791a), and this is compared with a process of "curing" frenzied Bacchic revelers that "replaces our mad dispositions with prudent habits" (791b). Exemplary for this forceful imposition of alien forms on the playful soul of the child is the Egyptian program of a rigidly enforced code of bodily posture, remarked in Book 2 as an excellent code (656d–e). The Egyptians are also noted in Book 7 as excellent pedagogues for their *use* of play, not as a *source* of education but as a "charm" to make studies in the formal, rigid science of mathematics more "palatable" (819b–c). In general, this is the tone of the entire educational program, using force to break the child of its natural attachments and tendencies and to construct an artificial "discipline" in the soul of the child, using play only as a deceptive, motivational adornment to lead the child along (Book 2, 660a).

What is striking in these passages is that the non-answerability of play to external standards is no longer recognized as autonomously self-disciplining, but is now judged by those very external standards it was supposed to have eschewed, in relation to which it now appears undisciplined.[13] In general, education is now understood as a contest between culture and nature in which the goal is the victory of culture over nature. What the Athenian Stranger says about their arguments about the impious in Book 10 captures this sense nicely (though the context of the remark is narrower than this larger point):

> [These arguments] were spoken, at any rate, rather vehemently somehow, on account of a fondness for victory over bad human beings. The reason, dear Cleinias, why they were animated by a fondness for victory was a concern lest the bad should believe that if they ever were stronger in arguments, they could act in the ways they wish, according to the sorts of notions they have about gods. It's on account of these things that an eagerness of spirit has prompted us to speak with youthful vigor; but if we've made some brief contribution to persuading the men in some sense to hate themselves, and to desire somehow the opposite dispositions, the prelude to the laws about impiety would have been spoken by us in a noble way. (907b–d)

Here the Stranger and his interlocutors have been aiming to achieve victory over "the bad," and to make them "hate themselves."[14] Similarly, the educational program they are designing is an attempt to stifle the nature of the child, and to induce in the child what can only be an attitude of self-hating. This is very far from the method of the good judge of Book 1, who aims at neither destruction nor submission, but at the peaceful friendship between those who were otherwise opposed. Indeed, what this indicates is that the Athenian Stranger has not, in fact, offered an educational model different from the Cretan or the Spartan, but has instead simply reproduced that same repressive, militaristic, and artificial regime in a new guise. The norm of reconciliation that they betray, however, can suggest to us a conception of education different in principle from that which the Athenian Stranger and his interlocutors entertain. Whereas nature and culture are set in opposition in the account of education that these speakers develop, we can conclude, on the contrary, that culture should be understood as that to which we naturally aspire—that toward which our ἔρως is naturally disposed to develop. (See 1.643d; compare 3.690c, "the natural rule exercised by law over willing subjects, without violence.")

I will not further develop this particular insight about the relation of nature and culture, but I do want to supplement it by returning to a neglected dimension in our earlier quotations, namely, the relation between the natural and the divine. In the quotations about the child that have been our central concern, we discerned the child's natural openness to rhythm and so on. We noted, though, that the Athenian also describes this natural grasp of rhythm as being "moved by the gods" (2.654a). Similarly, in Megillus's praise of Athenian goodness, he describes the Athenians as being both good by their own nature and good by a divine dispensation (1.642d). I want to note here simply the complexity to the notion of "own" here. On the one hand, the natural motion of the young soul— playing—is a self-motion rather than an imposed motion; on the other hand, though, this motion is a reception of the divine, which, inasmuch as it is received, is not identical with the child's soul *simpliciter*. What this points to is the strange proximity of the divine: inasmuch as it is "own" to the soul, it is not alien—this is its proximity; but inasmuch as it leads, it is outside the scope of the soul—this is its strangeness. The god would thus seem to be a stranger, but a stranger who defines what is most intimate to one. Play is the child's welcoming of this stranger, the enacting of its most intimate natural reality in making itself open to the spontaneous emergence within it of an order or form it did not create. This means, first, that the child is thus naturally open, a point reinforced in the recognition that children are easily persuaded (2.663e–664a). It also means, second, that it is children's play that naturally enacts the relation the Athenian Stranger identifies as characterizing the true law-giver (1.624a; 4.713e, cf. 709a–c).

II. Education and Opposition

In our first section, we saw an introduction of opposition into a situation in which opposition should not be operative: spontaneous, self-organizing play was wrongly understood as agonistic competition. We will now see how, in the actual account of education, opposition is forcibly removed where its presence should naturally emerge. Let us begin by simply noting some situations of the removal of opposition.

In Book 7, there is a substantial and shocking discussion of the important role of nurses. We already noticed in passing that nurses were to be rocking babies non-stop, day and night to suppress the "mad motions within" their souls (790c–791a). In that same discussion, and in accordance with the requirement that children develop "the straightest possible posture from youngest infancy" (788d), the Athenian Stranger specifies that the nurses are to hold babies all the time until they are three years old, so that the children will not risk damaging themselves through walking:

> Shall we compel nurses, by legal penalties, to somehow carry the children about continually ... until the babies have become capable of standing, and even then to be very careful lest the children, being still young, should distort their limbs by somehow putting too much weight on them? Shall we command the nurses to keep carrying the children until they've reached the age of three? (789e)

In the very situation in which the children, who, like colts, would naturally be inclined toward constant motion and, indeed, dancing, the Athenian Stranger prescribes a complete and forceful suppression of that natural bodily activity, aiming for stillness and secure self-reserve, rather than movement in engagement with the alien world of space and, indeed, with the alien world of one's own limbs.[15]

This steering clear of the embrace of opposition is also seen in the discussion of studies in music, in which the musical curriculum is simplified by the removal of any polyphony, melodic variation or variation in tempo or rhythm. This is prescribed on the grounds that "[t]hings that contradict one another are disturbing, and produce difficulty in learning" (812e). And even more clearly still, the removal of opposition is in fact to be an *end* and not just a *means* of education, in that in education any opposition between right and left is to be effaced in favor of ambidexterity (794d–795d), men and women are as far as possible to be educated equally (6.781b; 7.804d–e, 805c–d, 806c), (though, strikingly, the Athenian Stranger insists on aggressively retaining the natural opposition of man and woman in matters of ἔρως [1.636b–d; 7.836c]), and, again, as far as possible, life is to be lived without regard to the opposition between day and night (7.808b; cf. 790c). In short, then, the method and object of education seems strongly to be oriented toward the evading or removing of opposition, (and, indeed, the removal of nature).[16]

As a method, however, the evading or removal of opposition seems directly opposed to the initial arguments introduced by the Athenian Stranger regarding education. In general, the central thrust of Book 1 was to argue that no one could be well educated in courage without learning to deal with both pleasure and pain, and the argument was that the one-sided Cretan and Spartan education was wrong for not making students learn to deal with that to which they are opposed (namely, pleasure) (see, e.g., 1.634a–b). Again, after Cleinias initially affirms the superiority of giving a child the educational path that is most free of suffering, the Athenian Stranger challenges him, ultimately winning his assent to the idea that it is pedagogically desirable to work through difficulties (7.792b–793a). Again, in the discussion of comedy, the Athenian Stranger remarks that "someone who is going to become prudent can't learn the serious things without learning the laughable, or, for that matter, anything without its opposite" (7.816de).

All these remarks effectively reconfirm again the principle already announced in Book 1, namely, that the good judge produces a result that reconciles opposed sides, rather than eliminating the opposition. If we reconsider the case of childhood walking, we can see the direct relevance of the story of the judge to matters of education. To learn to walk is to engage actively with that to which one is initially opposed: the spatial environment is pointedly *not* the body and, indeed, it is a sort of opponent in that contact with it can be painful (as is discovered through falling, bumping, scraping, or even falling asleep on a rough surface). In actually learning to walk, the child learns to cooperate with this oppositional environment, rather than to fight against it. Further, in establishing this relationship in which the two former opponents—body and earth—are reconciled, a new order of powers emerges for the child, powers unanticipatable in the terms of its earlier bodily relationship to the world. And, in this new, and newly powerful, relationship, the very character of the child's own body is changed for the child: the child comes to inhabit its own body in a new way, releasing its latent power only in and by developing a reconciled relationship to the spatial environment that was formerly its opponent. In the example of walking, then, we have an exemplary case of learning as precisely the incorporation of opposition.[17] We can see a similar structure in the Athenian Stranger's discussion of critique as a gentle remedy rather than an assault (1.635b, 634c). If we are open to reason and to truth, challenges to our beliefs are not enactments of antagonism, but are welcome opportunities precisely for learning and growth.

These examples of learning through opposition also reveal that learning is inherently risky. Inasmuch as one is engaging with that to which one is opposed, one has the hope of developing a new relationship only by entering into relationship with that which is still currently an opponent. The child can, indeed, damage its body through a fall, and criticism, even if well-intentioned, can be more than one can take, resulting in a crippling of one's self-esteem. An education that makes security primary, however, evades this risk only by eliminating the real possibility of growth.

And, finally, let us note again what we saw at the end of section 1: the new, reconciled situation into which one grows cannot be anticipated in the terms from which which one is growing. Education, therefore, inherently depends on an openness to the new. Through critique one discovers the view one had not anticipated, but one now recognizes it as one's own. In the case of the child learning to walk, the new relationship releases to the child a natural form within its behavior that it could not otherwise imagine. Here again we see the "strange proximity" we spoke of earlier. In embracing the strange, in being open to what it cannot anticipate, the child discovers its own native powers, and the one criticized discovers her or his own natural beliefs.[18]

III. Education and Difference

I want to end, now, with a brief articulation of a further problem with the educational program outlined by the Athenian Stranger, a further way in which his proposals seem to violate his principles. Most simply, the Athenian Stranger seems to confuse the appropriate use of mathematical and proportional equality.

In Book 6, the Athenian Stranger distinguishes between two types of equality (757b–d). There is a familiar kind of equality which amounts to a distribution of quantitatively identical parts. If, however, the parties to whom the distribution is being made are themselves of unequal worth, the shares will not be equal to the participants. Political justice, therefore, calls for a distribution in which shares are equal to the worth of the members, which is an equality of proportion (757c). "It is for this," the Athenian Stranger says, "that we should now strive, and to this equality that we should now look, Cleinias, to found the city that is now growing" (757d).

It is striking that in the educational regime outlined in Book 7, education, on the contrary, is based entirely on a non-proportional equality. The prescriptions of the educational system are utterly uniform for all students, specifying, for example, that, all students will study written things for three years starting at age ten, and lyre-playing for three years, starting at age thirteen (809e), and that,

> [n]either for the father nor for the child himself, whether he be a lover or a hater, will it be permissible to prolong or shorten, with more or less time, this lawful period of study. (810a)

This rigidity makes no allowance for differences in aptitude or interest—again, an overriding of any natural difference—aiming to produce a uniform result (just as it would be best to have all sing with one voice the same song, best if all called the same things dear). Even if such uniformity were desirable— and surely it is not—the Athenian Stranger's claims about proportional equality should already have led him to realize that this method could not produce such uniformity. Indeed, he himself recognizes that not all will learn to write with equal speed and beauty (810b).[19]

Finally, it is also a striking feature of the *Laws* that the old men are the ones who set the terms for children's play.[20] In Book 2 the Athenian Stranger maintains that the pleasure and satisfaction the old receive from hearing Homer recited is truer than the pleasure and satisfaction that children receive from watching puppet shows or that middle-aged men receive from watching tragedies performed. In Book 7 the Athenian Stranger maintains that the philosophical argument he, Cleinias, and Megillus have been making is the most suitable story for children to be told.[21] Both of these arguments seem to me again to have missed the point of proportional equality. The pleasures of puppetry are proper to children as the pleasures of Homer are proper to old men: there is not a single pleasure that is best *simpliciter,* but, instead, pleasures are distributed appropriately, and are always "pleasures for . . . ," that is, pleasures defined in relationship to a specific nature. This is true both for matters of form—puppetry, tragedy, etc.—and for matters of content; that is, it is not the case that translating the old man's story into a children's format would be an appropriate children's story. It is not the case that Homer is inherently better than puppets—it is rather that Homer speaks to the needs of an older person's perspective, while puppets speak to the needs of a child's perspective.

In short, the principle of proportional equality points to the need to respect the autonomy of different ages and different perspectives, and also to the need to offer a flexible educational system, responsive to the different needs, interests, and abilities of those who would be educated. Just as openness is required for the child to be educated, so is openness required if the educational system is to be educating.[22]

Conclusion

This emphasis on openness and responsiveness points to an educational system that can never have a finally fixed form.[23] Partially, the system must be responsive to the different needs of its different students. Even more importantly, though, the system must be open to the newness that naturally emerges through any real process of education. The power behind education, and, indeed, its very *raison d'être* for education, will always be found in our φύσις, our spontaneous power of self-emergence; though learning answers to our nature, it is also (and definitively) the case that through learning we come to identify with what we could not anticipate, and therefore we ourselves will be changed through education. Our educational systems must themselves change to respond to such unanticipated developments.[24]

Educational systems will always have to propel students into alien domains—domains that do not simply "come naturally" to the child—and educational systems will always have to be instituted in one determinate way or another. Education, therefore, can never be simply a matter of passively "letting nature happen," and educational systems will therefore always be (rightly) imposing artificiality and uniformity on playful, spontaneous natures to which such systems do not fully fit.[25] For this reason, educational systems will only ever be "controversial" in the sense defined in Book 1, because they will always be enforcing a determinate stance whose significance as helpful or hindering cannot be adequately settled by the terms of the system alone, but must be determined, rather, by how they do or do not fit with the dynamic and varied natures of those who participate in these institutions. Education will thus always involve a significant degree of opposition and risk for students, and it is therefore incumbent upon those systems to be committed to self-transformation and innovation. For both the student and the educational system, the norm must be that which the Athenian Stranger identifies with true justice: rather than being governed by matters of force and fear, they must encounter the future with an awe toward its revelatory power.[26]

Notes

1. For the significance of this dramatic context for interpreting the dialogue, see especially the contributions to this volume of Eric Salem and Catherine Zuckert.

2. See *Laws* 7, 800a. On the reality behind the idea that Greek cultural education was accomplished through song and dance, see Herington 1985; Calame 2001; Nagy 1994, chap. 13. See also Ostwald 1969.

3. The issue of proper method is raised in *Laws* 1 at 638b, 638e.

4. All translations are from Pangle 1980.

5. On the problem of "victory" as a criterion, see the discussion of the "tyrannical" use of force that lies behind law in Laks 1990, esp. 222.

6. He does this by "laying down laws." See Seth Benardete's discussion of this conversation in Benardete 2000a, 14–16. Benardete argues that the notion of peaceful reconciliation can equally be the notion of watered-down compromise.

7. Compare *Laws* 1, 643e–644a: an education that aims at strength, rather than ruling and being ruled with justice is "vulgar, illiberal, and unworthy to be called education."

8. This consequence connects with the sense of "ἀμφισβητήσιμον"—controversial—as it is initially introduced at 636a, where a measure is called controversial because it can harm as well as help.

9. Contrast the "useless love of victory" in *Laws* 7 at 796a.

10. Compare Aristotle, *Posterior Analytics* 2.19, on the "σύμφυτον κριτικὴν δύναμιν." On the importance of the theme of the innate musicality of children, see Laks 1990, 227–228. I have taken up this theme in Russon 2009, especially in chapter 1. These passages from the *Laws* are of paramount importance for interpreting the theme of ἀνάμνησις in the Platonic dialogues.

11. Compare Dewey 1997, chapter 4, "Social Control."

12. This phrase in the quotation from Megillus is excised by Valckenaer.

13. Compare *Laws* 2, 672a–d, where the non-answerability of play is closely associated with the greatest good bestowed by Dionysus, which is the awe [αἰδώς] in the soul that comes from wine.

14. Note that the speakers themselves rely on "youthful vigor."

15. Benardete offers an insightful discussion of this program of upbringing in Benardete 2000a, 190–195.

16. Ibid., 196–198.

17. Compare Benardete's example of the beautiful and strong body, ibid., 16.

18. See Benardete, ibid., 76.

19. As David Roochnik rightly notes in his discussion of *Laws* 7 in his contribution to this volume, there is something absurd about trying to legislate, as Roochnik puts it, "how many rocks per minute a baby should receive." There is a certain "comic" aspect to the Athenian's law-making—and perhaps, thus, to human law-making in general—inasmuch as it seems to live in denial of this absurdity, trying to substitute its "rational" planning for the rationality that is the self-developing nature of things themselves (see *Laws* 7, 822d–e). The failure of the Athenian Stranger and his interlocutors to recognize this absurdity sufficiently leads to their establishing of a repressive regime of laws. On the other hand, Socrates' remark in *Republic* 4 (425a–b) to the effect that laws surrounding social propriety are not necessary for "gentlemen" demonstrates an opposite and complementary failure to recognize that the forms of developed human relations are not simply "natural," and it is from this fact that the necessity for the forceful intervention of law could be established. See also Catherine Zuckert's discussion, in her contribution to this volume, of the impossibility that the law fully form persons, and Eric Sanday's discussion, in his contribution to this volume, of the idea that the lawmaker's project cannot fail to fail.

20. Noted by Diskin Clay, in Clay 2000, 276. The whole of Clay's contrasting of the *Laws* and the *Republic* (271–277) is worthwhile reading. For a powerful contrast of the political positions of the *Laws* and the *Republic*, see Zuckert 2004. See also Laks 1990.

21. *Laws* 7, 811c–d, but see Roochnik's discussion of this passage at the end of his contribution to this volume for the possible ambivalence of this passage.

22. Clay 2000 (277–278) notes that, unlike the *Republic* for which it is a central issue, the *Laws* pays no attention to the theme of the education of the philosopher. ("Philosophizing" is mentioned only twice in the dialogue, at 857d and 967c, a point discussed prominently in Catherine Zuckert's contribution to this volume.) Perhaps a conversation oriented more toward the educational conditions that would allow for the arising of a philosopher would have produced a different vision of childhood education than this conversation that is oriented significantly toward the conditions that produce obedient perpetuators of tradition. Clay writes: "It is remarkable that philosophy enters the dia-

logue from an alien culture of the poets, the sophists, and the materialists so well known to Athens. In addressing the young atheist, the Athenian Stranger seems to be speaking not in the new colony of Magnesia but in his own native city. The atheists of Magnesia will be taken care of by the Nocturnal Council proposed in *Laws* 12. The members of this council belong, unlike other Magnesians, to the world outside the island of Crete" (278). Compare Zuckert 2004, 389, 393–394, and her contribution to this volume in general. See also the brief discussion by Despland 1985, 195.

23. Compare Patricia Fagan's contribution to this volume, regarding the way in which the regime in the *Laws* is built upon the premise that "what comes from outside can only be harmful to us," and in general regarding the theme of "openness to the divine." Compare also Eric Salem's contribution to this volume, regarding the xenophobia of the Cretan society that provides the dramatic setting for this dialogue.

24. Eric Sanday, in his contribution to this volume, makes a comparable point about laws overall, when he argues that the "finishing" of laws can only be enacted as an ongoing part of life within the laws.

25. For a rich and insightful discussion of these themes in the context of contemporary philosophy of education, see Dewey 1997, chapter 1, "Traditional vs. Progressive Education," and 1944, chapter 6, "Education as Conservative and Progressive." I have discussed related issues in Russon 2003, chapter 6.

26. See *Laws* 1, 630c: "πιστότης ἐν τοῖς δεινοῖς"; compare *Laws* 1, 644c–d, 647b; *Laws* 2, 671d. I am grateful to Catherine Zuckert, Michael Zuckert, and the Liberty Fund for the invitation to the seminar on the *Laws* in which the ideas behind this paper were first developed.

5 On Beginning after the Beginning

John Sallis

Almost always, it seems, one begins after the beginning. So it is with Socrates when, in the *Phaedo,* he tells of launching a second sailing, as sailors, in the absence of wind to fill their sails, take to the oars. What prompted Socrates was the recurrent failure of his efforts to grasp things directly and the consequent entanglement in intractable aporias. Thus finally, as he explains, he turned away from things, forsook immediate vision of them, and, instead, had recourse to λόγοι, seeking to discover therein the truth of things.

Today, too, it is difficult to begin otherwise than after the beginning and in such a way that this posteriority is decisive. For, despite all efforts and claims to the contrary, we continue—we cannot but continue—to draw on linguistic and conceptual resources that originated in the Platonic texts. Even when what is sought is another beginning that would divert thinking from the first beginning, there is no escaping the necessity of reanimating and interrogating the Platonic beginning. Even in the present instance, in which a discourse focused otherwise than on the beginning of a dialogue is inserted into a sequence of discourses, the beginning—in whatever way it is launched—will be made after the beginning. The discourse will not only take as its theme beginning after the beginning but also will enact beginning in such a manner.

Yet I will begin even farther afield from the beginning, turning first not to the *Laws* but rather to a dialogue that is even more permeated by the question of beginning. In this dialogue, the *Timaeus,* the orientation to the beginning is even more explicit. Near the beginning of the first of his three long discourses, Timaeus declares: "With regard to everything it is most important to begin at the natural beginning" (29b). And yet, one of the most remarkable and decisive features of the *Timaeus* is that it itself violates this prescription about beginning. Though, to be sure, Timaeus's first discourse proceeds as if—that is, under the pretense that—it begins at the beginning in tracing the god's fabrication of the cosmos, there are dissonances to be heard in the course of this discourse, disorders within this cosmology. Eventually it is revealed that, not having begun at the beginning, the discourse must be interrupted and a new beginning launched, a beginning after the beginning that is, on the other hand, more attuned to the most archaic beginning. This figure of interruption and new beginning in which the discourse turns back to a more archaic beginning is repeated at various levels and stages of the *Timaeus*. This palintropic figure attests that it is perhaps even imperative to begin after the beginning, especially when it is the beginning as such that is under interrogation.

In these formulations it is evident that with the word *beginning*, as with its near-synonym *origin*, my intention is to translate ἀρχή in such a way as to keep in play both the substantive sense and the verbal sense sustained by its affiliation with the corresponding verb ἄρχω. This differentiation as well as the interplay it opens up is one that subsequently proves extremely persistent and consequential; indeed it is still echoed when in the *Science of Logic* Hegel responds to the question "With what must the science begin?" by distinguishing between objective and subjective beginning, while also insisting on their essential connection.

In its classical signification, ἀρχή designates the whence, that from which something comes to be or simply is. Aristotle defines it repeatedly with the word ὅθεν. Yet it is important also to keep in mind that, for the most part, an ἀρχή is not just a starting point that would subsequently be left behind; rather, it is such that it continues, beyond the mere point of origin, to sustain or determine what it originates. The wonder that Socrates discerns in the face of the young Theaetetus and identifies as the ἀρχή of philosophy is no momentary occurrence but rather is an openness, an attunement, to questioning that remains in force throughout the extended conversation with Socrates.

The *Laws* is also, like the *Timaeus*, an interrogation of beginnings. Though it may seem less persistently, less exclusively, oriented to beginnings than the *Timaeus*, one should bear in mind that even the extensive legislative program that commences in Book 4 is linked directly to a beginning, namely, to the task of founding a colony in Crete, a task entrusted to Cleinias and nine of his fellow citizens. Yet, indisputably, the beginnings to which the two dialogues are, respectively, oriented could hardly be more diverse: whereas the theme of the *Timaeus* is the beginning of the cosmos, the *Laws* is dedicated to interrogating the origin of cities. More precisely, the concern is with the origination of the πολιτεία of the πόλις; let me, with all due reservations, translate these words as *constitution* and *city*.

Such is, then, the question with which, in only slightly different terms, the *Laws* begins. What the Athenian asks about in the opening sentence is the *cause* (αἴτιον), indeed in a sense that immediately proves to be affiliated with that of *origin*. The question concerns the originating cause of the legal arrangement in the cities of the two strangers whom he addresses. Yet the legal arrangement, the body of laws in their interrelatedness, is nothing other than the constitution of the city, its makeup as a political entity.

The very first word of the dialogue proposes an answer to the question of the originating cause of constitutions. This answer, expressed in the single word *god* (θεός), is immediately affirmed by the two strangers. And yet, in the question as the Athenian poses it, god is proposed not simply as the answer but as the first of two alternatives. Here is the question as the Athenian poses it in the first sentence of the dialogue: "God or some man, which do you, strangers, take to be the cause of your legal arrangements?" (624a). Not only do the strangers affirm that god is the cause but furthermore one of them, Cleinias of Crete, identifies the particular god that in their respective cities is taken as origin of the legal arrangements. In Crete—so says Cleinias the Cretan—it is Zeus; in Sparta, from which hails the other stranger, Megillos, it is Apollo. The response of the two is neither affirmed nor denied by the Athenian Stranger. Though, to be sure, the Athenian will later invoke the god to help in fashioning the city and its laws (712b), he will also distinguish between what in this regard is of godly origin and what is of human origin (732b). Indeed, in significant stretches of the discourse in the early books, the theme is how humans themselves, in response to their conditions, originate and transform the constitution of cities. The initial disjunction is thus played out as a perhaps undecidable conjunction.

Yet my charge is not to focus on the beginning of the *Laws* but to leap ahead to Book 3, beginning thus at this distance from the beginning. By the time Book 3 begins, the three old men will have made their way some distance along the road leading from Knossos up to the cave and temple of Zeus on Mount Ida, the legendary birthplace of Zeus. In making this journey they are enacting the μῦθος to which, referring to Homer, the Athenian draws attention near the outset of Book 1, the μῦθος according to which Minos, legendary king of Crete, went to hold converse with his father Zeus regarding the laws to be laid down. Since in the *Laws* it is the founding of a Cretan colony that prompts the discussion, such an enactment—such a repetition in deed of the mythical beginning— is appropriate as setting the scene for the discussion.

Yet by the time Book 3 begins, this enactment will already be well under way, and the three travelers will have left the Minoan city of Knossos behind. Since near the end of Book 4 (see 722c) the Athenian observes that they departed shortly after dawn and that by this time it is high noon, one may suppose that the conversation in Book 3 takes place around mid-morning. It is noted also that the time of the summer solstice is almost at hand (see 683c). Both the light and the heat will be increasing in intensity, and the shady resting places along the way will have become more indispensable. It is likely too that by this time they will have crossed the coastal plain that extends from Knossos and will have headed up into the mountains. The relative ease and comfort with which they would have made their way during their early morning discussion of pleasure, wine, music, and symposia will now have given way to the strenuousness of traversing a steeper way in the mid-morning summer heat. One cannot but suspect that there is considerable mirroring between the way they are traversing and the course of the λόγος in which they engage.

Thus, at the opening of Book 3, the beginning of the way will have been left behind. The Athenian says: "This much, then, for that" (676a). With these words he marks a break with what has preceded, and indeed at this point the conversation turns entirely away from the themes of pleasure, wine, music, and symposia that dominated most of the first two books. Now a fresh start, another beginning, is to be made. And yet, this new beginning is also a repetition of the first beginning, a renewal of the question that appears to have gotten lost in the conversation that ensued. But now, at the outset of Book 3, the question is posed more precisely, or, at any rate, in a formulation that conforms more closely to the way in which it is to be taken up. The Athenian asks: "Now, what are we to say about the origin [ἀρχή] from which a constitution comes to be?" (676a). In other words, how do the constitutions of cities originate? How do they begin? From what beginning?

One thing is readily ascertained: the absolute beginning is inaccessible. The Athenian observes that the time since cities first came to be is indefinitely long, virtually limitless, so vast and immeasurable that it cannot be spanned by our understanding. During this time myriads of cities have come to be and myriads have perished; and so, if the cause of such change could be discovered, then the origin of constitutions might also come to light.

Yet limits are needed if there is to be genuine determination. One cannot go back to the indefinitely removed beginning. And so, at this point the Athenian devises a most ingenious way of proceeding: instead of the vain attempt to recover the absolute beginning, his recourse is to begin after the beginning, to begin with a beginning after the absolute beginning. He takes this beginning to be indicated by the truth contained in certain ancient λόγοι, namely, those that tell of the destruction wrought by floods, plagues, or other disasters, destructions of such scope that only a small portion of the human race survived. He proposes that they consider one of the many such destructions, one that resulted from flood. This cataclysm would have spared only herdsmen high in the mountains, people unskilled in the various τέχναι. These people would have retained virtually no implements or inventions. Most of the animals would also have been destroyed, leaving the human survivors only a few herds of oxen and a few flocks of goats. Most decisively, these people would, according to the Athenian, have retained no memory of the very things that are the subjects of the present discourse, namely, cities, constitutions, and legislation. The Athenian concludes that from these people in that situation there developed the whole of what we now possess: cities and constitutions, crafts and laws.

It is, then, from this beginning after the beginning that the Athenian will begin his account of the constitutions of cities. And yet, according to the ancient λόγοι, there have been many such destructions, indeed many such cataclysms by which development was interrupted, most humans and their institutions were destroyed, and a new beginning from the scant remains became necessary. If the account that the Athenian has proposed is to have any basis, there must be a connection between the cataclysm being considered and the extant political institutions of his own day. The cataclysm being considered must be the most recent destruction, and the new beginning that came in its wake must be the beginning from which—as indeed the Athenian says—all present-day institutions have arisen. The genealogy, if it is not to be mere fancy, must take its bearings not only from the beginning but also from concrete present-day institutions, which must therefore be connected to precisely this beginning, which must contain within it their own actual beginning.

In the sequel the Athenian will actually demonstrate this connection by tracing the history from the meager beginning up to present-day Sparta and Athens. But even before this genealogy gets under way, a remark by Cleinias comes to bridge the gap mythically. He formulates it, interrogatively, as a paraphrase of and supplement to what the Athenian has said. Remarking initially that the many things that were lost through the cataclysm remained then unknown for myriads upon myriads of years, he adds that one thousand or two thousand years ago some of them were finally revealed again. He proceeds then to enumerate a series of seven largely mythical figures all of whom were in some sense inventors who through their inventions revealed to humans certain of the things that had been lost. First comes Daedalus, who invented carpentry and other crafts and who was capable of fashioning statues that actually moved; his long and complicated affiliation with Minos, including his construction of the labyrinth, is good reason for his coming first in the present context, linked, as it is, from the outset to the story of Minos. The second to be named is Orpheus, whose music for the kithara could charm even wild beasts. Third comes Palamedes, who invented the alphabet. Next is mentioned Marsyas, the satyr who first invented music for the aulos, and his lover Olympus, inventor of melodies. Next in the series is Amphion, whom Cleinias credits with lyric; he was an inventor of music for the aulos and was reputed to have built the walls of Thebes by using the power of his music to move the stones. The last in the series is alluded to by the Athenian and then called by name by Cleinias: he is Epimenides, the only real historical figure, a doctor who invented certain miraculous drugs and who was closely associated with the Cretan worship of Zeus.

By enumerating this series of inventors, Cleinias construes this span of time as a history in which a very long period of oblivion is followed by a time of recovery in which these mostly mythical figures bestow upon humanity the fruits of their inventiveness. Since these figures belong to the living memory carried by μῦθος, the enumeration serves also to attest to the continuity of this history with present-day institutions. Furthermore, by recalling the mythically attested gifts of these inventors, Cleinias adds credence to the Athenian's claim that all these things had been lost as a result of the cataclysm.

And yet, what is most curious are the actual gifts, the inventions by which these figures allegedly revealed again to humanity the things that had been lost and forgotten. Admittedly, the first and last of the seven, Daedalus and Epimenides, seem to have re-endowed humanity with certain useful τέχναι, though in both cases the products of the τέχναι are marvelous, miraculous, rather than simply useful for satisfying ordinary needs. Furthermore, both of these figures are conspicuously linked to the μῦθος of Minos and his relation to—hence the Minoan worship of—Zeus. Thus, by naming Daedalus and Epimenides as the first and last in the series, Cleinias in effect sets the entire series within the frame of the μῦθος that is being enacted by the three old men on their way to the cave and temple of Zeus.

Still more remarkable is the fact that none of the other figures practice or reveal ordinary, useful τέχναι; neither do any of them appear to bestow on humanity a gift having to do with cities, constitutions, and legislation. None of the things, then, that it would seem most important to reveal again to humanity seem to be revealed through the inventions that these figures bring forth. Indeed, with the exception of Palamedes, none of these figures brings forth anything but music. What they invent is music for the kithara or the aulos; and even if, as with Orpheus and Amphion, they accomplish some marvelous feat such as gaining entrance to Hades or building the walls of Thebes, they do so only through the magical power of their music.

Thus, the inventiveness of the seven figures, the revelations that they bring to humanity, has little to do with the useful τέχναι by which the needs of the city are served. Even less, so it seems, do their gifts contribute to the proper constitution and legislation of the city. What they produce and in turn enable humanity again to produce seems to have no bearing whatsoever on the question to which the *Laws* is from the outset devoted, the question of the origin of the constitutions of cities. Or could it be that music somehow has a bearing on the constitution of a city, that how the kithara and the aulos are played has something to do with the norms and practices that determine the character of the city?

Such is, then, the mythical frame, as it were, articulated by Cleinias of Crete, the soon-to-be cofounder of a colonial city. Within this frame the Athenian resumes his account, proceeding now to the genealogy. The development from the situation of those who survive the cataclysm to the institutions of the present day involves four primary stages, a distinct kind of constitution corresponding to each.

The first is that which took shape with those who had survived the destruction. Their memory of this event prevented them from leaving the highlands. Between them exchange was minimal, as metal, timber, and tools were extremely rare. On the other hand, they were so few that there was minimal conflict and no great lack of food and clothing. Being neither extremely poor nor, in the absence of precious metals, extremely rich, they were less inclined to quarrel with one another. They were largely unskilled in τέχνη, especially in that of war. They were—says the Athenian—good, both because of this situation and because of their simplicity (εὐήθεια), in the double sense of mildness of disposition and also simple-mindedness or naiveté. Thus, in the words of the Athenian: "They accepted as true what was said about gods and men and lived according to these things" (679c). For this reason, living as they did by custom and ancestral laws, but also because they did not yet possess writing, there was no need for a lawgiver who would set down a body of laws. Nonetheless, their situation, which the Athenian, citing Homer, compares to the rather primitive household of the Cyclops, amounts to a kind of constitution. It is a kind that, according to the Athenian, is still to be found here and there, a constitution best designated by the word *dynasty* (δυναστεία). It is a constitution in which the eldest rule with an authority handed down from the parents.

At the second stage these small clans congregated together to form larger communities, each bringing into the mix its own peculiar customs and laws. The Athenian identifies this mixing of different laws within the larger community as the origin of legislation. Legislation must now begin in order to establish which of the laws brought along by the various clans are to be adopted. Thus certain members of each clan will need to be chosen as legislators; not only will they render the laws uniform but also from the chiefs of the various clans they will fashion an aristocracy or even a monarchy, thus transforming the dynasties into a constitution of an entirely different kind.

Though no mention is made of it, one would presume that this transformation could occur, that there could be genuine legislation, only after the recovery of writing. According to the operative μῦθος, it would be Palamedes, the inventor of the alphabet, who bestowed on these people the gift of writing. It would follow that by the time of this second constitution the long initial period during which people were oblivious to what had been lost would have passed, and the time of recovery through the inventive figures would have arrived.

The third form of constitution came about, according to the Athenian, when people became forgetful of the cataclysm and so moved from the mountains down onto the plain. Most remarkably, however, the Athenian says not a word about this constitution, about how it was formed or about the laws that it involved. What he does say is that this city formed by those who moved down onto the plain was Ilium. Thus, quite suddenly, the genealogy is connected to actual history, at least as kept in memory through Homer's poetry. For it is solely by way of a citation from Homer that refers to a time when

> sacred Ilium was not yet built
> upon the plain, a city for humans
> (*Iliad* 20.216f.)

that this crucial connection is made. Thus it is hardly surprising that the Athenian, referring also to the earlier citation about the Cyclops, underwrites these citations by declaring that here the poet speaks according to god and according to nature. Once Ilium is introduced, the Athenian moves quickly to the Trojan War, observing that many other cities had also been founded, that they made attacks on Ilium, and that finally the city was sacked by the Achaeans. Yet when—so the Athenian's account continues—those who had fought against Troy returned home, they were not nobly and justly received. Because of sedition on the part of the young men, many of the returning heroes were murdered or exiled. Yet those who survived were eventually gathered together by a leader named Dorieus and so came to call themselves Dorians. Now directly addressing Megillos the Spartan, the Athenian remarks that the further events that ensued are told about fully by the Spartans. This fourth city that was thus formed was of course Sparta itself.

At this point the Athenian abruptly breaks off the account in order to comment on the course that the discussion has followed. He says: Now we have been brought, as if by a god, back to the point at the beginning of our dialogue about laws where we digressed and fell into the topics of music and drunkenness; but now, after our wandering, the λόγος is letting us get a hold on it again. The reference is to the point in Book 1 where the interrogation of Spartan institutions and their banning of symposia led off into the discussion of the drunkenness occasioned by such events and eventually of music and the Dionysian chorus. Now that that discussion and the subsequent genealogy of the cities have been carried out, indeed up to the point where Sparta makes its appearance as the fourth city, the discourse has returned to the point from which the digression was made. Once this wandering course is recognized as such, then it becomes evident that the dialogue indeed began after the beginning and that, especially in the genealogy in Book 3, it has carried out a turn back to a beginning prior to the beginning, a palintropic turn to a more archaic beginning.

Now, again, the Spartan constitution is to be interrogated, again, from the beginning; the Athenian proposes that in thought they put themselves back to the time when Sparta, along with Argos and Messene, was founded. Thus the account, the history, is resumed and eventually, though not without minor digressions, advances to the time of the Persian War. The contrast with the Persian freedom-crushing monarchy provides the Athenian finally with a pretext for speaking of his own city.

His account is a kind of genealogy in reverse; it is intended to show how a certain excess of freedom has led to the ruin of the city. The account begins by reporting that at the time of the Persian threat the Athenian constitution involved a division into four classes with corresponding magistrates. At that time, he observes, there was a sense of shame or honor that served to bind Athenians to the existing laws, and in the face of the Persian threat they were bound even more firmly. Without these bonds and the fear of defeat by the Persians, the Athenians would not, he attests, have come together to defend and ultimately save themselves.

It is against this background that the Athenian sets out to explain, as he puts it, "the origin of the excessive development of the free way of life" (700a). Up through the time of the Persian War, there were, he observes, firm laws in Athens to regulate music. The various forms of music were clearly differentiated. One form consisted in prayer to the gods; these were called hymns. Another form concerned the birth of Dionysus; these were called dithyrambs. There were also dirges, odes, and many other forms, each distinct from the others. The laws prohibited misusing one form of music for another. Also, at this time music was judged by the musically educated, not by the clapping and whistling of the unmusical mob.

But then, after a time, there appeared—so the account says—poets who were ignorant of music. They introduced unmusical lawlessness into music by jumbling everything together, mixing hymns with dithyrambs, using the sound of the kithara to imitate the sound of the aulos, and so on. Even worse, they asserted that there was no such thing as correct music and that the only criterion for judging music was pleasure. Both the assertions and the practices of these ignorant poets served to instill in many Athenians a lawlessness regarding music and to foster in them the opinion that they too could judge the excellence of music. What arose, as a result, was a democracy in music, replacing the earlier aristocracy.

Yet even this, says the Athenian, would not have been so bad, had it been only a democracy *in music*. But from this change regarding music, there arose and spread the opinion that all are entitled to judge everything. Shamelessness and lawlessness became rife as people refused to be governed by rulers and eventually rejected even governance by parents and elders, seeking finally to avoid having to obey any laws at all, seeking even to avoid being subject to laws. Then, finally, says the Athenian, comes the ultimate freedom: "they cease to give heed at all to oaths and pledges and to everything pertaining to the gods" (701c). Thus swept up in the spread of lawlessness, they slip back toward a pre-Olympian state of harshness and evil. As the Athenian says, they come "to imitate the nature of the Titans of old," reverting to a state to which even the rule of Zeus is alien.

This spread of lawlessness thus produces an extreme regression of the city, a reduction of its constitution to a stage even more primitive than the dynasties, since governance even by parents and elders comes to be rejected. Yet what is most remarkable about this spread of lawlessness is the origin assigned to it: for it is *from music*, from the lawlessness introduced into music, that lawlessness spreads throughout the city, disrupting its constitution and reducing it to a condition anterior to that of even the most primitive cities. What this entire passage elaborates corresponds precisely to what Socrates says in the *Republic*: "For beware of change to a strange form of music as endangering the whole. For never are the tropes of music changed without the greatest political laws being changed, as Damon says, and I am persuaded" (424c).

But then, if changes in music are capable of bringing about such profound changes in the constitution of cities, music must have an essential bearing on the makeup of cities, on the way in which its laws are arranged and its citizens are governed on the basis of those laws. Just as music is capable of insinuating itself into the soul in such a way as to shape its dispositions, so music must permeate the constitution of the city in such a way as to shape it, for better or for worse, depending on the correctness, the lawfulness, of the music. But this is to say, then, that music belongs to the origin of the constitution of cities, that it is an essential moment in the origination and sustaining of the makeup of cities. It is to say that music belongs to the beginning of the constitution of cities both in the beginning and after the beginning. One could say—with only the slightest ellipsis—that cities begin musically.

6   It is Difficult for a City with Good Laws to Come into Existence: On Book 4

Michael P. Zuckert

I. Prologue

The subtle action of Book 4 can be appreciated only when it is seen in relation to Book 3. Only at the end of Book 3 does Cleinias divulge to the Athenian that he and nine others have been charged to form a new colony. This is perhaps the most decisive and surprising moment of the dialogue. He seeks the Athenian's aid in his enterprise. It is an amazing coincidence that one of these three idle talkers about laws actually has the opportunity to legislate. But more amazing is the observation we cannot help but make that Cleinias has been walking with this apparently knowledgeable Athenian since dawn and it is only now, three-quarters of the way to noon, that he divulges to the Stranger his task and only now attempts to enlist the Athenian in the enterprise. That new task sets the tone for the rest of the *Laws,* but most immediately for Book 4.

But why does Cleinias only now divulge his task and enlist the Athenian in it? There seem to be two possible answers. He might not have thought that the Athenian had much to contribute—he might not possess any particular wisdom about legislation. Alternatively (or in addition) he might not have trusted the Athenian—he might have respected the Athenian's wisdom but not have trusted him to use it for the good of the Cretans.

On the trust front (and perhaps on the wisdom front as well) the Athenian gets off to a shaky start: he praises the drinking parties of Athens, a practice Cleinias was prejudiced against and one that is emphatically Athenian and not Dorian. For the Athenian to praise an Athenian institution seems to be an act of loyalty and attachment to his native city, a sign that he favors his own culture and cannot be entrusted with the task of legislating for Cretan Dorians. Cleinias's hesitations about the Athenian are no doubt further fed by the latter's critique of Dorian laws in Book 1 as aiming only at a part of virtue and not the whole of it.

What then happens during the course of Book 3 to lead Cleinias to disclose his mission as a lawgiver? Most immediately preceding Cleinias's divulgence is an exchange between Megillus and the Athenian concerning the growth of liberty in Athens. That exchange is persistently punctuated by the Athenian's raising the question, why are we having this conversation about laws? At 699e the Athenian says, "But consider now . . . if what we're speaking of is pertinent to lawgiving. . . . That's why I'm going through all this, I'm not doing it for the sake of the myths." At 701c he asks, "why, again, have all those things been said by us?" and adds immediately: "I must once more repeat my question and ask— 'for the sake of what have all these things been said?' " (701d). And finally, just before Cleinias speaks up, the Athenian once again emphasizes that "all these things have been discussed for the sake of understanding how a city might best be established sometime and how in private someone might best lead his own life. But what sort of a test in conversation might we ever set for ourselves in speech, Megillus and Cleinias, to reveal whether we have been making 'something useful'?" (702b). As if by divine coincidence Cleinias just happens to furnish the perfect "test"—his new colony.

Unless we have here a particularly artless kind of writing by Plato, it is difficult not to see the Athenian's persistent raising of the question of "what is our point here" and his constant hammering away at the practical aims of their conversation (in real contrast with Socrates in the *Republic*) as fishing. The Athenian seems to know or somehow divine that Cleinias has just such a charge and is not so subtly urging him to bring it forward. If that is so, and it certainly seems much more likely than the alternative, then we might think of Book 3 (or perhaps the whole of Books 1–3) as an effort by the Athenian to win Cleinias's confidence so that he can become a partner, or at least a trusted advisor, in the founding of the new city.[1]

If we look at the Athenian's words in that light, then his argument in the last half of Book 3 appears to be very much tailored to winning over the two old Dorians, largely by overcoming the impression he made earlier by criticizing their laws and praising an Athenian practice. The last half of Book 3 presents almost the reverse of that strategy. The Athenian praises the Dorian cities and political orders as superior to Athens (683e), strongly condemns the Athenian attachment to liberty (698a), and in particular blames the prototypically Athenian institution of theater as responsible for the corruption of Athens (700aff.). Early on he crossed the prejudices of his interlocutors. In Book 3 he plays up to them.

But it is not merely a strategic retreat, for the situation at the end of Book 3 is not quite the same as the situation at the very beginning of Book 1. The Athenian put off his Dorian fellow travelers by blaming their laws and lawgivers for concentrating too heavily on the inculcation of courage and for slighting or completely ignoring the rest of virtue. Just prior to the Athenian's embarking on the topic of the relative merits of Athens and the Dorian regimes he convinces Megillus the Spartan of the proposition that courage is but a part of virtue and that courage without other virtues is vicious (696b–c). The decisive argument setting the stage for this major event in the dialogue appears to have been the Athenian's tracing the history of the three Dorian cities, Argos, Messene, and Lacedaemonia. One thrived and two were ruined: the Dorian political experience was mixed. The Athenian attributes the success of Sparta to the blending that occurred in that constitution as opposed to the purity in the other two. He argues that "the cause of the destruction of the kings, and of the whole plan, was not cowardice, nor a lack of knowledge of war on the part of the rulers or of those for whom it was fitting to be ruled. The corruption was caused by all the rest of vice and especially ignorance regarding the greatest of human affairs" (688c). Courage is perhaps a necessary but not a sufficient condition of political health, as the history of the three Dorian cities shows. Only Sparta, which, perhaps unwittingly, mixed in other virtues—especially moderation—succeeded.

The Athenian thus rehabilitates Sparta, the leading Dorian regime, while at the same time modifying and successfully challenging the Spartan self-understanding and preparing his interlocutors for founding a political order very different from their home cities. Only then does the Athenian turn against Athens and praise Sparta. He flatters his interlocutors, but not without at the same time trying to draw them toward his own perspective. Nonetheless we might draw two conclusions regarding the Athenian's preparation of Cleinias (and Megillus) to invite him to share in founding the new colony: he had to win their trust in his wisdom and he had to win their trust in his good-will or loyalty to their project. The Athenian was willing to pay the price—praise of the Dorians and blame of his own city.

II. The Action and the Problem of Book 4

The action of Book 4 extends the trajectory of Book 3 for it continues the Athenian's efforts to gain and keep the trust and support of the Dorians. But by the end of Book 4 he has led them quite far from where they were at the end of Book 3, by getting them to support the practice of preludes, a practice completely foreign to Dorian practice. And they know it: Megillus points out that the Athenian's emphasis on wordy preludes is contrary to "the Laconic way" (721e). In short, the action of Book 4 proceeds by the Athenian continuing his (qualified) pro-Dorian position that he arrived at by the end of Book 3, but by the end of Book 4 winning the assent of the Dorians to a turn away from the Dorian model. The arc of the action of Book 4 thus poses the following problem: what happens between the opening and the closing of the book that makes possible or requires the shift away from Sparta on the part of the two Dorians?

Although other considerations are surely at work in the Athenian's presentation of the ideal or desirable conditions for a city, the endorsement of the Spartan way certainly seems to be among them. The chosen location for the planned colony is not all that the Athenian would wish for—it is too near the sea, for one, but it has many qualities of which he approves, qualities that are more characteristic of Sparta than of Athens or of Cretan cities. It can produce most or all of what it needs for itself, so it will not be driven to import goods from elsewhere. Though it can produce all that it needs, the terrain is such that it is unlikely to produce a surplus and so it will not be possible to produce for export. It will not be a commercial city (as Sparta is not); it will not exchange or sell goods and thus will avoid an "infection of silver and gold money," again as Sparta does (705b). It has a harbor but no natural resources for shipbuilding. It will be a land-oriented city, like Sparta, not a sea-faring city like Athens, or like Minoan Crete.

The sea, argues the Athenian in a very non-Athenian way, is a very bad preceptor. By encouraging commerce, it "engenders shifty and untrustworthy dispositions in souls; it thereby takes away the trust and friendship a city feels for itself and for the rest of humanity" (705a). Rather than binding men together, the sea and the commerce it fosters divide them. The sea harms the souls of sea-faring peoples through its effects on their fighting men. The Athenian contrasts infantrymen with marines. The latter are quick to retreat because they can jump into their ships and be off. The former are more steadfast. On Dorian standards of war-making capability the landed are superior to the sea-going.[2]

Since the Athenian supports this last point only by a distorted quotation from Homer, one begins to suspect that he is exaggerating his support for Spartan over Athenian virtues, in line with the rhetorical strategy pursued in Book 3.[3] He goes so far in the direction of this strategy that he slaps down Cleinias, citizen of sea-faring Crete, when the latter objects to the Athenian's depreciation of the sea and of marines: "We Cretans at least assert that it was the naval battle of the Greeks"—mainly the Athenians—"against the barbarians [Persians] at Salamis that saved Greece" (707b). The Athenian responds that rather it was "the land battles at Marathon and Plataea" that saved Greece. Military historians may disagree over which of these victories was most important, but all would agree that the Athenian too summarily dismisses the importance of Salamis, perhaps the peak of Athenian military achievement. His argument proves that he is no partisan of his own.

At the same time, much more clearly than before, the Athenian is creating a wedge between the two Dorian regimes and thus in principle between the two Dorian interlocutors. Even though Cleinias is his main conversation partner, and even though it is Cleinias who is to be part of the team of legislators to found the new city, the Athenian consistently favors Megillus and Sparta over Cleinias and Crete. Minos is singled out as the source of the "evil" example Athens followed to its own peril (706a–b). The Athenian explicitly joins Megillus against Cleinias in valuing Salamis beneath the land battles of the Persian War.

By the end of the discussion of the very first topic of Book 4 the dialogue has reached its high point—an obviously exaggerated high point—in its rehabilitation of the Dorian regimes. By the end of Book 4 as we have already noted, the discussion will move very far in another direction toward a novel and very un-Dorian and especially un-Spartan practice. That move is made with the full support of both Dorians. The Athenian has them both overcome their attachment to their own perspectives in offering the notion of a very different kind of political order, and he has apparently healed any rift between the Dorians that his strategy may have caused earlier in Book 4. The problem in understanding Book 4 is to trace this movement.

The basic dynamic present in Book 3 and the earlier parts of Book 4 does not change as Book 4 progresses. The method the Athenian uses is a form of flattery but a more subtle form than he had used before. The decisive strategy is his introduction of the metaphor of the free and slave doctors treating the free and slave patients. He gets Megillus and Cleinias to identify themselves with the free doctor and patient and thus to accept the persuasive ways of the preludes rather than the simply commanding ways of the laws characteristic of the actual Dorian regimes.

The successful use of the free vs. slave doctor image allows the two old Dorians not only to identify with the "good" pair as against the practices of their home cities, but also to embrace the yet more enticing view that politics might be pacified to the extent that persuasive argument replaces force. This is the hope with which the Athenian beguiles them—and with which Plato beguiles many readers of his *Laws*.

But a seemingly small detail at the end of the discussion of preludes indicates that the hope for a radically different kind of politics is hollow. The detail to which I refer is the seemingly picky question: Are the preludes part of the laws or are they prefaces to laws? The answer the Stranger gives is that they are not part of law proper—law remains coercive command (722d–e). There is a common theme underpinning the great variety of topics in Book 4. That theme, in brief, is the tension between the legislative art and the conditions that art faces, conditions that resist its application. So far as the conditions of political life resist the application or sovereignty of the legislative art, then to that extent politics resists being remade according to that art, i.e., resists being remade in the best way.

This relationship is not simply one-sided, for as the Athenian reveals, like all human arts, the legislative art supplies means by which those forces in the external world that resist human purpose can be partially surmounted. This side of the legislative art is brought out well in the discussion of the site for the new city. Nonetheless, the Athenian puts forward his claim about the preludes as prefaces at high noon i.e., at the moment of maximum light, and thereby signals that command and coercion will not disappear into persuasion, rational or otherwise (722c). Book 4, having raised our and the Dorians' hopes, ends with this moderately pessimistic conclusion.

III. "Location, Location, Location": Siting the New City (704a–707d)

The Athenian asks about the siting of the new city. This is, for him, a given, the Cretans having already selected the site, but he nonetheless clearly has strong opinions about how the new city should be sited. All human things are not matters of chance, but the "given," which from the point of view of human aims and plans is chance, always plays a large role in political action and perforce in thinking about political action. Although one can formulate an "ideal," one must appreciate that the "given" always intrudes: "the best laid plans of mice and men" always run into a more or less recalcitrant reality.[4]

However, reality may be more or less recalcitrant, as the Athenian reveals in his discussion of the arts: human beings can develop knowledge and techniques that allow them to accomplish their aims and plans more or less well in the face of the recalcitrant "given" (709c). The Athenian does not specify the limits of art in overcoming chance, but the example immediately at hand is suggestive: the new city is not sited in the best way, according to the Athenian's political understanding. The site is for him an immovable given, but was it such for those who actually decided on the site, including, we should presume, Cleinias? The siting committee has decided on a location eighty stades from the sea (about eight or nine miles). It is an abandoned area of Crete and has no nearby neighbors: almost certainly the city could have been located farther from the sea (704c). Had the siting committee possessed the Athenian's knowledge of the political art, it would have located the colony elsewhere. The "givens" are often not simply given, but are the result of human choice, the quality of which depends on the wisdom of those who choose. Although he does not say it aloud, the Athenian leads the reader to believe that the power of the "given" may be much weaker than it appears to be—if the practitioners of the arts can prevail upon other human beings to act wisely.[5]

This conclusion brings us back to one of the overall features of *Laws:* an Athenian who is apparently wiser than his two interlocutors attempts to convince them of his opinions on politics and legislation. The book as a whole shows a largely successful effort by the Athenian—he has by the beginning of Book 4 persuaded his fellows to listen to him, which is better than Socrates often does in similar situations. Yet, so far, he has done so in part by appealing to their prejudices in favor of their own. But if such is the method of persuasion, then we must conclude that the limits of persuasion are severe when knowledge and prejudice point in different directions, as they appear to do in the case of the siting of the colony. The Athenian thinks the sea is bad and to be avoided; the Cretans are a sea-faring people and favor it. It was not a mere accident that led them to locate their city where they did, a compromise between their Dorianness and their habitual use of the sea.

The Athenian puts much weight on location, not so much in and of itself but for the way of life the location will foster. Location will determine or nearly determine the economic character of the city and that in turn will determine or nearly determine the way of life and character of the citizens. Plato and other Greek thinkers are often accused of being insufficiently attentive to the role of economics and other sub-political elements in giving shape to a community. We see here that this is not at all true of the Athenian.

The primary standard by which the Athenian condemns commerce is "the trust and friendship a city feels for itself and the rest of mankind" (705a). He is obviously no friend of the commercial republic that Montesquieu, Hume, Madison and other early moderns favored. Rousseau, very much influenced by classical republicanism, is much closer to the Athenian than the commercial republicans whom he opposed. But the Athenian also sees commerce as hostile to "well-born and just dispositions" and, as we have seen, to courage (705b, 706c). Commerce, the Athenian believes, is hostile to individual virtue and to the virtue (friendly unity) of the city. He clearly has a model of an isolated and inward-looking polity, devoted nearly single-mindedly to the whole of virtue (705d). Perhaps we ought to see his doctrine on location as an important step along the way toward transcending Sparta. The isolated location and the completely self-sufficient character of the city would produce some of the qualities of a Sparta-like community—unity among the citizens, closedness, stability—but this community with no neighbors and no commerce would have less of a reason to devote itself predominantly to matters of war. To found a city that does not glorify war and courage, the Athenian is saying, one must either model it on Athens, which is more open to the world, or on the isolated city he projects as ideal—in principle, the only city on earth.[6] The Athenian option has already been rejected—it is considered less virtuous than the imperfect Dorian regimes. But the condition for success that the Athenian lays out points to the deep limitations of the Spartan path; for a successful Sparta, one that would be free to pursue the whole of virtue, would require a kind of isolation unusual to human communities.[7]

If this line of thinking is correct we see a certain complexity and perhaps irony in the opening stages of Book 4. On the one hand the Athenian continues on his track of rehabilitating the Dorian regimes, especially Sparta, but at the same time he subtly shows the limitations of this path. The simultaneity of these two tracks accounts for the noticeable exaggerations of the Athenian's rhetoric—only by distorting and overstating his argument can he make the case for the Spartan path.

IV. "Look at all the lonely people": Populating the City (707e–708d)

After location the next important question the Athenian poses is about the colonists—will they be from one place, with pre-existing connections to each other, or will they come from all over Crete, or even from the entirety of Greece? Cleinias informs him that the settlers will come from Crete, although some will come from the Peloponnese. Athenians, Ionians, and others will not be welcome. It is to be a kind of mean between homogeneity and heterogeneity.

The Athenian does not have so clear an opinion on this as he had on location. He raises one consideration favoring a homogeneous settlement: "the tribal unity, the similarity of language and of laws, since they imply a sharing of the sacred things and all such matters, create a certain friendship" (708c). That is, applying the standard of civic unity and friendship that had been so important in the discussion of location and way of life favors homogeneity of population. In the context it is difficult for the interlocutors and the reader not to be reminded of a basic fact about Sparta: it has that sort of homogeneity among its citizenry but as a whole the city lacks it, for the ruling Dorians sit atop a conquered and enslaved helot population of different origin. Sparta is an armed camp not only because it lacks the desired isolation from neighbors, but also because it lacks internal homogeneity.

Heterogeneity of origin, while it does not produce spontaneous "friendship" among the citizens, has a certain advantage as well: it is easier to introduce new laws to a heterogeneous population. Therefore, the conditions of settlement of the new city should fall somewhere between the two extremes of heterogeneity and homogeneity. The Athenian seems to lean closer to the heterogeneity option, however (708b).[8]

The Athenian distinguishes between two pairs of alternatives—homogeneity combined with resistance to reform or heterogeneity combined with receptivity to reform—both of which may present a great difficulty in producing civic unity (708d). The absence of an optimal alternative leads the Athenian to conclude that "lawgiving and the founding of cities is the most perfect of all tests of manly virtue" (708d).[9] The unspoken premise behind his conclusion, however, is that both reform and civic unity are requisites of a healthy political order. That premise is clarified immediately following when the Athenian brings out the role of art in relation to the "given." The sub-political "givens" that form a solid basis for unity are not themselves the result of the art of the legislator; therefore it follows that all communities grounded on those "givens" will most likely require reform in accord with the precepts of that art.

V. Rulers (708e–715e)

The discussion of site and population has served to underline the difficulty of legislating. The Athenian would not himself go so far as to say that "no human being ever legislates anything" because circumstances or necessities determine all, but he can see how one might be tempted to say so (709a). The Athenian resists that pessimistic conclusion because he believes that there are arts that allow human beings some control over events despite external forces. The chief political need then is for "a lawgiver who possesses the truth," presumably, the political or legislative art (709c).

But possession of the legislative art is not enough. Just as the Athenian's political art remains purely theoretical (so long as he does not have Cleinias and his fellow founders as partners), so the legislative artisan in general requires an alliance with political power. The Athenian comes close to Socrates' conclusion in the *Republic* that justice requires that rulers philosophize or philosophers rule, i.e., that there be a conjunction of philosophy and political power. The Athenian's position differs from that one in two ways, however: he speaks not of philosophy but of an art of legislation parallel to piloting or medicine. It is not evident that this legislative art need be philosophical anymore than sailing or piloting need be philosophical. Perhaps more noticeably, the Athenian does not call for the identity of rulers and legislative artisan, merely for their cooperation. He thus avoids the difficulty posed by the *Republic:* how to engineer that convergence of philosophy and political rule in the same individual. The Athenian's alternative raises difficulties of its own, however: how to engineer the *cooperation* of the political ruler and the possessor of the legislative art.

The Athenian's procedure in discussing the rulers of the new city is strikingly different from his procedure in discussing the other elements of the city. With regard to both location and population the Athenian began with the situation on the ground—with the already settled location, with the preexisting plan for recruiting citizens—and moved from those particulars to general considerations of place and people. Had he proceeded in the same way in regard to the founders, he would have begun with Cleinias and his committee. Instead he begins with what a possessor of the political art would pray for.

The Athenian calls for a "tyrannized city" as most likely to further the project of instituting the innovations the possessor of the political art will wish to introduce. Given his general hostility to tyranny this preference may seem odd.[10] The previous discussion of population provides a clue for why the Athenian does so. The citizens on whom the legislative art–inspired reforms are to be worked are used to a more imperfect regime. They will always require more or less forceful "reshaping" from above, for they cannot be presumed to be able to impose reforms on themselves or even to be particularly receptive to the reforms required.

The tyrant needed for reforming the city must be a man of very special qualities, one who has the intellectual strengths that would make him an apt student of the legislator and the character strengths that would allow him to bring about the reforms the legislator prescribes (709e–710a). More than anything, the tyrant must possess moderation if his "other qualities are to prove beneficial" (710a). The moderation the Athenian has in mind is a "natural" quality of "self-restraint with regard to pleasures." He does not explain why this quality is particularly necessary but it is easy to surmise. Unless the tyrant has this kind of self-restraint it is unlikely that he will accept the legislator as his partner and guide. This type of cooperation requires a very special kind of ruler. The problematic nature of the Athenian's proposal comes to light when one asks how likely it is that a tyrant would possess the qualities of self-restraint and deference required for the partnership to work. Tyrants generally do not fit that description (compare especially the tyrant at 661d–e).

It Is Difficult for a City with Good Laws 95

But, on second thought, if the possessor of the legislative art is parallel to the possessor of the medical or piloting arts, why are special qualities required in the one who would employ him? Do people not voluntarily call on the services of the medical doctor, the pilot, the trainer, who possess skills from which they will benefit and for which they are even willing to pay? Why does this not extend to the legislative art? The Athenian calls attention to the fact that the legislative art may be different from the other arts. The tyrant, when ill, does not need special traits of character to call on a doctor. But only a special kind of tyrant will work with the legislator. It seems that rule means something to people that piloting their own ships or self-medicating do not. The ordinary tyrant derives too much pleasure and pride from his preeminence and from ruling to share power or take comprehensive guidance from a legislative artisan.

After having brought out the great unlikelihood of the partnership between legislator and established rulers, the Athenian posits an option closer to the Socratic position in the *Republic:* "when this greatest power coincides in a human being with prudence and moderation then occurs the natural genesis of the best regime and laws to match; but otherwise it will never come to pass." The Athenian can only think of one instance in which such qualities were found in the same person and that was a long time ago and "never among us" do we see such a person (711e). Thus the Athenian concludes that his remarks on the rulers needed for proper reform are "like a myth pronounced in oracular fashion revealing . . . that it would be difficult for a city with good laws to come into being" (712a).

This conclusion particularly applies to the possible cooperation between the Athenian and the Knossan Committee of Ten. Contrary to Cleinias's expectation he judges a group of oligarchs the most difficult kind of rulers for the legislator to work with (710e). They are most conservative and least likely to give way to the radical plans of the legislator. The general line of this argument in Book 4 reinforces what we have been inclined to conclude from observing the relationship between the Athenian and Cleinias. The Athenian had to win Cleinias's confidence by making many concessions to his prejudices and desires. Although the *Laws* is often said to be a more practical and practicable plan for a polity than the *Republic,* we see as early as this moment in Book 4 that this is not so. Either the plan outlined in the *Laws* is not for "a city with good laws," or the Athenian is signaling that it will not come to be. This is one of the most decisive or revealing moments in Book 4.[11]

In order to move his argument along the Athenian posits a god in place of the noble tyrant. Cleinias is delighted: "Let him come indeed" (712b). A god is surely more convenient than a noble tyrant to have as a silent partner in founding the city. This god is to play an active role in the founding, for he is to be the "true ruler" (713a). The notion of a god as ruler at the founding is agreeable to Cleinias, for it is equivalent to the founding of Crete as described in the opening lines of the *Laws:* Zeus, with Minos, founded Crete.[12] The unnamed god plus the Athenian plus the Committee of Ten will found Magnesia. This god is conjured out of thin air to satisfy the need for a primary source of authority. Neither the Athenian nor Cleinias has any good reason to believe that such a god exists, much less rules.[13] Cleinias is happy accepting the god as a mythic co-founder, which may explain his statements about Zeus as founder in Book 1 (644a–b).

Having conjured a founding god, the Athenian then asks about the regime or constitution they are to set up for the city thus founded. The question about rulers shifts from the ruler who will help found the city to the post-founding rulers (712c). The Athenian is seeking a regime where the ruler does not despotize over the city, as is the case in most of the extant regimes. In place of such a regime he would have a city where the "god who truly rules as a despot over those who possess intellect" rules (713a).

Cleinias unsurprisingly wants to know who this god is (713a). The Athenian replies with a "little more . . . of myth." He tells a version of the myth of Cronus. In the age of Cronus there was "peace and awe and good laws and justice without stint." People in that age "were without civil strife, and happy" (713d–e).

The age of Cronus is past, however, but the Athenian concludes "that we should imitate by every device the way of life that is said to have existed under Cronus . . . We should obey whatever within us partakes of immortality. . . ." What should rule then is "the distribution ordained by intelligence" which is "law." (714a) That is to say, the Athenian brings his long discussion of the rulers needed for the new city to the tentative conclusion that the "law" should rule, a not altogether satisfactory answer. But Cleinias is content and does not press the issue.

All the elements of the city are now in place—the location, the population, the rulers. It is now time to move on toward the promised legislation. But the Athenian again postpones things. Legislation proper must be preceded by a prelude, a prelude about preludes. The last half of Book 4 is devoted to further preliminaries to legislating, but preliminaries of a very different sort.

VI. Prelude: Political Theology: (715e–719a)

With the city's people in place, the Athenian begins to speak directly to them rather than merely speaking of them. He speaks to them first of "the god."

This must be the very god whom he conjured as the legislator's aid in founding, the god who replaced the tyrant. The god was second best to the tyrant, but given the Athenian's specifications for the tyrant, apparently more readily found. When he introduced the god (712b) he did not specify in what way the god would "take part with us in the ordering of the city and the laws" (712b). The speech to the citizens of the new city fills in what was left out there. The god does not so much act as serve as the subject of the Athenian's speech. What the Athenian says about the god "would contribute something to making the hearer listen in a more tame and agreeable mood" to the "legislation" laid down by the legislator (718d). A little later we learn that what is said of the god, i.e., the aid the god gives in founding, is a "prelude" to the laws. It is what the Stranger presents as a general prelude to all the laws.

It is difficult to judge how seriously to take the speech about the god. The Athenian does not present it as true but rather as useful in preparing the citizens to receive the laws. Given the way in which the god was first introduced that is not at all surprising, for first the tyrant and then the god were brought out as aids to the founder-legislator in his work. According to this perspective the speech about the god could be the equivalent to the "noble lie" in the *Republic*. Political theology replaces the naturalistic myth of the *Republic*. (Or rather, if we accept Catherine Zuckert's conjecture about the *dramatic* order of the dialogues, the naturalistic myth of the *Republic* replaces the political theology of the *Laws*.)[14]

The speech about the god is to be an aid to legislating but the Athenian leads us to believe it will be of only limited efficacy. It is only effective in a soul that is "not entirely savage" and the Athenian suggests it is not very effective there either: "even if these words have no great effect but only a small one, still insofar as they make the one who listens to them more agreeable and a better learner, that is in every way desirable" (718d). The speech appears to be both useful—even necessary—and of limited use, for the same reason: "there is no great plenty or abundance of persons who are eager in spirit to become as good as possible in the shortest possible time" (718d–e). The god to whom he refers is not addressed by name, although according to the scholiast he is described by a phrase that is used of Zeus.[15] Nonetheless, the Stranger's account of the god's activities does not fit Zeus: the god "completes his straight course by revolving according to nature" (716a). The god sounds more like a natural body than like a god, for it runs its course "according to nature."[16] The Athenian attributes neither intelligence nor will to his god. The "god" therefore is not identified as the giver of the laws.

Accompanying the god—the sun perhaps?—is personified Justice or Right (Δίκη) (716a). She too does not legislate but takes vengeance on "those who forsake the divine law" (θεῖος νόμος). The "divine law" does not appear to be a law the god lays down but the law the god follows, the law "prescribing" the regular circular course of nature. The god does not appear to have any choice in following the course of nature; Justice follows the god, whether by choice or not is not clear, and human beings may or may not follow Justice and the god. Human beings are the first beings in this account to be identified as having a choice or as being free to follow (or not) the natural motion of the god. Human beings deviate from the divine law, deviate from "humility," when they get "puffed up," "boastful," "insolent," thinking themselves capable of ruling others rather than in need of being ruled. Human beings appear to naturally take pride in their powers and self-sufficiency and to seek to "seem to be somebody" in the eyes of others. Their "natural" course is anything but orderly and regular.[17] The Athenian asserts that the man who acts like this "undergoes the blameless vengeance of Justice, bringing complete ruin to himself and his household and city as well" (716b).

The Athenian is bringing out what a stranger, a misfit, man is in the cosmos. The heavenly bodies operate according to "divine law," which is the natural course that they follow. Man lacks this natural orderliness largely, it seems, because of the human phenomenon of mind: man is aware of himself as "something" and wishes to be "somebody" in the minds of others. But man, who, by nature, does not automatically behave like the god, nonetheless pays the price; the Athenian affirms that happiness and success on the individual, family, and political levels require that kind of orderliness. The Athenian presents a philosophized version of the vision of man presented by tragedians: man's hubris, his tendency to puff himself up, and lord it over others, leads to disaster. But the Athenian sees this as the human way: men are strangers in the universe for they do not follow the natural order.

Happy and successful life requires that men live according to a certain natural order as the god does, or "become a follower of the god," despite the great differences between men and the god (716c). They must make the god "the measure" of their lives, not each other as they naturally tend to do. The virtue of the one who achieves this way of being is moderation (716d). Moderation is *the* virtue of virtues. The Dorian cities elevate courage as the highest virtue: the Athenian aims at a moral revolution.

The revolution the Athenian is attempting to effect in his interlocutors must be the basis for the changes he makes in Dorian political theology. The Dorians see Zeus and Apollo as their founding gods and lawgivers. Zeus and Apollo are like men, however: self-conscious, concerned with the opinions of others, irregular and willful in their behavior. They are not models or measures of the moderation that the Athenian demands of men. A god who resembles the heavenly bodies replaces the gods who resemble men. The Athenian offers this idea not as a philosophically truer account, but because it can or might promote the moral reform he seeks.

From all that he has said thus far the Athenian rather surprisingly concludes that "the noblest and truest of principles" is that good men must sacrifice to and commune with the gods, specifically the Olympian gods (716e). The celestial god is the measure but the Olympians must receive men's worship. With the reintroduction of the Olympians we also see the reintroduction of the intelligence and will that the celestial god did not possess. Men can only worship beings with intelligence and will, but only a being without intelligence and will can be "the measure." The Athenian's political theology contains a deep cleft between these two elements. This cleft is not accidental, however, and in various forms recurs regularly in the monotheistic theologies of the post-Platonic world. God is both unchanging and perfect, and sensible and responsive. The Athenian's theology is marked by a deep tension, but he strives to overcome that tension through the subordination of the Olympians to the celestial god and an accompanying reinterpretation of the Olympians. The Athenian goes to some lengths to set up a hierarchy of "targets" for "pious reverence" (717a–b), ranging from the Olympians (not "the god") at the top to human parents at the bottom. The explanation he offers for the inclusion and ordering of these "targets" is brief but suggestive:

> It is just that one in debt pay back his first and greatest debts, the eldest of all his obligations, and that he consider all his acquisitions and possessions as belonging to those who engendered and nourished him; he should strive with all his power to devote these things to their service. (717b–c)

The Athenian's view is very similar to Nietzsche's in *Genealogy of Morality* (2.19–21). The origin of worship of gods is the sense of debt, perhaps originally to parents but projected backward to gods. The gods so understood are not the same as "the god" of whom the Athenian has been speaking; but his emphasis on debt, obligation, and subordination to larger cosmic powers is attuned to the larger moral task he has outlined of overcoming the human tendency to "puff up." Human beings who recognize and worship the gods (and lower beings) as the Athenian suggests will not feel themselves to be self-sufficient "somebody's." They will experience humility and thus be encouraged to behave with moderation. Piety is particularly connected to moderation; thus the Athenian's dedication to producing a human order devoted to moderation is at the same time directed in an eminent way to piety toward beings understood to be the very source of the good and of existence itself. Thus the god must be supplemented by the Athenian's version of the Olympians.

Yet the Athenian also implies that his political theology will be of limited efficacy. The closest the Athenian comes to explaining the limitedness of his political theology is his insistence to the two old Dorians that parents must be treated with particular respect (717d). Even the old are spirited and given to anger—how much more so the young. Human beings are too much creatures of spirit to take entirely well to the counsels of humility, reverence, and dependence. The general prelude about the god and the gods is thus both necessary and of limited use. The Athenian appears to have muted hopes for constructing a good society on the basis of piety or divine law.

VII. Law (719a–724b)

The Athenian has shown himself to have a certain poetic bent. He has composed a speech for a character named "the legislator" to deliver to a set of characters called "the people." This speech is so much not his own that it has "an effect" on him, which he wishes to share with his companions. The speech takes the form of a "dialogue with the lawgiver." Once again he plays the poet, but this time he does not speak as the lawgiver but rather to the lawgiver, and "on behalf of the poets." Just as the three companions had earlier criticized and set bounds to what the poets could say (656c), now, speaking for the poets, the Athenian criticizes the speech of the lawgiver. The "poets" speak of their tendency to "contradict" themselves by composing different speeches for different characters as suits those characters. The lawgiver does not have the luxury of doing this—he must say the same thing to everybody. The lawgiver, however, has acted more like a poet (as does the Athenian) and less like a proper lawgiver, for he laid down a rule (not yet quite a law) that addressed different things to different individuals. He prescribed moderate funerals for everybody, but what is moderate for a rich man is not moderate for a poor man. It is not entirely clear what the Athenian's point is, however. Is it that the lawgiver has been a poor draftsman in this case, that he needs to be more precise in specifying what a moderate funeral is, so that there is a clear and unambiguous definition of the legally permissible funeral? That is, should the legislator be less like the poet, in that he must truly say only one thing to everybody? Or, is his more subtle point the obverse, that proper treatment of individuals does not recommend the unambiguous speech to which the lawgiver aspires? Is the Athenian's point, as speaker for the poets, that the legislator needs to be even more rather than less the poet?

The Athenian perhaps takes the point in the latter direction, for his "reply" on behalf of the poets leads him to introduce the idea that all (or most) laws should contain a speech of sorts and not merely be commands. The speech is to be an explanation of the command, a giving of the reason for the law. But judging from the example he gives of a marriage law, it is to be an explanation of a very far-reaching kind. The bare-bones marriage law specifies the age at which a man is to marry and the penalty for not doing so. The accompanying speech places the law and its command in the context of a story about human life that gives an account of the intent of the law. The speech is poetic in a double sense. It tells a story of the sort both philosophers and poets might tell (compare this speech to "Diotima's speech" in the *Symposium*), but it does not give the kinds of proof a philosopher would give. It has the character the Athenian attributes to all pronouncements of the poets—they are inspired and do not know the reasons for what they say (719c). The speech, in explaining the point of the law, makes the law better able to speak to different persons in different ways. It allows the addressees of the laws to understand better how the laws apply to them, what the laws mean for them. If this is a proper reading of the little dialogue the Athenian constructs, then it implies that there is a necessary place in his city for the poets and for poetry, although the Athenian does not withdraw his earlier suggestion that the poets must not be free to say just anything. If necessary to proper legislating, they must still be subordinate to the legislator.

Perhaps the ultimate point of this discussion, however, is to contribute to what we might identify as the overriding theme of Book 4: "no mortal ever legislates anything, but that almost all human affairs are matters of chance" (709b). Or, perhaps better put: mortals cannot legislate successfully. One cannot expect much from legislation. In the present case the problem is that law must both say one thing as a command and address different individuals and circumstances appropriately. The Athenian appears to share a view of the limits of law with other Platonic philosophers; both Socrates and the Eleatic Stranger express views similar to this. No matter how much the Platonic philosophers may otherwise disagree, they seem to agree on this.

The introduction of the poetic dimension of law leads to a back and forth exchange between the three old men about whether the speech is properly part of the law or a prelude to the law. The Athenian concludes that it is not a proper part of the law but a prelude (722e). As we have noted, this is the conclusion they reach at high noon (722c), suitable to the hour at which it is pronounced, for it gives a new understanding of what law is. Law is "tyrannical command," i.e., command backed up by force. The poetic or persuasive element is "prelude," i.e., a speech aiming to put the addressees of the law proper "in a frame of mind more favorably disposed and therefore more apt to learn something" (723a–b). It makes the people more likely to accept the law but does not alter the essential character of law: coercion and command. The Athenian thus definitively revises the way he had characterized law near the beginning of the conversation. Law is not "soft and gentle" (See 645a).

The Athenian had implicitly promised to indicate what makes up for the limited effectiveness of his (or any) political theology. Law, understood as he presents it here, seems to be the answer. All the discussion of preludes and speeches and poets has the temporary effect of obscuring the harsh character of law and thus of political life. The preludes, represented by the free doctor in contradistinction to the slave doctor, raise for a moment the hope that law can be replaced by persuasion. Just as the "free doctor" explains to his patients the nature of their illness and the reason for his prescription, and just as the free patient accepts the treatment voluntarily, so the Athenian momentarily holds out the hope that the people can be guided to accept governance voluntarily, as advice rather than command.

It is that prospect—flattering to the people and optimistic about what political life might be—that wins the assent of the two Dorians. The action of Book 4, as we have noted earlier, is a movement from the affirmation of Dorian ways, a flattery of the Dorians for the excellence of their laws and institutions, to a rejection by Megillus of the "Laconian way" and an acceptance by Cleinias of the innovation of preludes that the Athenian proposes (723b). The Athenian has succeeded in persuading them to accept not only the innovation of preludes to law, but the particular prelude to the entire code—the legislator's speech about the god, piety, and moderation. He has moved them to the opposite moral pole from that of their native cities. Like a wise poet he has cast them as the free patients of the free doctor, and holds out the hope for a free politics.

By retreating from the preludes and leaving us the harsh knowledge that law is command and coercion and not speech (poetic or otherwise) the Athenian punctures the hopes with which he has beguiled the two Dorians. Once again, he shows the limits of the legislative art. The resistances with which the legislative art must struggle are not only in the external world, but in humankind itself. Hence the main point of Book 4 is that it is indeed "difficult for a city with good laws to come into existence."

If, then, Book 4 is a prelude meant to prepare its audience for legislation, then it serves its purpose by, in effect, working to reconcile us to politics more or less as it is, as we might say, to politics—warts and all.

Notes

1. This conclusion has much in common with Eric Salem's subtle and thoughtful analysis of *Laws* 1. I am more skeptical than he is, however, about the degree of success the Athenian has in winning the two Dorians over in *Laws* 1. Also see Catherine Zuckert, 2009, 62.

2. See Patricia Fagan's contribution to this volume.

3. Benardete 2000a, 128–129. The relevant Homeric passage is *Iliad* 14.65–102.

4. See C. Zuckert, 2009.

5. See Fagan, 2–3.

6. Cf. Fagan: "Virtue in the new city will depend upon the city's isolation from all other peoples," 3.

7. Thus I see the idea of the city's isolation to be quite the opposite of what Fagan infers from the Cyclopes. See Fagan, 7–8.

8. Consider the discussion of the origin of legislation: 681c–d.

9. Cf. *Laws* 5 where the Athenian suggests some practices of population selection that extend beyond these alternatives (735bff.).

10. But consider C. Zuckert 2009, 71, on Cleinias and tyranny.

11. See Strauss 1975, 57; C. Zuckert 2009, 83.

12. Perhaps there is more irony at play here on the part of all participants in the conversation than Fagan allows (Fagan, 8).

13. See Sara Brill, on *Laws* 10, in her contribution to this volume.

14. C. Zuckert 2009, ch. 1.

15. Pangle 1980, ad loc.

16. Cf. C. Zuckert 2009, 85–86.

17. Ibid., 87.

7 "He Saw the Cities and He Knew the Minds of Many Men": Landscape and Character in the *Odyssey* and the *Laws*

Patricia Fagan

The opening discussion of the constitutions of Crete and Sparta in *Laws* 1 (624a–626b) reveals two features central to the creation of laws, constitutions, and education: they are received from a god through a human intermediary (Zeus through Minos in the case of Crete, Apollo through Lycurgus in the case of Laconia). Second, aspects of the constitution develop out of the interactions of human groups with the terrain they inhabit. The Athenian stranger asks Cleinias, why does your law demand the common messes and the γυμναστική and weapons you employ (625c)? Cleinias replies that their γυμναστική has emerged from the landscape of Crete: it is not flat, so the Cretans do not use horses, but run. When running, light arms like bows and arrows are necessary. So, because of the landscape they inhabit, the Cretans have developed a particular set of military practices and a γυμναστική that supports that military practice. This paper traces a part of the working-out of these two themes, the relation between terrain and political character and the role of the divine in a πολιτεία, in the earlier and central books of the *Laws*. My discussion begins from the point about the relationship between constitution and terrain. I will examine here the opening of Book 4, where the stranger explains the significance for the development of virtue in the new city, of the city's having a proper location and the right type of productive land; the new city's virtue will depend upon her being isolated from other cities and agriculturally self-sufficient. I will discuss this analysis in light of the Cyclopes of the *Odyssey*, another isolated and agriculturally self-sufficient group, whom the stranger invokes in Book 3 as an example of the most just type of rule. The landscape the Cyclopes inhabit and the landscape the new city will inhabit, I will argue, indicate that the citizens of the new city will, like the Cyclopes, be characterized by hostile and closed-minded stances toward what comes to them from outside. I will turn next to a discussion of how the very opening of the *Laws* (as I have noted above) points to the crucial necessity of openness to the strange for the creation of laws and constitutions through its mention of the divine and mortal lawgivers of Crete and Sparta. Openness to the strange reveals itself here as openness to the divine, a theme that the *Laws* pursues through the figure of Dionysus. In the final section of the paper I will examine what I take to be the key features of Dionysus for the *Laws*: his ability to drive humans to madness in his rites and his violent punishment of cities that refuse to be open to the divine. Plato's use of the *Odyssey* and of Dionysus-myth, then, invite us to challenge some of the claims that the Stranger so authoritatively makes about the sources and nature of virtue in a city.

When concrete discussion of the construction of the new city begins in Book 4, the Stranger, following the precedent of the conversation with which the *Laws* begins, first asks Cleinias, at 704a–b, "What must one think the city is going to be? . . . I'm not asking what name it has at present or what it will be necessary to call it . . . What I mean to ask about it now is rather this: whether it will be on the sea or inland."[1] Cleinias answers that the city will be eighty stades from the sea and will have access to very good harbors along the coast. Further, the land around it is very productive, lacking in nothing (704b). There is no neighboring polis near it, because "an ancient migration from the place has left the land deserted for an incalculably long time" (704c).[2] Further, the terrain overall is rough, as is the rest of Crete, and does not provide any good stands of fir, pine, cypress, pitch pine, or plane trees, the trees used for shipbuilding (705c). The new city, then, will be inland, isolated from other cities, surrounded by land rich for agriculture but lacking ships' timber.

Since the goal of any constitution is the rearing of citizens who possess all the parts of virtue (a point developed in the early pages of Book 1, 630a ff.), the Stranger's response to the information Cleinias provides addresses how this terrain will assist in or interfere with the developing of virtuous citizens: "it would not be incurable, at least, as regards the acquisition of virtue" (704d). He elaborates this statement as follows: the new city will be closer to the sea than it should be, but its distance from the sea will provide some protection from dangers from the sea. The dangers from the sea are other people, primarily. Other people come to cities by sea and fill a city with trade and money-making, which give citizens untrustworthy and παλίμβολα (reversible, unstable) habits (705a–

b). Other people also provide citizens with examples of behavior to imitate, as the Stranger indicates in his discussion of the imitating of enemies at 706a–d (I will discuss this section in more detail below). So, being some distance from the sea will protect the new city from a variety of outside influences. Further, that the land is capable of producing all the agricultural product a city could need will be good for the city, since, presumably, the city will not need to import anything from outside. That the terrain is rough, that there is not an *over-abundance* of productive land, is also good, as the city will not then have an excess of goods that she will export to the outside (705b).

The absence of trees used in ship-building is good, because it will prevent the city from easily imitating the practice of building ships and sailing around. The Stranger tells Cleinias and Megillus that the people of Attica, who did not have good ship timber growing in their territory, did not learn the practices of ship-building, sailing, and naval warfare from the Cretans when Minos attacked them and took the annual tribute of the seven youths and seven maidens (706b–c). At that time they were unable to defend themselves against Minos, which was a good thing for them, since, now that they have learned all of the practices of the sea, and, in particular, of warfare at sea, the Athenians have created among their citizens wretched habits (706d) of cowardice and changeability. The people of Attica have, in effect, become παλίμβολοι, reversible. Notice the discussion of how marines behave: they attack, they run back (πάλιν—the first element of the adjective παλίμβολος) to their ships, they drop their weapons and flee (706c)—they are constantly in motion, unstable, reversible.[3]

Key for the Stranger here is the isolation of the new city from the outside. Agricultural self-sufficiency will ensure that the city does not need to seek contact with other cities, other people. Absence of near neighbors will ensure that other people do not happen to come to the city by land. Distance from the sea will ensure that other people do not happen to come to the city from the sea. Virtue in the new city will depend, first of all, upon the city's isolation from all other peoples. The laws of people in isolation have already been discussed in Book 3, as part of the overview of the history of constitutional development. Over the course of cosmic time, the Stranger says, many thousands of cities have come into being and passed away (676b–c). The old stories tell us that disasters, such as flood and plague, have destroyed humans and left tiny groups behind (676c–677a). These tiny groups lived in the mountains, kept sheep and goats, and did not possess any of the arts of city-dwelling nor any of the vicious habits of city-dwelling (677b–679e). These people lived under the type of πολιτεία, the stranger says, that we would call a δυναστεία, a dynasty, following πατρίοις νόμοις, ancestral laws (680a–b). They were, in fact, the Stranger says, just like what Homer describes when he discusses the Cyclopes (680c); here the Stranger quotes *Odyssey* 9.112–115:

> These people have no institutions, no meetings for counsels;
> rather they make their habitations in caverns hollowed
> among the peaks of the high mountains, and each one is the law
> for his own wives and children, and cares nothing about the others.[4]

Such people, the Stranger says a bit later, are found scattered in single houses and by tribes because of the lack of resources caused by the destructions, living under ancestral laws and living under kings (βασιλευόμενοι), under a kingship that is most just (δικαιοτάτην) (680d–e).

Note already two resonances with the material from *Laws* 4 I have just discussed: the isolation of the units and the land abandoned after a disaster (compare 4.704b–c—the site will be eighty stades from the sea and without neighbors because of "an ancient migration"). Note also the dissonance of uttering the word δικαιοτάτην (most just) in a context describing the practices of the Cyclopes, whom the Stranger explicitly identifies at 680c. The text does not merely rely on our recognizing the precise context of the quote, but makes a point of *naming* the Cyclopes, renowned, because of the *Odyssey*'s Polyphemus, as examples of idiosyncrasy and violence, two qualities opposed to the possession of δίκη.[5] So this quote and the claim that this kind of regime is the most just kingship stand as a problem demanding more scrutiny and more thinking.

To understand what the text could be asking us to think about here, I turn to the section of the *Odyssey* that the Stranger quotes. These lines are part of Odysseus's description of the land of the Cyclopes as he relates his wanderings before the court of Alkinoös, king of the Phaiakians (*Odyssey* 9.106–141). The lines that the Stranger quotes appear close to the beginning of this passage. What I want to establish here is that the terrain of the land of the Cyclopes and the terrain of new city have two important characteristics in common. Given that Book 1 and the Stranger's discussion of terrain in Book 4 have told us that terrain determines constitution, which determines the character of the citizens, it should be the case that similar terrains lead to similar characters.

First of all, at 9.107–111, the poem tells us that the Cyclopes, outrageous and lawless (ὑπερφιάλων ἀθεμίστων, line 106),

> ... putting all their trust in the immortal gods,
> neither plough with their hands nor plant anything,
> but all grows for them without seed planting, without cultivation,

wheat and barley and also the grapevines, which yield for them 110
wine of strength, and it is Zeus's rain that waters it for them.

This land, like the land of the new city, is lacking in nothing in terms of agricultural produce, although here, of course, there is no agriculture. The Cyclopes and the new city are both self-sufficient (compare *Laws* 4.704b). The Cyclopes, further, are isolated. Their isolation depends not simply on their being in that part of the world that is off the map, the part of the world in which Odysseus's wanderings take place, but on their not having the ability to use the sea to travel. They live across a stretch of sea from an island that is perfect for habitation: it possesses forest, goats, arable land, meadows, a good harbor (*Od.* 9.116–139). The Cyclopes do not come to this island because (*Od.* 9.125–130) they do not have ships or ship-builders; if they had they could sail to other cities as men do, crossing the sea with their ships to each other. The Cyclopes are kept to one place because they cannot leave it. The Stranger hopes that the citizens in the new city, in the same way, will not be able to leave the city because they, like the Cyclopes, will not have ships. Ships, in the *Odyssey* passage, are explicitly linked with two things: contact with other cities and peoples and the foundation of new settlements (the Cyclopes, if they could sail to the habitable island, could make it a well-founded dwelling, *Od.* 9.130). Contact with other humans is precisely the thing that the stranger wants the new city to avoid. In both the *Odyssey* and the *Laws*, then, we see the same themes, self-sufficiency and isolation, emerge.[6]

What, then, are the Cyclopes like and how can their practices be said to be related to the terrain in which they dwell? Our understanding of the Cyclopes depends largely upon the behavior of Polyphemus, visited by Odysseus and twelve of his companions. Polyphemus, of course, kills some of Odysseus's companions and eats them raw, trapping those left alive inside his cave with a great boulder. In Polyphemus's behavior we see the greatest violation of the practice of hospitality that the *Odyssey* offers. Polyphemus himself does not explain his behavior, except insofar as he says, when Odysseus beseeches him for a guest-gift and appropriate hospitality in the name of Zeus, protector of strangers (*Od.* 9.266–271), that the Cyclopes, being better than the gods, do not worry about Zeus; he would not spare Odysseus simply out of fear of retribution from Zeus if he felt like doing them harm (*Od.* 9.273–279). So the Cyclopes are not bound by the same divine laws, the laws of *xenia*, hospitality, that bind human beings. That freedom does not explain *why* Polyphemus acts as he does, though. It explains *how* he can act as he does without fear of the gods. In part, I think, we see why Polyphemus eats Odysseus's companions in the opening description of the land of the Cyclopes at *Odyssey* 8.106–141. In this land, the earth produces for the Cyclopes everything that they need out of the soil, grains and grapes; for other needs they herd goats and sheep. The Cyclopes are beings in whose world everything that appears is *for their use*. Earth produces, they eat what it produces. Animals are there, they eat the animals. Their only experience of life that is not Cyclopean life is that it is to be exploited and destroyed. When, returning from a day spent herding his flock, Polyphemus finds Odysseus and his companions waiting in his cave, what he finds is another version of earth producing for him from itself. He knows that Odysseus and his companions must have come to his land from across the sea and asks them why they have come here (*Od.* 9.252–255), but displays no particular interest in Odysseus's reply, other than to say that he will treat the strangers as he sees fit. Then he kills and eats two of the companions (*Od.* 9.287–293). The strangers are present and vulnerable or open to him, just as a sheep is vulnerable or open to him, or a grapevine, and he treats them as he would treat other life that comes beneath his hand: he eats them. The land that produces in itself all of our needs leads us to regard everything that appears before us as for *our* needs. The world exists *for us*, not for others, not for itself.[7]

It is precisely this stance toward others that Cyclopean isolation encourages. Not having access to the rest of the world means not having access to, as the poem tells us, the cities of human beings (*Od.* 9.128).[8] The proem of the *Odyssey* tells us that it will sing the man of many ways who wandered much and saw the cities and knew the minds of many men (*Od.* 1.1–3); the wanderings themselves, as Odysseus narrates them in the central books of the poem, insist on his travels forcing him to develop a new understanding of how he sees his own relationship to strangers. We see a progression from the marauding pirate as whom he begins his wanderings, as he and his companions fall upon and sack the city of the Kikones, killing the people and taking their wives and possessions as spoil (*Od.* 9.40–41)[9] to the assimilable gracious guest of Alkinoös and the Phaiakians. Contact with strangers, with the cities and minds of others, has forced Odysseus to cease to regard the world as *for him*.[10]

The self-sufficiency and isolation of the Cyclopes, then, leads them to destroy what comes to them by eating it. This is their habit, their not-quite-immediate response to what is not themselves. In the same way, when we turn back to Book 4 of the *Laws*, we see a similar habit developing: what comes from outside, what is not us, can only be harmful to us. The Stranger argues that the city's isolation is what will ensure its virtue because the influence of outsiders through trade and warfare will only be harmful to the city. We in the new city, rather than seeing the world as *for us,* will see it as *not* for us. In either case, we do not let what comes from outside tell us what it is. We already know.

So, in light of the invocation of the Cyclopes in Book 3, we see that the new city's terrain already indicates that she will foster citizens who are not *open* to the strange, insofar as they will know what the strange, the ξένος, is before they meet it. It is that which we must reject and fear. The discussion in Book 4 does not regard this prejudice as problematic; indeed, it will serve as the motivation for many of the laws concerning education, trade, and the like, that the Stranger goes on to articulate. It is nonetheless the case that the *Laws* itself has already indicated at least one way in which openness to the strange is critical to a city and her laws: laws, constitutions, are not things that human beings simply make up themselves. Rather, laws come to us from the gods and come to us through human intermediaries. The opening of the dialogue, as I noted at the beginning of my discussion, reminds us that the Cretans received their laws from Zeus through Minos and the Spartans received their laws from Apollo through Lycurgus. To the first humans to receive these constitutions, they must have seemed a radical change from current ways of thinking and acting.[11] In order for these divine utterances to become constitutions, laws, for human beings, the people of Crete and Laconia must have been *open* to accepting them. The new, the strange, coming from outside, from a god, had to be something they could accept.

Keeping these things in mind, when we turn again to the new city in Book 4, we see that the Stranger argues as follows: at 709a–c he says that god, chance, opportunity, and art guide all human affairs; human beings themselves are not simply self-directing, but depend on these other forces, especially for the framing of laws. The good lawgiver, faced with installing his laws in a city, would ask to have a city governed by a tyrant (τυραννουμένην πόλιν) (709e). Under a tyrant (710b) the lawgiver's laws would be accepted most quickly and easily. At 711b–c the Stranger notes that the tyrant, of all rulers, can most effectively serve as an example to the people of his city, so that he may turn them toward virtue through praise if they follow his example, and through dishonor if they do not. Cleinias wonders at this point why citizens would follow the tyrant, who would be using a combination of persuasion and violence (πείθω and βία) to govern (711c). The Stranger replies that no one could ever change a constitution more quickly than an all-powerful ruler (711c). So in *one* specific instance—tyranny—the openness of citizens to change is not important. The tyrant will change things as he sees fit, using whatever method he chooses, persuasion or violence. He can impose his will. In any other type of city, then, it must be the case that citizen openness to transformation of the laws is necessary and crucial.

Further, the Stranger has argued in Book 3 that the lawgiver must aim at three things: that the city be free, that the city be a friend (φίλη) to herself, and that the city have intelligence (νοῦς) (701d). The laws should, then, create a city that participates in the hallmark of the divine, reason and understanding.[12] The gods, then, in the stories of Minos and Lycurgus, and in the very notion of law itself, are the sources of law for humans. We receive law from the gods through other human beings, lawgivers, and so we must be prepared to accept, to be open to, the divine as it comes to us through humans. We can recall Polyphemus, who marks himself as lawless, particularly concerning hospitality, when he tells Odysseus that he has no fear of Zeus and the gods and so will not restrain himself in any way out of respect for the gods' laws. If we are not to be like Polyphemus, we must, in the end, be open to the divine.[13]

This point about the necessity of openness to the divine as the provider of law is not merely implicit in these stories of Minos, Zeus, Apollo, and Lycurgus, nor in the account of the ease with which a tyrant can install the constitution of the lawgiver; openness to the divine is a thread that runs throughout the *Laws*. I have seen it at play most clearly in the use the dialogue makes of Dionysus. So it is to Dionysus I now turn.

The god first appears in Book 1, at 637b–c, as one of his festivals, the Dionysia. Megillus complains that people use the Dionysia (not Spartans, of course) as an excuse to yield to all sorts of pleasures once they get drunk; he has seen this behavior at Athens and at Taras, Sparta's colony in Italy. The Stranger's response here is interesting: he notes that any stranger amazed at (θαυμάζων) what he is not used to at home should be reminded that this is how law is *here* and that maybe the law is different at home (637c). I note two things here initially: what causes amazement, θαῦμα, is strangeness, lack of familiarity, and the response to θαῦμα, as evinced by Megillus, can be to condemn what is not familiar and what is not understood.[14] The *proper* response, articulated by the Stranger, is to see that the unfamiliar can be law, νόμος, that it has its own meaning, history, and place. In the example here, the Dionysia at Athens and Taras, we see that the rituals of a place, the way one city honors a god recognized and shared by all Greek cities, can cause amazement to a stranger.[15] He can be closed to the divine as it manifests itself outside his own home. Second I note that this expression of open-mindedness occurs in a context involving Dionysus.

We next meet Dionysus in Book 2, in the discussion of the importance of holidays and festivities that opens the book. Holidays are necessary, the Stranger says, to help us resuscitate what we learned over the course of our education about good attitudes toward pain and pleasure (653c). The gods give us periods of rest from work and they have given us the Muses, Apollo, and Dionysus as the gods who will, as fellow-celebrators (συνεορταϲταί), set us back upright again (653d). The gods mentioned here are of course the gods in charge of musical performance. What is being invoked especially is choral performance. Dionysus oversees choral performance as the god of group identity; the Muses as performers are always a chorus; Apollo is here called μουϲηγέτηϲ, leader of the Muses, indicating that he is chorus-leader of the Muses, a typical performance role for him.[16] It is of course choral music that is discussed over the course of Book 2. The Stranger also refers to these gods as fellow celebrators, συνεορταϲταί, implying that these gods are present to us when we celebrate. This implication is odd for Apollo and the Muses: in our world we do not meet these gods face to face.[17] For Dionysus it is commonplace, as he alone among the gods is conceived as present with his worshippers at their festivities; he is one of the celebrating group.[18] The Stranger installs Dionysus here as crucial to education and crucial to the maintenance of the lessons of education in later life. His chorus of elders in the revised drinking curriculum of Books 1 and 2 will serve as models for appropriate singing and as singers of the best and most beautiful things (665a–d).

Toward the end of Book 2, another aspect of Dionysus is raised: his role as the god of *mania*, madness (672a–c). Drunkenness is a variety of madness that, the Stranger says, people misinterpret and condemn when they should not.[19] He tells a story, an aetiological tale about the origins of *mania* among humans, which he also says we should perhaps not tell (672b). The story goes as follows: Dionysus's sense was struck out of his soul by Hera; as vengeance the god inflicted Bacchic *mania* along with choruses and wine on human beings. *Mania* is what causes sensible things to cry out and jump about randomly when they are young. This crying out and jumping are what give rise to μουϲική and γυμναϲτική and are also what allow us to perceive rhythm and harmony (672d). Μανία, then, produces the two central planks of education. So μανία in this basic but important way is not something to condemn.

The story the Stranger tells here is significant: Hera made Dionysus lose his senses, and so he installed important aspects of his own worship among human beings. We seem to have here an allusion to and an adaptation of the most common type of myth of Dionysus, in which the god is not recognized and so punishes people (the recognition myth). The association of Hera and madness and Dionysus seems to point to a particular myth, the myth of Lycurgus;[20] the best-known version of this myth appears at *Iliad* 6.130–140. The common features of the various versions are roughly as follows: Hera instigates Lycurgus to attack Dionysus, who is on earth with a group of women and is mad. Dionysus flees before his attacker. Lycurgus is punished in a variety of ways, none of which involves the installation of rituals.[21] The Lycurgus myth, in its extant formulations, does *not* follow the pattern of the recognition myth, which includes, as *its* concluding moment, the installation-of-ritual function. Euripides' *Bacchae* provides the most thorough working-out of the Dionysiac recognition-myth pattern, which contains the following five elements:

1. Dionysus appears *in disguise* among humans to ask for recognition of his rites.
2. The group or representatives of the group refuse to acknowledge the god; they resist the new and innovative relationship with the divine that he offers.
3. The god drives the offenders mad and drives them out into the wild.
4. The god has humans destroy children within their own household.
5. The god, now recognized, installs his rites within the group of humans.[22]

The Stranger's story of the introduction of *mania* to humans by Dionysus, then, takes one fairly common myth, the myth of Dionysus and Lycurgus, and adds a final element, the institution of a ritual, from the dominant Dionysus myth-type. This invocation of the recognition myth reminds us of the violence of the god's anger at humans who refuse to be open to the strange.

Dionysus is the god of the mask, the ξένος, the stranger *par excellence*. Dionysus is the god who reminds us always of the crucial importance of not rejecting the one who comes to us from outside and who, as he does in the *Bacchae*, upsets us.[23] He overturns the customary order of the city, driving women out of their homes, out of the city, to dance in the wild places. He intoxicates, he unifies, he terrifies. He is not moderate and he demands that we not be moderate, too. The recognition myth insists on the god's hostility to the staid order of the city-state, manifested in part through his driving us to dance. Book 7 of the *Laws* discusses the dances of Dionysus briefly. The Stranger enumerates the different types of dance: warlike dance, like the Pyrrhic dance that imitates combat (815a), and peaceful dance in honor of the gods (815d–e). These are dances of a πολιτικὸν γένος, a political type, unlike *Bacchic* dancing, in which drunken people imitate ritual and members of the Dionysiac retinue, like satyrs (815c). This dance is not warlike, not peaceful, not πολιτικόν. Like the god in whose honor it is performed, Bacchic dance is not *of* the city.

Dionysus is the god who manifests himself as hostile to city order, as *not* πολιτικός; yet he is a crucial god for every Greek city-state, as he is for the new city. His function in the city is to refresh, to allow us to turn from the everyday world of work to festivity and to madness. His madness allows us to see the new, to jump, to dance. His madness also comes in a more violent form as punishment—punishment in which we humans are the agents—when we refuse to be open, when we take up the stranger only as dangerous, as abusable because of his danger. Dionysus is the god who tells us not to manifest the Megillan response to θαῦμα at the unfamiliar, rejection and condemnation. Dionysus is, further, the god who, as the one who drives us out of our households and out of the city, overcomes the tendency of city-dwelling humans toward introversion and isolation.[24] He is the god who enforces our openness to each other, to other households, other cities, to the new; he ensures that we not isolate ourselves in our comfortable, familiar, homely understanding of the world.

The two planks of law-creation in *Laws* 1, then, that laws be received from a god and that laws emerge from humans' relationships with their landscape, tell us that the new city—built in a land that will ensure her hostility to strangers due to her belief in her own self-sufficiency—will not achieve the primary goals of law-giving in a city. She will not be free, but closed; she will not be a friend to herself because her closedness will cripple and endanger her; and she will not have intelligence because she will refuse to countenance the possibility that the world is anything other that what she already thinks it is, the possibility that she needs to attend to what is outside herself and regard it as anything other than amazing. She will not be capable of seeing the law-abidingness in what does not abide by her laws.[25]

Notes

1. All translations of the *Laws* come from Pangle 1980.
2. See Nicholas F. Jones, 1990, 473–492. Jones notes (475) that the new city is a reconstruction on an old site, a fact that points to the πολιτεία constructed in *Laws* being a reconstruction of the cities upon whose laws the laws of the new city are based.
3. Morrow 1960 (96–97) sees the criticism of naval warfare here as a manifestation of late fifth- and fourth-century criticism of Pericles' strategy for the conduct of the Peloponnesian War (to avoid infantry battle with the Spartans by abandoning the agricultural territory of Attica to the Spartans and to withdraw into the walls of the city, fighting primarily by ship), which troubled many Athenians because this policy manifested "unwillingness to preserve the sacred soil of Attica." Inherent in this criticism is Athenian reverence for and attachment to their land, their territory. Compare Jim Roy, 2002, 191–202. At 191–200, Roy locates the discussion at *Laws* 4.704a–707d within an Athenian debate about the Piraieus (the main commercial port of Athens) as a location that undermined the Athenian citizen body because it provided a place for groups of Athenians to engage in bad behavior, such as prostitution and dishonest business prac-

tices. Morrow and Roy both point to Athenian discomfort with Athens' reliance on its navy and ports and the opposition between Athens proper (including her sacred soil) and those parts of the polis associated with the navy.

4. All translations of the *Odyssey* are my own. Jones 1990 notes that the πολιτεία constructed by the Athenian Stranger promotes the introversion of the demes, in particular, through their being coherently internally organized and kept out of the work of government (492). This isolation and internal coherence are parallel to the isolation and internal lawgiving coherence of the households of the Cyclopes.

5. Compare Hesiod's account of the coming end of the Iron Age at *Works and Days*, 174–201: there will be no agreement among people, no respect for oaths, but violence and praise for violence.

6. The passage in *Laws* 4 under discussion here is, of course, very much concerned with ships as providing contact with other cities and peoples. Given that many of the new settlers are supposed to come from mainland Greece, in particular the Peloponnese (708a), the role of ships in city-foundation is also relevant to *Laws* 4.

7. Compare Erwin F. Cook, 1995. Cook argues (97–100) that the *Odyssey* marks the Cyclopes as being without the social laws associated with the agora, the site of counsel and "corporate political memory." He notes, further, that their living, essentially, in a paradise in which everything they need comes spontaneously from the earth is what causes their excessive violence, their hubris.

8. Cook 1995 (108–109) remarks on the association in the account of Polyphemus and the Cyclopes of ships, commerce and culture as lined up against the Cyclopes.

9. The poem indicates that this attack is not part of any plan of warfare, but is simple opportunism, when it says, "carrying me from Ilion the wind brought me near the Kikones at Ismaros" (*Od.* 9.39–40).

10. Odysseus's transition from simple violent exploiter to guest of course depends also on his increasing vulnerability before those he meets· over the course of his wanderings he loses all of his companions. To understand himself as vulnerable, open to the wills of others, is to cease to see the world as for himself.

11. Compare Plutarch's account of Lycurgus's introduction of his constitution to Sparta in chapter 5 of his *Life of Lycurgus*. Lycurgus wins over supporters secretly and then, with thirty armed elite men, occupies the Spartan agora—his reforms come as part of a coup. He then announces his new πολιτεία, claiming that it was given to him by Pythian Apollo.

12. See, for example, *Laws* 1, 645c—a city should take over a logos from the gods and set that logos as a law for itself. Compare *Laws* 4, 715eff.—the god holds the beginning (ἀρχήν) and end (τελευτήν) and the middle of all the things that are.

13. See Pangle 1976. His discussion focuses on *Laws* 10 and the arguments there about theology and the nature of the soul. His point (1059) is that all the laws the Athenian proposes are "proposed with an eye to the god at all times." He notes further (1060) that a healthy political life, for Plato, must include myth and religion. My point here is that god is central to the idea of the πολιτεία already in *Laws* 1.

14. That is, the response can be a rejection similar to the fear of the strange encouraged by isolation.

15. Megillus's response to the rituals of other cities reminds us that the first generation of citizens in the new city will be in the same position as Megillus with respect not

just to ritual within the new city, but to all its institutions. They will be people who grew up under other laws. Compare Morrow 1960 (547), who notes that a major project of the new πολιτεία articulated in the *Laws* is to "harmonize" laws drawn from a variety of cities to create a single homogeneous citizen body out of settlers from several different cities. Jones 1990 (473–475) remarks on the same point: he sees the primary problem of the new foundation to be overcoming the "rootlessness and disunity" of a new city whose settlers come from multiple cities.

16. See Calame 1977, 100–103, 140–143.

17. See Burkert 1985, 146–147.

18. Compare the choral entry-song in Euripides' *Bacchae* (64–167), in which the chorus of Lydian maenads describes the god participating, as celebrant, in the rituals in his honor.

19. Marcel Detienne, 1989, 23, notes that the drinking of unmixed wine by the old men in the new city has wine in Dionysiac ritual take the place of mania in Dionysiac myth.

20. This Lycurgus is not the lawgiver of Laconia, but a king, son of Dryas, in Asia Minor.

21. According to *Iliad* 6.130–140, Zeus grows angry with Lycurgus and blinds him. Apollodoros's *Bibliotheca* 3.5.1 tells us that Lycurgus, mad, kills his own son, Dryas, with an axe, thinking that he is cutting vines; the people of his city then, on the orders of Dionysus, kill Lycurgus.

22. Other versions of this pattern include the myth of the daughters of Minyas and the myth of Dionysus's introduction of wine to Attica through the mediation of the farmer, Ikarios.

23. See Detienne 1989, who notes (23) that Dionysus-myth consistently portrays the god introducing his own worship to humans in his role as the Stranger; these myths insist, Detienne argues, on violence and defilement (brought on by the god's imposition of madness) followed by purification (achieved through accepting the god).

24. See Seaford 1993. Seaford argues here that Dionysus is the divine opponent of a tendency on the part of the city and especially of the household toward a false sense of self-sufficiency, manifested mythically, for example, as the endogamy of incest in Sophocles' *Oedipus Tyrannos* (see especially 138–141).

25. It will be apparent from my arguments here that I disagree with Nightingale 1993, who argues (in many regards compellingly, in my view) that the *Laws,* through the way it is written, provides no discursive strategy to challenge or undermine the authority of the Stranger as lawgiver. Through the inclusion of mythic material, Plato precisely opens up the Stranger's authority to question.

8   On the Human and the Divine: Reading the Prelude in Plato's *Laws* 5

Robert Metcalf

In the opening pages of Plato's *Laws*, Cleinias advances the thought that all human beings are "enemies" [πολεμίους] one to another, and each human being to himself, so that, within each of us, there is a war [πόλεμος] being waged of the self against itself [ἐν ἑκάστοις ἡμῶν . . . πρὸς ἡμᾶς αὐτοὺς] (626d–e). This thought determines the discussion that follows, insofar as ἀρετή is understood in terms of attaining "victory over oneself" [τὸ νικᾷν αὐτὸν αὑτον] (626e) after fighting off [διαμάχη] fears, pains, longings, and pleasures (633c–d), and thus, after "withstanding" [καρτερεῖν] pleasures rather than being enslaved or compelled by what is shameful [τῶν αἰσχρῶν ἀναγκάζεσθαι] (635c–d).[1] Victory within this πόλεμος of the soul amounts, therefore, to what is superior within us exercising control over what is inferior, and ἀρετή, accordingly, is understood as being able to rule over oneself—the Athenian specifies "those who are good" [οἱ ἀγαθοί] as the ones able to "rule themselves" [ἄρχειν αὑτῶν] (644b). This polemical orientation toward ἀρετή, and particularly with respect to pleasures and pains, is a theme for which the Athenian has recourse to the lines from Hesiod, quoted also by Adeimantus in Plato's *Republic*: "Vice in abundance is easy to get; / The road is smooth and begins beside you, / But the gods have put sweat between us and ἀρετή."[2]

This polemical orientation toward ἀρετή is philosophically significant in and of itself, but it also has implications for the composition of the prelude in Book 5. First of all, in order to make sense of ἀρετή as a "victory over oneself," it establishes a hierarchy within the soul of the superior over the inferior, and maps onto this a hierarchy of goods, namely, the "divine" goods over the "human" goods. The Athenian distinguishes between these two types of goods early in the text and assigns them their relative importance as follows:

Now the good things are twofold, some human [ἀνθρώπινα], some divine [θεῖα]. The former depend on the divine goods, and if a city receives the greater it will also acquire the lesser. If not, it will lack both. Health [ὑγίεια] leads the lesser goods; in the second place is beauty [κάλλος]; third is strength [ἰσχὺς], both in running and in all the other motions of the body; and fourth is wealth [πλοῦτος] ... Practical wisdom [φρόνησις], in turn, is first and leader among the divine goods. Second after intelligence comes a temperate disposition of the soul [σώφρων ψυχῆς ἕξις], and from these two mixed with courage comes justice [δικαιοσύνη], in the third place. Courage [ἀνδρία] is fourth. All of these last goods are by nature placed prior in rank to the first, and this is the rank they should be placed in by the legislator. (631b–d)

The second, key implication is that this establishment of the higher (the divine) in relation to the lower (the human) can be articulated mythopoetically, as we find in the myth of Cronus presented in Book 4. There, the Athenian says that, in the time of Cronus, human nature was not sufficient by its own power to direct human affairs without becoming filled with hubris and injustice [ἀνθρωπεία φύσις οὐδεμία ἱκανὴ τὰ ἀνθρώπινα διοικοῦσα αὐτοκράτωρ πάντα μὴ οὐχ ὕβρεώς τε καὶ ἀδικίας μεστοῦσθαι] (713c).[3] Cronus knew this about human beings and carried out a bit of philanthropy, appointing a race of daemons to exercise mastery over us, just as we exercise mastery over sheep, goats, and oxen (713d). That is to say, Cronus devised a political solution for our all-too-human incapacity for self-governance, as the daemons were made the kings and rulers of πόλεις in place of humans. Thanks to Cronus, the human races were taken care of [ἐπιμελούμεον], provided with peace and a sense of shame, good order and justice plenty [εἰρήνην τε καὶ αἰδῶ καὶ εὐνομίαν καὶ ἀφθονίαν δίκης παρεχόμενον], thus making for happiness without strife (713d–e).

The Athenian then announces the "present-day" moral of this story[4] to be the following:

What this *logos* is saying, making use of the truth [ἀληθείᾳ χρώμενος], is that there can be no rest from evils and toils for those cities in which some mortal rules rather than a god. The *logos* deems [οἴεται] that we should imitate by every device the way of life that is said to have existed under Cronus; in public life and in private life, in the arrangement of our households and our cities [δημοσίᾳ καὶ ἰδίᾳ τάς τ'οἰκήσεις καὶ τὰς πόλεις διοικεῖν], we should obey [πειθομένους] whatever within us partakes of immortality [ἀθανασία], giving the name "law" to the distribution ordained by intelligence. But if there is one human being, or some oligarchy, or a democracy, whose soul is yearning for pleasures and desires, and needs to be filled with these, and retains nothing, but is sick with endless and insatiable evil [ψυχὴν ἔχουσα ἡδονῶν καὶ ἐπιθυμιῶν ὀρεγομένην καὶ πληροῦσθαι τούτων δεομένην, στέγουσαν δὲ οὐδὲν ἀλλ' ἀνηνύτῳ καὶ ἀπλήστῳ κακῶν νοσήματι ξυνεχομένην]—if such a one rules a city or some private individual, trampling underfoot the laws, there is, as we just now said, no device for salvation. (713e–714a)[5]

In other words, while it may be true the gods have put sweat between us and ἀρετή—it requires, after all, an ongoing πόλεμος to achieve ἀρετή—still, it is thanks to the gods that we accomplish even this much. For the gods help us manage our own affairs by offering a model to which we can look, and in becoming "like" them to the extent possible, achieve the victory that is ἀρετή.[6] We are enjoined to imitate however we can the happy life that was provided for us in the age of Cronus, which I take to mean that we may think of ἀρετή and the "ruling ourselves" conceived as ἀρετή in the mythopoetic terms of being ruled by beings higher than ourselves. The mythopoetic lens through which we can see things affords us some inroads into an understanding of the prelude in Book 5.

But before we turn our attention to this prelude, we should note the fact that Book 5 begins just after the Athenian and his interlocutors have come to a greater sense of clarity as to what they have been discussing, and how they should be discussing, the matters at hand. The Athenian remarks that they have been in discussion since about dawn and it is now high noon (722c), and only now does it become clear that they have been composing preludes to the laws—which, as with preludes in music, are "composed with wondrous seriousness" [προοίμια θαυμαστῶς ἐσπουδασμένα] (322d–e). The preludes, then, that they have been composing with respect to gods and ancestors, and are now about to compose on how one should comport himself with respect to soul, body, and property (724a–b), are delivered "so that he who receives the law uttered by the legislator might receive the command [τὴν ἐπίταξιν]—that is, the law [ὁ νόμος]—in a frame of mind more favorably disposed and therefore more apt to learn something [εὐμενῶς καὶ τὴν εὐμένειαν εὐμαθέστερον . . . δέξηται]" (723a). The Athenian then appears to gloss the emphasis on learning, μανθάνειν, in the significance that he attaches to memory, μνήμη: "What is going to be said after this is of no small significance, and it makes no small difference whether or not the things are remembered clearly or unclearly" [σαφῶς ἢ μὴ σαφῶς αὐτὰ μνημονεύεσθαι] (723c). As we shall see, this attention to memory in how the preludes are composed may be key in accounting for their most distinctive features.

As for an initial impression of the prelude in Book 5, it is difficult to not agree with the various commentators who have said that the entirety of it reads like a long sermon.[7] Perhaps what is most striking about it is its non-dialogical character, as it stretches twenty-one Stephanus pages, at the end of which Cleinias says merely the following: "O, Athenian Stranger, what you have said is altogether excellent [παγκάλως], and I must do these things [ἐμοί τε ὅυτω ποιητέον]" (747e).[8] For some commentators, the non-dialogical character of Book 5 points to its "un-Socratic" character, inasmuch as the prelude does not appear to invite readers to practice philosophy.[9] As Andrea Nightingale puts it, "[I]t is one thing to believe that the gods endorse the truths that a person has discovered for himself by way of philosophical inquiry; it is quite another thing to encourage people who have not discovered these truths to accept them as divinely authorized rather than to seek out the truth for themselves."[10] On the other hand, as we have seen, the Athenian makes clear that the point of this and the other preludes is to *persuade* the auditor. Harvey Yunis offers the following comment on the persuasion at issue:

> The preamble is meant to be a persuasive statement that will induce the
> citizen to comply with the terms of the law on his own, without regard to
> the sanction included in the law . . . Essentially the preamble aims at the
> psychological state of the citizen, for it is a means to directed action. In the
> first try at a preamble the Athenian states the law, then adds διανοηθέντα
> ὡς . . . with the persuasive statement following (721b7) . . . He will do what
> the law enjoins if he bears in mind such and such. If the citizen believes the
> preamble, he will fulfill the terms of the law because of what he believes.
> The law and its sanction become otiose (cf. 822e–823a). By supplying the
> beliefs which suffice to bring about the action envisaged in the law, Plato
> has attempted to bridge the gap between belief and action.[11]

This interpretation accounts for how the preludes, even if non-dialogical, nonetheless contribute to the uncoerced law-abidingness of the citizenry through persuasion. The monological format, on this reading, would be appropriate given the uni-directionality of the instruction: the speaker presents those beliefs that the audience is to be persuaded of, and, bearing these in mind, to act on. However, this does raise the question of how such preludes are supposed to be persuasive. Are the preludes to persuade only by way of the authority of the speaker, as Yunis and Nightingale read it?[12] Alternatively, is it the case that the persuasiveness of, in particular, the prelude in Book 5 lies chiefly in its reformulation of the moral education sketched out previously in Plato's *Laws?*[13]

In any case, apart from this indeterminacy as to what is supposed to make the prelude persuasive, the prelude itself is remarkable for its language. Notice, first of all, that the first section of Book 5 begins with a sentence that, in Greek, has a solemn, percussive sound to it: πάντων γὰρ τῶν αὑτοῦ κτημάτων ψυχὴ θειότατον, οἰκειότατον ὄν, "Of all one's possessions, soul is the most divine, being most one's own" (726).[14] Leaving aside the question whether such language is likely to make the auditor "well-disposed" toward the law, it certainly is a memorable way to introduce the laws regarding property, and so perhaps is justifiable in part because of its mnemonic value.[15] Following this opening line, the Athenian says that we must honor the soul next after the gods (727a), and the proper way to do this is to honor that about oneself [τὰ . . . αὑτοῦ] which is better and stronger—what should exercise mastery [δεσπόζοντα]—above that which is weaker and worse, which should be subservient [δοῦλα] (726). The problem, he explains, is that none of us human beings accords honor in the right way, despite supposing [δοκεῖ] that we do.[16] Rather, we end up aggrandizing ourselves by way of words or bribes or obeisances, or praising ourselves or permitting ourselves the license to do whatever we wish, or by holding others responsible for our mistakes and exempting ourselves from blame (727a–c). In all of these ways we suppose that we are conferring honor on the soul, when in fact we do it harm. Here we might understand the famous claim that is made shortly after this passage, namely, that the greatest of evils is something that grows naturally in the soul—excessive love of oneself [ἡ σφόδρα ἑαυτοῦ φιλία]—as explaining, in part, our systematic misconstrual of proper honor. This claim also goes to show the practical implications of the admonishment to "cleave to what is better": "So every human being should flee excessive self-love, and should instead always pursue someone who is better than himself, without putting any feeling of shame [αἰσχύνη] in the way" (732b).

As to the specific harm that is done to the soul by the various ways of dishonoring it, the Stranger offers an example in what immediately follows: "Further, when a man gives way to pleasures that run afoul of the *logos* and commendation of the lawgiver, by no means does he confer honor upon his soul, but rather he dishonors it by filling it with evils and regret [ἀτιμάζει δὲ κακῶν καὶ μεταμελείας ἐμπιπλὰς αὐτήν]" (727c).[17] He then goes on to list a number of ways, similar to this one, in which one dishonors the soul: namely, not enduring [καρτερεῖν] the toils, fears, hardships, and pains that are commended by the lawgiver (727c); supposing that life is a good thing no matter the cost (727d); honoring beauty above ἀρετή—this last case being a "true and complete dishonoring of the soul [ἡ τῆς ψυχῆς ὄντως καὶ πάντως ἀτιμία]" since "this *logos*, by saying that body is to be honored more than the soul, tells a lie: for nothing earth-born is to be honored more than that of Olympus, and whoever holds a different opinion about the soul is ignorant of how wondrous a possession he has but neglects" (727d–e). By this point in the speech, it has become clear that the speaker seeks to persuade the hearer, above all, of the *incomparability* of the goods in question: in this case, honoring the soul requires an understanding that the soul is incomparably worthier of honor than anything "earth-born." In the case that follows, someone who lusts to obtain money in a dishonorable way is described as "giving away what is beautiful and honorable about the soul for a little gold—and yet, all the gold upon the earth and beneath the earth is not worth ἀρετή [πᾶς γὰρ ὅ τ' ἐπὶ γῆς καὶ ὑπὸ γῆς χρυσὸς ἀρετῆς οὐκ ἀντάξιος]" (727e–728a). The language that is used here, of that which is "upon the earth and beneath the earth" is meant to emphasize, I take it, the incomparability of all that is earth-bound to that of Olympus. For the absurdity of exchanging the one for the other is a recurrent theme in Plato's writings—consider, for example, Socrates' words in the *Phaedo* (68e–69b), or what Socrates is reported to have said to Alcibiades in the *Symposium* (218d–219a) and so on.

Furthermore, we learn in what follows that the measure proper to goods of the soul is altogether different from that proper to goods of the body and what belongs to the body. As to the former, the Stranger makes clear that whoever is not prepared to "make every effort [πάσῃ μηχανῇ]" to refrain from what is wrong and shameful and to practice all that is good and noble "to the extent of his ability [τὰ δὲ ἐπιτηδεύειν ξύμπασαν κατὰ δύναμιν]" is, in fact, dishonoring his soul (728a–b). To say it differently, honoring the soul requires a relentless dedication to ἀρετή, for "honor," he says, "is following the better, and doing our utmost to make as perfect as possible what is worse [τοῖς μὲν ἀμείνοσιν ἕπεσθαι, τὰ δὲ χείρονα γενέσθαι δὲ βελτίω δυνατὰ τοῦτ' αὐτὸ ὡς ἄριστα ἀποτελεῖν]" (728c). By contrast with this "perfectionistic" measure with respect to the soul,[18] the goods of body and material goods are to be measured according to the mean. For example, the Stranger says that we are not to aspire to having a body that is extremely beautiful or extremely strong or so on, nor certainly to have one that is extremely ugly, extremely weak, etc. Rather, we should aim at having one that lies in the mean [ἐν τῷ μέσῳ] with respect to these various qualities, precisely because the mean with respect to bodily goods is the one that is "most temperate and most stable [σωφρονέστατα ἅμα τε ἀσφαλέστατα]" whereas the extreme conditions make for boldness and boastfulness, on the one hand, and lowliness and lack of freedom on the other (728d–e). The same measure holds in the case of money and property: the mean is to be aimed at, in other words, because it is most conducive to goods of the soul, whereas extreme conditions are least conducive (728e–729a).[19] But of course, to say that the measure for goods of body and of what belongs to the body is to be determined by goods of the soul is just another way of saying that the soul is incomparably worthier of honor than all that is "earth-born."[20]

At this point we should pause in our examination of the prelude in Book 5 to observe that the entire framework of the prelude, foregrounding the proper relation between gods and human beings, between soul and body, the goods of the soul and the "earth-bound" goods of the body, is something for which only the prelude in Book 10 seeks to present what we would call an argument.[21] No doubt it is in part because of this reliance upon Book 10 that the latter discourse is called "a prelude that would be noblest and best [κάλλιστόν τε καὶ ἄριστον προοίμιον ἂν εἴη]" (887c). The prelude in Book 10 addresses those who call the entire framework into question by denying that there are gods, for it is by thinking that "the gods are not as the law commands us to think of them" that the younger generation has become persuaded to live according to nature, which means "living in control over others in truth, not being a slave to others according to *nomos*" (890a). Counteracting these impious theories, the prelude goes so far as to correct the shortcomings of traditional theology which, in effect, undermine the moral framework of Book 5 by persuading people that what is most important is not so much abstaining from wrongdoing [τὸ μὴ δρᾶν τὰ ἄδικα] as making up for one's wrongdoing by bribing the relevant gods or goddesses (885d). Rather than dispensing with inherited religious belief altogether, the Athenian's aim is to reform it, preserving what is indispensably important within it, as he asserts that the greatest issue of all is that of correctly thinking about the gods and thus living nobly or not [τὸ περὶ τοὺς θεοὺς ὀρθῶς διανοηθέντα ζῆν καλῶς ἢ μή] (888b).[22] This theological framework of the *Laws* in general, and for the preface in Book 5 in particular, must always be kept in mind, for, as one commentator put it, "The laws . . . are surely not revealed by god; but, just as surely, they are proposed with an eye to god at all times."[23]

Most relevant for our focus on Book 5 is the way in which ancient myths of retribution are brought into the account so as to provide an example of the way that the gods care for or "give thought to" [φροντίζειν] human beings. Here, the Stranger calls it "the greatest judgment for wrongdoing [τὴν γὰρ λεγομένην δίκην τῆς κακουργίας τὴν μεγίστην]":

> to become like men who are evil [τὸ ὁμοιοῦσθαι τοῖς οὖσι κακοῖς ἀνδράσιν], and in becoming like them to be separated from good men and their *logoi*, while seeking to attach oneself to the other kind and keep their

company; and he that is joined to such men inevitably does, and has done to him, what the evil say and do. (728b)

This greatest "judgment"—or, rather, "punishment [τιμωρία]," as the Athenian is quick to correct (728c), is something that "hardly anyone takes account of" [οὐδεὶς ὡς ἔπος εἰπεῖν λογίζεσθαι] in determining how to honor or dishonor his soul (728b). Indeed, the Athenian goes on to call this punishment a "condition following from wrongdoing [ἀδικίας ἀκόλουθος πάθη]" (728c), which underscores the claim that this punishment is something undergone inescapably by the person who does wrong. It is impossible not to hear an echo of this in Book 10 of the *Laws,* in what the Athenian sets forth as the "just sentence of the gods that dwell on Olympus" (904e)—a sentence that no one can ever escape (905a)—"to go join worse souls as you become worse and better souls as you become better [κακίω μὲν γιγνόμενον πρὸς τὰς κακίους ψυχάς, ἀμείνω δὲ πρὸς τὰς ἀμείνους], and alike in life and in every death to do and to suffer what is befitting that like should do toward like" (904e–905a).[24] It is, we learn, a testament to divine providence that the gods have contrived the universe in such a way that we are in fact always ascending or descending through our actions, no matter whether we are oblivious to how our actions assimilate us to one sort of life or the other (903c). However, to the degree that these myths involve a "threat" of sorts, we may ask whether they approximate the ideal of persuasion *rather than coercion.*[25] This is especially vivid in Book 12's mythic account of the soul leaving the body so as to answer to the gods, with the comment given on this: "To the good man this is heartening, but to the bad man very frightening" [μάλα φοβερόν] (959b).

Of course, the account of "punishment," along with the account of the soul in how it is to be honored vis-à-vis the body and its belongings, is what the Stranger refers to as the "divine" part of what is to be expounded on what practices should be followed and how we ought to live, as opposed to the "human" part. In turning to the human part, he offers a very strange reason for doing so—namely, because "we are in dialogue with human beings, not gods" (732e). He then introduces the distinctively human part of what is to be expounded with a famous passage:

"By nature, the human consists above all in pleasures and pains and desires [ἔστι δὴ φύσει ἀνθρώπειον μάλιστα ἡδοναὶ καὶ λῦπαι καὶ ἐπιθυμίαι]. To these every mortal animal is, as it were, inextricably attached and bound in the most serious ways. The noblest life should be praised not only because it is superior as regards the splendor of its reputation, but also because, if someone is willing to taste it and not become a fugitive of it because of his youth, it will prove superior in respect to that which we all seek [κρατεῖ καὶ τούτῳ ὃ πάντες ζητοῦμεν]—namely, having more delight and less pain throughout the whole of one's life [τῷ χαίρειν πλείω, ἐλάττω δὲ λυπεῖσθαι παρὰ τὸν βίον ἅπαντα]." (732e–733a)

Presumably what is specifically "human" about this human-oriented part of the prelude is that it approaches pleasure not as something that in and of itself will lead one away from the road of ἀρετή, but as something naturally bound up in all human pursuits: ἐν τούτοις ἐνδεδεμένοι πεφύκασι (733d).[26] This insight signals a return to a point made by the Athenian in Book 1, when pleasures and pains are portrayed as the two springs that "flow forth by nature, and he who draws from the right one, at the right time and in the right amount, is happy . . . [but] he who does so without knowledge and at the wrong time lives a life that is just the opposite" (636d–e). The Athenian's aim in Book 5 is to recognize this fundamental point, and address the question as to what "correctness" amounts to when we praise the noblest life for correctly experiencing pleasure [γεύηται . . . ὀρθῶς] (733a).

The Athenian now sets about to determine more carefully what it is that we want when our pursuits have an eye to pleasure and pain. This sort of examination is familiar to us from other texts of Plato, since often Socrates devotes attention to the various ways in which our pursuit of pleasure is not at all a pursuit of pleasure *per se,* but the pursuit of highly determinate pleasures whose determinacy is not evident until after examination. For example, Callicles praises—at least in very general terms—the life dedicated to indiscriminate pleasure-seeking, yet upon examination it turns out that the pleasures he extols do not include the twisted pleasures of the catamite that Socrates imagines (*Gorgias* 494e–495a). Similarly, Glaucon is made to recognize that his conception of a pleasant life—a life involving "relish [ὄψον]," as he puts it (*Republic* 372c)—is not the bucolic one of reclining on beds strewn with yew and myrtle, enjoying desserts of figs, chick peas, and beans, with maybe some roasted acorns thrown in (372b–d), but rather requires the determinate pleasures of reclining on proper furniture, and enjoying a whole range of delicacies, oils and incense, prostitutes and pastries (373a). What the Stranger is concerned to detail is not an inventory of desiderata such as this, but the more general structure to our desire for pleasures. For example, he says: "Now we want pleasure for ourselves, while we neither choose nor want pain; we don't want what is neither pleasant nor painful instead of what is pleasant, but we do want it in exchange for pain; we want less pain with more pleasure but we don't want less pleasure with more pain . . ." (733b), and so on, with impressive detail. Upon examination, it will turn out not only that our conception of a pleasant life is highly determinate in ways we may not have recognized, but that the life that turns out to be most pleasant, all things considered, is different from the one we took to be most pleasant at the outset.

To make evident this latter finding, the Athenian asks us to compare in hedonic terms the life of one who is temperate [σώφρων], wise [φρόνιμος], courageous [ἀνδρεῖος], and healthy [ὑγιεινός], side by side with the life of one who is licentious, foolish, cowardly, and diseased (733e–734a). Bracketing for the moment the foolishness, cowardice, and poor health of the second candidate mentioned, his licentiousness might of itself appear to guarantee that his life will prove to be more pleasant than that of the other candidate. Not so, as the Athenian explains:

> "Now he who knows will set down the life of temperance as a life that is mild in every way, with gentle pains and gentle pleasures, a life characterized by desires that are mild and loves that are not mad . . . In the temperate life, he will say, the pleasures outweigh the pains, while in the licentious life the pains are greater and more numerous and more frequent than the pleasures. From this it follows, necessarily and according to nature, that the one life is more pleasant for us and the other more painful; and he at least who wants to live pleasantly will no longer, voluntarily at any rate, permit himself to live licentiously. Indeed, it is now obvious—if what is being said now is correct—that every licentious man must necessarily be living this way involuntarily. The whole mob of humanity lives with a lack of moderation because of their ignorance or their lack of self-mastery or a combination of both." (733e–734b)

Not surprisingly, the Athenian is then able to argue without much trouble that, on balance, pleasures prevail for those who are wise, courageous, and healthy, while pains prevail for the foolish, cowardly, and diseased (734b–d). "In sum," he says, "the life that possesses ἀρετή, of body or also of soul, is more pleasant than the life possessing vice, and that in other respects—beauty, correctness, ἀρετή, and good reputation—it is far superior to the life of vice. Thus it makes the one who possesses it live more happily than his opposite, in every way and on the whole" (734d–e). This all sounds reasonable enough, given the parameters of the prelude being composed, but nonetheless there are some questions to raise, even if Cleinias does not see fit to raise them here in the text.

Perhaps most disconcerting about the account of pleasure in these passages is that it entirely occludes the *skiagraphic*, or "shadow-writing," character of pleasure and pain, as it was articulated earlier in Plato's *Laws*. The passage in question occurs right on the heels of the Athenian's claim that, to make some citizens willing to live the pious and just life, the lawgiver must not "split the pleasant from the just, and the good from the noble" (663b). He then says the following:

> Looking at things from a distance produces a dizzying obscurity [σκοτοδινία] in everyone, so to speak, and especially in children; but our lawgiver will do the opposite to opinion [δόξα] by taking away the obscurity [τὸ σκότος], and will somehow or other persuade, with habits and praises and arguments, that the just and unjust things are shadow-glyphs [πείσει ἀμῶς γέ πως ἔθεσι καὶ ἐπαίνοις καὶ λόγοις ὡς ἐσκιαγραφημένα τὰ δίκαια ἔστι καὶ ἄδικα]. From the perspective of the unjust and evil man himself, the unjust things appear pleasant, the opposite of the way they appear to the just man, while the just things appear very unpleasant. But from the perspective of the just everything appears entirely the opposite. (663b–c)

After this, Cleinias and the Athenian agree that the better sort of individual is really the one to judge with authority on matters as to pleasure and pain (663c–d), and furthermore they agree that a lawgiver would be justified in lying to the citizenry in order to persuade them toward living a life of ἀρετή (663d–e). If we are to take the idea of *skiagraphia* in this passage seriously, it would follow that a given auditor of the long prelude in Book 5 may be in no position to judge the truth of the argument presented, namely, that the life of ἀρετή is at the same time the life most pleasant and good, all things considered. Is an auditor supposed to *trust* that, although the dissolute life appears more pleasant to him from his perspective, it is the "better sort of individual" who is authoritative for making such judgments?

Perhaps the Athenian's proposed regime of moral socialization will be sufficiently effective that the audience will recognize the argument of the "human" part of the prelude to be consonant with their own experience of pleasures and pains, and this "consonance" [ξυμφωνία] will be adequate for the education that the prelude is intended to serve—I take it, at least, that the discussion of such "consonance" as ἀρετή and παιδεία in Book 2 can be read to support this interpretation.[27] Nonetheless, the *skiagraphic* character of pleasure in pain, coupled with the *polemical* orientation toward ἀρετή in Plato's *Laws*, may lead us to the conclusion that something other than a lengthy non-dialogical prelude may better serve the purpose of persuading the audience toward choosing a life of ἀρετή. By contrast with the prelude of Book 5, delivered at "high noon"—the time of smallest shadows—other texts of Plato's afford readers the opportunity to appreciate the interplay of light and shadow that makes up the drama of arguments about ἀρετή. Here we should recall that it is on account of Plato's great artistry as a philosophical writer that, in robustly dialogical texts like *Protagoras* and *Gorgias*, readers of the text are presented with well-crafted and highly persuasive speeches that have the effect of making the opposing perspectives on pleasure and ἀρετή vivid—sometimes captivatingly so. Thanks to Plato's artistry, we as readers can inhabit for a time the perspective of a Callicles, who regards only intense bodily pleasures as moments of really living, and regards the life of self-control and temperance extolled by Socrates as the life of a stone (*Gorgias* 494a–b). Were there nothing persuasive, at least on some level, about Callicles' view of pleasure and ἀρετή, there would be nothing especially significant about Socrates' triumph in showing him up before sympathetic bystanders. But there is something persuasive: in fact, Socrates says that Callicles is admirable in his willingness to say openly what many others think but do not say (*Gorgias* 486d–487e). Thus Plato has constructed these dialogues in such a way that they are able to persuade about matters of pleasure and ἀρετή by first allowing the auditor within the text or the reader of the text to experience the persuasiveness of an opposing perspective (like Callicles') and only then undergo a shift toward a perspective that is more persuasive, all things considered. In this way, understanding how Callicles is overthrown by Socrates in the dialectical *agōn* of the text is, at the same time, being persuaded that one ought to pursue a life of ἀρετή rather than a dissolute life.

Furthermore, one might say on behalf of this dialogical approach to persuasion elsewhere in Plato's writings that, in fact, it does greater justice to the polemical orientation to ἀρετή sketched out earlier in the *Laws*. If, indeed, ἀρετή requires a πόλεμος of the self against oneself, there will always be within us something that is not altogether persuaded—for example, persuaded that the life of ἀρετή is the life that is most pleasant and good. By writing dialogues of argumentative contestations between opposing perspectives on these issues— and ones that can be read and reread with pleasure—Plato allows us the opportunity to engage in the very struggle, the πόλεμος, that is key to ἀρετή, and hopefully be persuaded anew. All of this is missing in the prelude of Book 5, and the fact of its omission has the effect of refocusing our attention on the central question of what Plato's texts are meant to do. It is no doubt a great irony that a text like the prelude in *Laws* Book 5, which is geared explicitly toward persuading an audience, should be sufficiently unpersuasive by comparison with other texts that it raises for us the more fundamental questions: just what is persuasion, and what sort of persuasion is philosophy (as exemplified by Plato) meant to accomplish?

Notes

1. The Athenian goes on to discuss how individuals will be made to fight against pleasures to achieve the victory that is ἀρετή; in this particular case the virtues in question are courage and temperance (647c–d).

2. The lines are from *Works and Days,* 287–289. See Adeimantus's quotation of these lines at *Republic* 364c–d.

3. Pangle 1980 rightly points out that the Cronus-myth attributes wickedness and unhappiness to human nature (442).

4. This mythic discourse is itself framed by the rhetorico-pedagogical discourse running across the first four books of the *Laws.* An "education in virtue," we have read, is made possible by channeling and directing pleasures and pains (643c–644c). Accordingly, virtue is understood as the "correct formation" of pleasures and pains, and education consists in the correct disciplining of them (653a–654d). Those who are educated according to this plan experience pleasure only in harmony with *nomos* (659d), and the wise person, we are told, "keeps pleasure and pain in tune with right reason" (696c). At the same time, this pedagogy in virtue is rhetorical: the lawgiver must persuade that the unjust life is less pleasant than the just (663c–d), and the persuasion involved must therefore not drive a wedge between the pleasant and the virtuous (662d–663a). The rhetoric is also in part specifically theological: the doctrine must be, we are told, that the gods say that the best life is the one that is most pleasant (664a–c). We are to understand that god is the measure (716c), and those who are virtuous are most like god (716d). While much of the literature on Plato's *Laws* debates whether the persuasion outlined above is properly *rational* or, on the other hand, *rhetorical* (where the latter is understood in a way that philosophers deem pejorative), the text itself does not instigate a quarrel between rational and rhetorical persuasion. Rather, persuasion is understood to be one technique—or, perhaps, a family of various techniques—at the lawgiver's disposal along with other sorts of techniques: the method of disseminating the laws is partly persuasion, partly compulsion, partly chastisement (718b–d). The fact that these techniques cooperate with one another within an integrated nomothetic system is evident when the Athenian says, first, that the lawgiver must set forth what is to be honored (697b–c), and then, that the lawgiver must see to it that the disobedient are dishonored (711c).

5. Admittedly, there are a number of things in this passage that call for our attention: for example, the sense of "truth" implied in the way that the mythic tale—here called a *logos*—is said to "deem" something of general application to be true; the implicit phenomenology of pleasure-seeking, such that in yearning for pleasures and desires/appetites, one "needs to be filled with these" [πληροῦσθαι τούτων δεομένην], and so on.

6. Pangle 1980 remarks: "The chief characteristic of god is not justice (or courage) but moderation and inner measure. God does not actively benefit men, he does not even reveal a law; he does men good only by providing a model for them to imitate," 444.

7. Yunis 1996 remarks: "The best way to describe what Plato does in the preambles is to say that the lawgiver *preaches* to the citizens," 229. Laks 2000 describes the beginning of *Laws* 5 as "an exhortation regarding one's duties towards one's parents, friends, fellow-citizens, and most importantly, towards one's soul. This long address to the new Cretan colonists is an impressive sermon . . . ," 264.

8. Strauss 1980 comments: "Apart from Cleinias' reply at the very end, the Athenian is the sole speaker in Book 5. This Book is the least dialogic of all Books of the *Laws*," 81.

9. See Nightingale 1993, 295–96, 300; and Weiss 2006, 183. Laks 2000 concedes that philosophy—which is mentioned only twice in the *Laws* (857d, 967c) "seems to have been reduced to a strictly subservient role," 260.

10. Nightingale 1993, 285.

11. Yunis 1988, 33–34.

12. Yunis 1996 explains, "With regard to content, the message that is preached in this radical way is essentially mere assertion; no form of ratiocination, however dilute or disguised, need accompany the message. Yet proclamation differs from assertion and can have a persuasive power far beyond assertion. The difference between proclamation and assertion lies in the authority with which the message is delivered . . . In preaching of this sort, instruction is a matter of amassing the moral authority to compel conviction in the auditor," 231–232. Similarly, Nightingale 1993 reads the preludes as issuing from "a lawgiver who is accorded almost divine status," and are "inscribed in monologues that cannot be questioned or challenged by the citizens," 293.

13. Cohen 1993 writes: "the 'model' preamble to the code of Magnesia (726a–34e) grounds the laws on a hortatory summary of the theory of socialization set out in the first three books . . . The preamble closes by exhorting citizens to choose (733d–e, 734c–d) this life of virtue over inferior paths of life by following a self-imposed law. . . . ," 310. Admittedly, these alternatives are not mutually exclusive: the audience may be persuaded by the prelude of *Laws* 5 because it reformulates the salient features of the theory of moral education sketched out earlier, or because of the authority of the lawgiver, or both.

14. Yunis 1996, 230, compares the preludes of Plato's *Laws* with the language of preaching in the Christian Era as they both seem to utilize 1) authoritative proclamation, and 2) the grand style of vehement, unadorned utterance. The grand style, he explains, "is solemn, dignified, dense and asymmetrical; it strives for vehemence and passion while addressing the most important subjects," 231.

15. Perhaps, too, the strangeness of calling the soul a "possession," κτῆμα, is something that can be explained by the fact that the prelude leads up to a discussion of communal property (739c–e).

16. Benardete 2000a tracks the verbs of thinking, supposing, etc. in this passage, and concludes that self-knowledge is the burden of this passage: "It requires paradoxically both a knowledge of the better and the worse in one's own makeup and a knowledge of ignorance. The Stranger, in turning from the gods to the soul, summarizes Plato's *Apology of Socrates*" (155).

17. See the afterlife myth of *Gorgias* for the claim that the soul is disfigured by its misdeeds—a possible way of picturing regret, μεταμελεία, as a disfiguring of the soul.

18. A further bit of evidence as to the "perfectionism" in the Stranger's account is the language used at 731a: Let us all be lovers of victory when it comes to virtue, and without envy—for the envious sort "makes the whole city a flaccid competitor in the contest for virtue and does what he can to diminish fame" (731a–b).

19. Further indication of this incomparability is the fact that the Athenian goes on to argue that children should be left an abundance of αἰδώς rather than gold (729b).

20. See the claims made earlier in the *Laws*, 660e–661c, a clear echo of which is found in these passages from *Laws* 5.

21. Interestingly, the prelude in *Laws* 5 relies upon the famous prelude to the impiety laws in *Laws* 10, just as the intellectual atheism that is critiqued in *Laws* 10 is itself motivated to a large degree by the misconceptions about pleasure which are addressed in the prelude of *Laws* 5. In other words, the preludes offered in Plato's *Laws* are not, upon reflection, fully distinct philosophically, even if they differ from one another in level of argumentative sophistication, targeted audience, and so on. While *Laws* 10, of course, focuses its attention on thinking correctly about the gods, *Laws* 5 focuses on "living nobly," ζῆν καλῶς, in light of the gods.

22. The argument against atheism in *Laws* 10 is nested within a larger aim of persuading an audience of three points: that gods exist, that they take thought [φροντίζειν] for the human race, and that they cannot be influenced by sacrifices or prayers (885b).

23. Pangle 1976, 1059. Pangle continues this thought as follows: "For Plato, political science and a kind of theology are inseparable," 1060.

24. The words used here are almost identical to what Socrates says in the so-called "digression" of Plato's *Theaetetus*, when he specifies the inescapable penalty for injustice [ζημία ἀδικίας], as follows: "Two patterns [παραδείγματα], my friend, are set up in truth: the divine one, that is happiest, and the godless one, that is most wretched. But the unjust do not see that this is so, and on account of their foolishness and lack of understanding they are unaware that through their unjust actions they become like the one and unlike the other [λανθάνουσι τῷ μὲν ὁμοιούμενοι διὰ τὰς ἀδίκους πράξεις, τῷ δὲ ἀνομοιούμενοι]. Thus they pay the penalty of living the life that resembles the one they are becoming like [οὗ δὴ τίνουσι δίκην ζῶντες τὸν εἰκότα βίον ᾧ ὁμοιούμενοι] . . . evil men living with evil ones [κακοὶ κακοῖς συνόντες]" (176e–177a). Notice that these passages are presaged by some sort of remark as to human beings' lack of understanding with respect to the judgment formulated in these similar ways. In the passage from Book 10 the judgment is meant to refute the false belief that the gods do not care for humans (904e). In the *Theaetetus* passage, what is foregrounded is the ignorance of the unjust to that of which they should be least ignorant (176d).

25. Laks 2000 writes that "the ancestral myths of retribution, which figure in most of the preambles attached to criminal laws, strangely if interestingly blur the contrast between persuasion and threat," 290.

26. Stalley 1983 points out that the Athenian's "rules of divine provenance bid us to struggle against pleasures in order to honour the reason and then subordinate ourselves to it" (66), but then, "in setting out the rules of human origin the Athenian is seeking to demonstrate not that pleasure is the good but that a creature subject to pleasures and pains can still be advised to pursue the same kind of virtuous life that would be recommended by the reason" (67).

27. See, in particular, the opening discussion of *Laws* 2: 653a–c.

9 Being True to Equality: Human Allotment and the Judgment of Zeus

Gregory Recco

At the beginning of *Laws* Book 6, the Stranger turns to the establishment of the administrative apparatus of the new city, identifying the number and kinds of official positions that are required, as well as the procedures for filling them. While the lawmakers still have as their primary goal to make the citizens good, they must also strive to ensure that the city should be free of faction. Accordingly, after detailing the procedure for selecting the 360 citizens who are to make up the council, the Stranger concludes that "the selection made in this way would achieve a mean between a monarchic and a democratic constitution" (756e9–10). There follows a digression concerning two kinds of equality, already alluded to in Book 5 when the class system of property qualifications was introduced. The thought about proportional equality, giving all their due rather than the same amount, is familiar enough from its various articulations in Plato and Aristotle and elsewhere, but the Stranger's treatment of the distinction is nuanced and in some ways unclear, and his way of weaving the concerns that motivate it into nearly every corner of the web of official regulations attests to the complexity of the issue. In what follows, I will present the discussion of the distinction; follow out its use in the establishment of the various offices, in the enumeration of their duties, and in the procedures for selecting them; and investigate how the treatment of equality in the city responds to the imperative to keep the constitution to a mean between monarchy and democracy as a means of avoiding faction. The way that these issues are handled raises questions about the meaning of civic friendship, particularly, about whether it is to be understood in the end as a stabilizing necessity or a substantial good.

The Stranger begins: "An ancient *logos* is true—that equality brings about friendship—and it has been quite correctly and harmoniously said. But just what equality it is that has this very power confuses us very much, for it is very far from obvious" (757a5–b1). Correctly and harmoniously as it may have been said, the Stranger is evidently already thinking of equality itself as irreducibly dual, as he confirms: "There are two equalities, alike in name, but in deed nearly opposite in many respects. The one any city and any legislator is able to work in through the assignment of honors—namely, equality that is equal in measure, weight, and number—by evening it out in distribution by means of the lot. But the truest and best equality it is not easy for just anyone to see" (757b1–7). Before considering the second form of equality, several things are to be noted here. To begin with, the confusion about the ancient saying could have lit upon any of its three terms: there is no particular reason to think that the meaning of either "bringing about" or "friendship" is any more obvious in itself than "equality." But it is equality that is the Stranger's focus, and the investigation of any confusion inherent in the other terms is deferred, perhaps indefinitely. Second, the duality of equality is said to occur in deed, in spite of a likeness in name. One might wonder whether the divergence in forms of equality stems more from how they are put to work than from how they are defined. A third, related point is that, from the very start, these types of equality are being considered from the perspective of the city, particularly in respect of its assigning honors and distributions. These "honors" include that of being admitted to an official post in the city, as the whole discussion immediately follows the description of the selection of members of the council. Thus in the most general terms, the specifically political practice of the first type of equality consists in a kind of simple adjustment or straightening out that the lot somehow provides.

A few words about the use of the lot that the Stranger proposes for the selection of councilmen are necessary. The laborious and complex voting procedures, to which we will return in greater detail later, produce a total of 720 candidates in four groups of 180 according to property class. Of the 180 from each property class, ninety are ultimately selected by lot. Just what is being equalized, adjusted, or straightened out in this way is not yet clear, nor yet how the lot achieves this.

A return to the discussion of equality brings the second form to light. This form was said not to be easy for just anyone to see, and this is no wonder, since, as the Stranger now tells us, "it is the judgment of Zeus and helps humans rather little, though everything in which it does help either cities or private individuals it makes turn out good. For it allots more to the greater and less to the lesser, and by giving to each of these in measures proportioned to their nature—namely, always greater honors to those who are greater in respect of virtue, and lesser honors to those whose share in both virtue and cultivation is the opposite—it portions out what is appropriate to each in accordance with ratio" (757b7–c6). The reference to Zeus marks a strong contrast to the city-bound and otherwise mundane framing of the first kind of equality. The importance of such affairs to this truest and best form of equality is clearly marked off as minimal and occasional. This rhetorical magnification of the second equality might have, or even be intended to have, a double effect: making the prospective legislator both long for and despair of the blessing of this divine apportionment.

However that may be, a sort of connection of this kind of equality with the selection of the council should already be understood. Since the numbers of citizens that belong to the four property classes are not likely to be equal, and since what is most probable is that the highest classes would contain fewer households, the representation of the higher classes in the council is proportionately greater, for they have the same ninety seats as the lower classes. Here we seem to have those who are greater in one respect being accorded greater honors. But what is not explicitly stated is whether this is meant to be an instance of the true equality, for in the first place, we have no reason to suppose that measures of wealth correspond exactly to measures of virtue. Also, it is not *as* great individuals that members of the higher property classes are given more seats, but merely as members of a class. Finally, even if the "equality" in this case bears some marks of the proportionality proper to the judgment of Zeus in giving more to the greater, the way in which it is brought to bear is one that "any city or lawmaker is competent to introduce," namely, by measure, weight, and number, the characteristic marks of the first kind of equality. We may have to look elsewhere for the divine assistance of true equality.

Now, this election of the council is the immediate context of the remark about the mean between monarchic and democratic constitutions, but several other appointments have already been discussed, namely those of the law wardens and the various military leaders. The selection of the councilmen is distinguished from these by the use of the lot, and since use of the lot is mentioned in the discussion of the first equality, it must play some role in the previously mentioned "selection made in this way" that the Stranger says is to make the city achieve a mean between monarchic and democratic constitutions. Perhaps we can understand the use of the lot by seeing its difference from the mode of the other selections and by considering what is said about the problems it is intended to alleviate.

The thirty-seven law wardens apparently constitute the most powerful official body; at this point in the text, the full extent of their powers and duties has not yet come to light, but the Stranger makes clear that their duties are already broad and will only grow with each new law. In other words, their authority is coextensive with that of the laws as a whole. It is no surprise, then, that their selection should be surrounded with a special degree of ceremony. "The selection shall be made in that temple which the city holds most in honor and each man shall set upon the altar of the god the nominee's name, father's name, tribe, and deme written on a tablet on which he has also inscribed his own name in the same respects in the same way. [. . .] The ballots judged to come first, up to three hundred of them, shall be exhibited by the officers before the whole city" (753b7–d1). A run-off election, conducted in the same way after the names have been displayed for at least thirty days, reduces this number to one hundred. These names, too, are to be displayed for the same amount of time. The final run-off, unlike the other two, is not compulsory. "The third time, let whoever wishes vote for whoever he wants to out of the hundred, passing between slain victims as he does so" (753d3–5).

In the light of the founding of our modern republics, it is perhaps a reflex to think of the liberty to elect leaders as a distinguishing mark of democracy. But the solemnity and publicity of the procedure just described—a publicity that the use of written and signed ballots makes potentially everlasting, always capable of being reviewed in the light of intervening events—must exercise particular pressures on the elector's choices, pressures that it will not be too difficult to concede are not clearly democratic in their effects or in their intent. Further pressure comes from having the election take place in the city's most honored temple, from having to choose to participate in the final round of voting, and, not least, from having to walk between portions of an animal slaughtered in honor of the god in order to cast one's vote. Whatever else is to be said about this strange form of election, these elements make it function as a kind of dramatic staging of the city's will to allot high honors and distinction to a select few. The legislator's art and artfulness are at work in this presentation, even if little explicit reflection on the reasons for his choices is given.

Before reflecting further on this manner of conducting the election of the law wardens and using it as a point of comparison for the use of the lot, we should consider the selection of another important post: that of the military commanders. For the highest posts, those of the three generals, nominations are made by the law wardens. But, "if someone thinks one of the men not nominated is better than one of the nominees, let him state the name of the one to be replaced and his own nominee, and make this counter-nomination by oath; let whichever of these wins a show of hands be put forward for judgment" (755c8–d4). (Apart from the general remark a few pages earlier that only suitable people ought to be put into office, this is the first explicit mention of a criterion to be applied *by electors* in the selection of officers.[1]) As in the case of the election of the law wardens, the swearing of oaths lends a certain solemnity to the whole affair, and one would think, would tend to discourage counter-nominations. In any case, the bar is set rather high; not only must one swear an oath in asserting that one's counter-nominee is a better man than a particular nominee, but one must thereby effectively assert that the choice of the thirty-seven most powerful officials in the city was inferior.

The generals, for their part, are to nominate taxiarchs for themselves (though a counter-nomination, which is less stringent, is allowed), and the various divisions—hoplites, knights, and infantry—are for the most part in charge of electing their own chiefs. While this seems in some ways freer, we should note that these selections are made in a place that is "the holiest" (though it is also to be the "roomiest," to hold all the soldiers, and so is probably not a temple), that the troops are arranged by the type of their service, and that the knights vote for their chiefs, the hipparchs, "in full view of the infantry." While the potentially permanent exposure that the written ballot imposes is not present here, all voting is done by a show of hands, and the publicity of this procedure is something the Stranger decides to underline in this case, particularly that of the noble cavalry before the common infantry.

To review, then, these first two elections are entirely free of the use of the lot and emphasize rather dramatically their own selective character, whether in the case of the law wardens by publicizing and sacralizing a drawn-out whittling-down of many candidates to a few winners, or in the case of the military commanders, by exposing electors presumably used to functioning as cohesive units to one another as representatives of their units in selecting candidates blessed by either the law wardens or the elected generals. Is this, then, the true equality, the judgment of Zeus? And if it gives more to the better, why introduce the lot for other offices at all? Let us consider the reasons the Stranger gives for resorting to the lot before considering how and why it is applied to the laws concerning the council and other offices.

After saying that their city must keep to the middle way between monarchic and democratic constitutions, the Stranger explains: "even if they were set up with equal honors [or "declared equal in honors"—διαγορευόμενοι²], slaves and masters would never become friends, nor would the insignificant [φαῦλοι] and the serious [σπουδαῖοι]. For equals given to unequals would be unequal, unless they were to hit upon due measure. And it is on account of both of these that cities are filled with factional strife" (757a1–5). In the first sentence, two kinds of differences between people are juxtaposed, with uncertain implications. It is not clear whether the impossibility of friendship between slaves and masters, on the one hand, and between the insignificant and the serious, on the other, is due to the natures of the persons or to their positions, and more generally, whether it is meant to be due to the same causes in the two cases. (In light of the later discussion of slavery at Sparta, it is at least clear that the Stranger does not assume those in the condition of slavery to be thereby inferior human beings.) In like manner, the hypothetical "remedy" that is alleged to be futile ("equal honors") is ambiguous, as it could be a matter either of *establishing* the otherwise unequal in equal positions or of *publicly declaring* them to be equally honorable, perhaps while privately holding them to be unworthy or actually behaving toward them as unworthy.[3] As for the second sentence, "equals given to unequals would be unequal, unless some due measure were hit upon," the double or triple use of "equal" raises a welter of questions about commensurability and heterogeneity of magnitudes and persons: In what respects and in what ways are people unequal? What or who can reckon those inequalities? Even if there is a uniform and combined scale of human goodness, how can the scale of honors be compared to it? These questions are in no way answered by the appeal to measure at the end. Indeed this appeal to hitting upon due measure is itself ambiguous, in that it is not clear what roles aiming and luck are meant to be playing: surely we can miss what we are aiming at; we can also hit what we were not aiming at; perhaps we might yet chance upon what we are not aiming at, and would not even know how to aim at. Can we aim at good luck? The stakes are high, as the final sentence warns, for faction, party, and civil war threaten the polity, presumably when those who think themselves superior will not settle for being treated equally (or should one say unequally?) to other citizens.

In the face of all these perplexities about equality, the Stranger is initially quite clear about what must be done, or at least about what must guide action: the legislator must aim at the other equality, which is now equated with justice, or at least "political" justice, at the same time that it is called natural. As he states, "if anyone is to found another city, he must aim at this very thing in legislating, and not at a few tyrants or one, nor at some 'power of the people,' but always at the just. And indeed what was just spoken of, the naturally equal given in each case to unequals, *is* the just" (757d1–5). While this may seem to solve the problem alluded to above, the mention of tyranny and of plural tyrants makes that danger more explicit. In striving to win due recognition for themselves, those who think themselves superior could end up inducing the legislator to set them up as tyrants. Despite the gravity of the threat, the Stranger has mentioned one possibility that could save them: φαῦλοι and σπουδαῖοι could never become friends, he says, "unless due measure were hit upon."

Some clue as to what that measure would have to consist in should presumably occur in the passage that follows. I will quote it in full and then review it in detail. After asserting that the just is the proper aim of the legislator, the Stranger adds: "Still, every city is sometimes constrained, if indeed it is going to avoid involving itself in civil wars in respect of one of its parts, to make use also [προσχρήσασθαι] of certain derived names [τούτοις παρωνυμίοισι]—for what is 'modest' or 'generous' [τὸ γὰρ ἐπιεικὲς καὶ συγγνώμον] is an infringement on what is perfect and exact that goes against strict justice whenever it comes to be—which is why it is a necessity to make use also [προσχρήσασθαι] of the equal by lot as far as regards the discontent of the many, calling upon the god and good luck in prayers to correct the lot for them in the direction of the just. And therefore what must necessarily be used [χρηστέον] are both equalities, in this way, but the one that stands in need of good luck is to be used as little as possible" (757d5–758a2). From the last few sentences, one might think that the Stranger is saying that the way to avoid faction is to placate the many by giving them a few greater honors than they are due. The legislator's art, then, would consist in resorting to this specious equalizing to just the right degree: enough so that the many will not revolt, but not so much that the excellent will revolt. But it is possible that what the Stranger is suggesting here, and what his proposals for the administrative structure of the state would actually put into practice, is somewhat more subtle, and probably less dependent on the legislator's being able to calculate precisely what degree of balance of honors is appropriate.

For what he says every city must make use of, in the first instance, is not this or that form of equality, but "certain names." Perhaps this is meant to work in something like the following way: however the city practices its various distributions, it must be possible for one who thinks any given allotment of honors, power, or wealth to be too meager to call it "modest," and, perhaps at the same time, for one who thinks it too great to call it "generous." Now, no citizen who calls the quantity of something allotted "modest" or "generous" thinks "strict," "perfect," or "precise" justice has been achieved, but neither must he think an injustice has been done. In fact, in using words like "strict," "perfect," and "precise" as limiting terms, he has enlarged the sphere of the just to include what has actually come into being. In fact, in applying whatever conception of justice in allotments one begins with, one is likely to call one's own standard "strict" and anything that goes against it an infringement.

But how, one might ask, can the lot help this? Again, I think it is not the use of the lot alone that the Stranger is proposing as a remedy, but also the use of certain names for outcomes one does not like. So, the question becomes: What supports this practice of naming, and what does the use of the lot have to do with it? After saying that the equality of the lot must be used "as regards the discontent of the many," he says "what must necessarily be made use of are both equalities, in this way." Now, again, "in this way" could just be referring to the whole previous section in which some slight deviation from true equality was identified as a necessity for the legislator, who must nonetheless always aim at justice. And indeed the lot does have some characteristics that can help reduce tensions surrounding the selection of officers: one cannot easily call the lot either "fair" or "unfair," but one can more easily call it "chance"; further, no person or party can be blamed or praised for making the selection by lot come out a certain way; finally, the lot seems to have something divine about it, or at least the legislator intends it to be taken that way in entrusting the selection of priests to it completely, allowing the god thereby "to see to his own good pleasure" (759b8–c1).

But it is in the specific way in which the Stranger recommends using the lot, and in other devices, that I propose the substance of his proposal lies. When the lot is used, to take the most salient example, it is mixed with voting. In fact, in the case of the selection of the members of the council, the mixture is effected in accordance with numerical equality: exactly twice as many as are needed are selected by vote, and half of these are selected by lot. The same procedure is used in the case of the city-stewards and in other offices.

What is not clear is whether even this mixed procedure that involves voting can properly be said to contain any element at all of natural equality, the judgment of Zeus. We have already seen that the imbalance that is introduced by giving proportionally more seats to those of the higher property classes is no guarantee that the council will contain a predominance of virtuous types. We might consider, too, that an implicit presupposition of voting is that each vote should be counted as a unit, equal in weight to every other vote. In other words, even the procedures intended to give more to the greater rely on a species of that equality which anyone is competent to deploy: equality in accordance with number. In the end, the mixed procedure might be described as a mixture of *seeming* equalities, such that neither the lot nor the vote is simply what it is intended to appear as to those who might otherwise be discontented. Indeed, in his one explicit mention of the kind of mixing actually practiced, the Stranger is peculiarly reluctant actually to name the element that is to predominate. In introducing the rest of the offices after the council, the Stranger says they must establish the selections by "mixing δῆμος with not-δῆμος for the sake of friendliness [μειγνύντας πρὸς φιλίαν ἀλλήλοις δῆμον καὶ μὴ δῆμον] in every part of the town and country, so that it may be as unanimous as possible" (759b6–7). His listeners might take this as an understated way of distinguishing the base from the noble, and that may be how it is intended to be taken, but we need not take it the same way.

If the lot and the vote are thus meant to function in relation to the threat of faction as publicly established signs of equality, then we may also interpret the Stranger's extensive use of number along similar lines. In general, and in all its details, it is not clear just what the Stranger takes number to be. While it is at one time denigrated as something which anyone is capable of, he later calls investigation of a specific number, the number of citizens, one of the "divine matters" (771a). The number 5,040 in the first instance was said to be useful for the number of its subdivisions. Modern mathematics calls 5,040 a "highly composite" number, for something like the same reasons the Stranger puts forward: in particular, he notes that it can be divided by all of the numbers up to ten.[4] The number of tribes is set at twelve, and this division of the people is also a division of all the territories of the city, including the country. The division is meant to be natural, corresponding to the number of months in the year, and the movements of the land-stewards as well as the rotation of the presiding twelfth of the council are also meant to follow these natural cycles. Each of the tribes is named after one of the gods, and festivals devoted to the gods recognized in the city rotate evenly throughout the countryside and the town over the course of the year.

The harmoniousness, evenness, or naturalness of the number twelve makes the use of it understandable enough. But the import of other numbers of potentially political significance cannot be explained in this way such as eleven and ninety, to take two examples, as well as the frequent use of odd numbers for bodies of officials, which might thus be prevented from ever coming to a deliberative deadlock. While the latter makes a kind of mundane practical sense, the Stranger's mention of eleven is not immediately intelligible. Additionally, the Stranger extols the wondrous virtues of the number 5,040, but also notes that while it cannot be divided by eleven, the subtraction of a mere two households yields a number that can. He seems to be imagining setting the division of the populace into twelve, alongside another division into eleven, which might produce a marvelously complicated division of loyalties—though for what purpose, it is not clear. As for the number ninety, the number of councilors from each property class, Benardete points out that it cannot be divided by twelve, with the result that the representation of *tribes* in any segment of the council defined by property class can never be equal. Before this discourse on numbers turns into numerology, let me just make the generic observation that the Stranger seems to be using number—or to put it differently, collection and division in accordance with a kind of equality—to create both equalities and inequalities. The city thus numbered is, as it were, polyrhythmic, or at least syncopated. It is divided, evenly to be sure, but also in multiple intersecting and non-intersecting ways, and in ways that are in some cases associated with the natural and the divine.

Perhaps more practically, the Stranger's extensive use of both number and the lot seem intended to confound and conceal the degree of agency of any positively identifiable party, and indeed of any particular conception of equality. While this can help make for a city that is free of faction, it would need the help of that disposition we mentioned earlier, which inclines people to make use of those derived names in speaking among themselves about how events in the city are going. The degree of friendliness that would be required to keep the city whole and appropriately unanimous in the face of electoral disappointments of various kinds is surely greater than can be made up for by any single merely procedural device. A network of such devices would probably provide greater aid, but whether the extensive and ingenious apparatus of state that the Stranger has laid out for his interlocutors in Book 6 has settled the questions about fairness, excellence, and equality that could threaten any community remains very much unclear, to me at least.

To recall the ancient *logos* we heard about at the beginning, and revisit the Stranger's perplexity about it, we should consider what the intervening discussion has brought to light concerning equality. When the distinction is first introduced, it seems that the city should practice proportional equality or justice for the most part and admit only as much of the other type of equality as is necessary to appease partisans of a radical democracy. But even at the start, this "equality of Zeus" is presented as remote and difficult. The mixed procedures for selecting various kinds of officers, it was shown, do not in fact employ mostly this equality and only sparingly the other. Rather, "the equal in measure, weight, and number" is, so to speak, dramatically inflected in different ways, giving some emphasis to selectiveness and some to broad distribution. Indeed the mixing itself is sometimes effected in accordance with this kind of equality: 180 councilmen (in each class) selected by vote, *exactly half* of these appointed by lot. In short, the sensitive and potentially disruptive issue of the allotment of authority to citizens seems to be one that the city deals with by deceiving itself; its own official story is that in order to promote friendliness it had to mix two types of equality, when in fact its procedures amount to a simulacrum of equality that is intended to dupe democratic partisans and would-be tyrants alike into thinking that their own preferred type of government is favored, or at least not disfavored enough to make revolt seem preferable. This is a tense and unstable kind of "friendship" that falls far short of the organic unity of pleasures and pains envisioned in Book 5 of the *Republic,* and the devices put in place to promote it would not stand up to close examination. It is not difficult to conceive why the Stranger, knowing what he knows, would not feel or be at home in such a city.

Notes

1. The δοκιμασία, or "scrutiny," to which candidates for office are subjected happens after election, and its criteria are not extensively detailed, which leads one to imagine it as something like a formality.

2. Pangle splits the difference, so to speak, by translating "held equal when it comes to honors."

3. LSJ are of no help here, since the use of the passive they cite is this very *locus,* and both translations are offered as alternatives for this very sense.

4. A "highly composite" number is one that has more divisors than any smaller number, and thus is more likely to have a long string of consecutive divisors. The Stranger's mention of the high number of *consecutive* divisors of 5,040 will become relevant when the divisibility of its near neighbor 5,038 by eleven is mentioned a short while later.

10 The "Serious Play" of Book 7 of Plato's *Laws*

David Roochnik

R. G. Bury begins the introduction to his translation of Plato's *Laws* by stating that this work "lacks the charm and vigour of the earlier dialogues . . . [it] is marked also by much uncouthness of style, and by a tendency to pedantry, tautology and discursive garrulity which seems to point to the failing powers of the author."[1] Even without acceding to his suggestion that the inferior quality of this dialogue is due to Plato's diminished abilities, it is tempting to acknowledge Bury's description of the work. For the *Laws* does lack the sparkling density and playful irony of other dialogues. The Athenian is indeed pedantic, and his long-winded discourse is remarkably laborious. Especially for a reader inspired by the endlessly provocative minimalism characteristic of Socrates in so many other dialogues, tackling the *Laws* is a terrible chore. For above all else, what characterizes the Athenian's speech is its sustained and relentless seriousness.

For this reason it comes as a surprise when, in Book 7, somewhere near the middle of the dialogue, the Athenian says this: "Of course, the affairs of human beings are not worthy of great seriousness [μεγάλης σπουδῆς]" (803b). A few lines later he continues:

> I assert that what is serious should be treated seriously, and what is not serious should not, and that by nature god is worthy of a complete blessed seriousness, but that what is human, as we said earlier, has been devised as a certain plaything (παίγνιον) of god, and that this is really the best thing about it. Every man and woman should spend life in this way, playing (παίζοντα) the most beautiful games (παιδιάς)." (803c)[2]

In this, the apparently least playful of all Plato's dialogues, we find what might be his most emphatic praise of play.

Now, as some readers may already have recognized, in the first citation above I truncated the line. For immediately after saying, "the affairs of human beings are not worthy of great seriousness," the Athenian finishes the sentence with, "yet (γε μήν) it is necessary (ἀναγκαῖόν) to be serious about them. And this is not a fortunate thing" (οὐκ εὐτυχές: 803b).[3]

Unfortunately, human beings are constrained by some sort of necessity to be serious about what is not worthy of being taken seriously: namely, ourselves. This assertion is odd. How can I take seriously what I know is not worthy of such treatment? I can, of course, fake it. At least according to Alcibiades in the *Symposium*, this is precisely what Socrates does. He "lives his whole life being ironic and playing (παίζων) with human beings" (216e). He pretends, for example, to be taken by, and so to take seriously, beautiful young men like Alcibiades (and Charmides and Euthydemus [222b]), while in fact he "holds them in contempt" (καταφρονεῖ: 216d) and counts them as "nothing" (οὐδέν: 216e). And it is arguable that in the *Republic* he pretends to be interested in developing a serious model of a just human city, whereas in fact his real intention in this dialogue may instead be to "found a city within himself." As he puts it, "it doesn't make any difference whether it is or will be somewhere" (592b). It is possible, therefore, that his genuine concern in this dialogue may be not for the πόλις, but for the well being of the individual philosophical soul.

The magnitude of the Athenian's speech, and his consistently painstaking and often painful demeanor, surely seems to militate against the possibility of him faking it. Furthermore, the Athenian is conversing with Cleinias, a man charged by his fellow Cretans with an important task: to establish the laws for a new colony (702c). Unlike the hypothetical city-planning of the *Republic,* a venture that Socrates likens to a "dream" (443b) and describes as "playful" (536c), a venture that is in explicit service not to a political project but instead to the task of convincing two young men, Glaucon and Adeimantus, that the just life is superior to the unjust life (368c), here in the *Laws* there is a genuine piece of city-business to transact: assisting the founder of Magnesia.

So, the question must be asked again: how, if he is not faking it, does the Athenian manage to take seriously what he knows to be unworthy of seriousness? What sort of "necessity" constrains him to maintain the earnest, grave, methodical approach he adopts, and how, from a psychological point of view, does he manage to pull this off?

Before pursuing this question by examining material from Book 7 of the *Laws,* consider another passage from the *Republic.* Recall that in telling his story of the cave Socrates insists that the liberated prisoners who have made it to the upper world and seen the sun will not be allowed to remain aboveground. Instead, he "compels" them to return to the cave and there to participate fully in political affairs. Variants of the word he uses here, ἀνάγκασαι (516c), are repeated at least six times in this passage (500d, 519e, 520a, 520e, 521b, 539e, 540b), and to its implication Glaucon forcefully objects: "What? . . . Are we to do them an injustice, and make them live a worse life when a better is possible for them?" (519d). As commentators have understood, "the fate of the *Republic* hangs" on how this passage is interpreted.[4] For Strauss, it implies a conceptual incoherence and therefore tokens the impossibility of the perfectly just city.

> Only the non-philosophers could compel the philosophers to take care of the city. But, given the prejudice against the philosophers, this compulsion will not be forthcoming if the philosophers do not in the first place persuade the non-philosophers to compel the philosophers to rule over them, and this persuasion will not be forthcoming, given the philosophers' unwillingness to rule. We arrive then at the conclusion that the just city is not possible because of the philosophers' unwillingness to rule.[5]

For Strauss, it is impossible to make sense of the "necessity" invoked in the story of the cave. As a result, the efficacy, and the seriousness, of Socrates' putative exercise in city-planning must, in his view, be called into question.

By contrast, the necessity to be serious invoked at *Laws* 803b is different, for it does not require the non-philosopher to compel an unwilling philosopher to rule. Instead, it emerges from a self-recognition on the part of the Athenian; it is self-imposed. Even if human beings are not worthy of the greatest seriousness, he must, the Athenian tells himself, take them seriously. If this is a misfortune, so be it. Once again the standard picture of an old Plato writing the *Laws*, one who, perhaps unlike the author of the *Republic*, is resigned to the misfortune of being human and being political, does not seem out of order.

In any case, in Book 7 of the *Laws* the Athenian explains why human beings are not worthy of great seriousness. Not only are we "playthings" of the gods, as he had said earlier, we are their "puppets" (θαυμάτα) and as such we share only "in small portions of truth" (804b).[6] To this statement Megillus replies with indignation: "Stranger," he says, "you are belittling (διαφαυλίζεις) our human race in every respect!" (804b5). The Athenian responds:

> Don't be amazed (θαυμάσῃς), Megillus, but forgive me! For I was looking away toward the god and speaking under the influence of that experience, when I said what I did just now. So let (ἔστω) our race be something that is not lowly (φαῦλον) then, if that is dear (φίλον) to you, but worthy of a certain seriousness (σπουδῆς δέ τινος). (804b)

In effect, the Athenian has just said to Megillus, "Okay, if that's the way you want it, I take it back. Let human affairs be taken seriously."

This line is reminiscent of the bit of banter that precedes Aristophanes' speech in the *Symposium*. The poet, you recall, has been hiccupping throughout Eryximachus's rather pedantic analysis of Eros. When the good doctor finally finishes speaking, Aristophanes starts to poke fun at him by recounting the sneeze cure that he has just successfully applied. Eryximachus objects: "Good Aristophanes," he warns, "watch what you're doing." Aristophanes cheerfully relents: "Well said, Eryximachus! So let (ἔστω) what was said by me be unsaid" (189b3–4). Perhaps this sentence can function as the motto for comedy itself. Anything said can just as easily be unsaid, because nothing said by human beings is worth being taken seriously.

In a similar fashion, the Athenian in the *Laws* is willing to "unsay" what he has just said; namely, that "human affairs are surely not worthy of the greatest seriousness." If this statement is so easily retracted was he, then, not serious when he made it? If so, then he is being deliciously self-referential. The Athenian does not treat his own statement, "human beings are not worthy of the greatest seriousness," very seriously.

However, a more nuanced reading is in order. In responding to Megillus, the Athenian does not simply retract his original statement, for he says that human beings *are* worthy of "a certain (τινος) seriousness." In other words, even if we do not merit the "greatest seriousness" it may still be both possible and necessary to treat human affairs with a qualified or second-tier seriousness. As with so many other matters in the *Laws*, seriousness can be hierarchically stratified. While it is true that when one "looks away toward the god"—in other words, when one is being maximally philosophical—human affairs can be dismissed as merely playful. But when one is faced with a tough, civic-minded Spartan, and a Cretan charged with founding a colony, when one's gaze is resolutely horizontal rather than vertical, then a "certain seriousness" is required. Indeed it is "necessary." And it is generated by the recognition of the essential predicament of the human race: we are, unfortunately, human. This means that although, as Cleinias strongly maintains in Book 1, we are a bellicose lot prone to fighting among and even within ourselves (see 625e and 626d), we must work hard to figure out the best way to organize our political lives.[7]

Keeping this in mind, we now can see that although the Athenian seemed to engage in a comic unsaying of what has been said, his invocation of the unfortunate necessity to apply a "certain seriousness" to human affairs might be better construed as tragic. Whether we wish to or not, we must squarely face the fate that fortune has allocated to us and take our humanity seriously.

Because the Athenian's remarks about play spark these kind of reflections, it should come as no surprise that later in Book 7 he has a bit to say about both tragedy and comedy. He imagines the tragic poets, whom he describes as "serious" (σπουδαῖος), coming into his city and asking, "Strangers, shall we frequent your city and territory or not? And shall we carry and bring along our poetry?" (817a). The Athenian is not particularly inviting in response. "Best of strangers," he says to the tragedians, "we ourselves are poets, who have to the best of our ability created a tragedy that is the most beautiful and best; at any rate, our whole political regime is constructed as the imitation of the most beautiful and best way of life, which we at least assert to be really the truest tragedy" (817b). Presumably the very "myth" (812a) of the laws that the Athenian has been reciting is the truest tragedy because it is generated precisely by the recognition that we must treat our humanity with a "certain," less-than-greatest, seriousness. Although we are equipped with reason and so, at our optimal state, we can theorize about matters divine, because we have bodies and so need to eat and sleep, because we must live in cities and our time on earth is short, we can never do this continually, fully, or even adequately. Hence, we must act as if human life, in all of its petty detail, is meaningful and beautiful, when, as one who looks away to the divine understands, it might not be. The Athenian recommends that we impose this recognition upon ourselves.

Because the city itself, or at least the Athenian's "sketch" (803a) of its laws, is already tragic, the tragic poets may well be superfluous. As a result, the Athenian forces them to audition for entrance. Their work will have to be approved by the city's censors and only "if the things said by [them] are evidently the same, at least, or better [than the song we have sung], will we give you a chorus" (817d).

By contrast, the comic poets are immediately granted admittance to the city. For they have an essential pedagogical and civic function to perform. The Athenian explains: "For someone who is going to become prudent can't learn the serious things without learning the laughable, or, for that matter, anything without its opposite" (816d). In this altogether serious city, comedy is required, even if for negative reasons: "one should learn about the ridiculous things just for this reason—so that he may never do or say, through ignorance, anything that is ridiculous, if he doesn't have to" (816e). As a result, comedies will be performed only by slaves and hired foreigners, so that serious-minded citizens will not be infected by the ridiculous behavior that is imitated on stage and the language that is there recited. To reiterate: comedy has a serious role to play. Citizens must learn what it is to be ridiculous so that they do not have to be. Therefore, the Athenian states "let the play (παιγνία) we all call 'comedy' be thus ordained in law and in argument" (816e).[8]

There is one odd note in this brief discussion of comedy: a citizen should never do or say anything ridiculous "if he doesn't have to" (μηδὲν δέον: 816e5). This suggests that there might be some circumstance in which it is proper or needful for a citizen to be ridiculous. There might be occasions when it is appropriate to occupy or imitate "a shameful (or ugly) body" or entertain a shameful or ugly or lowly "thought" (816d). But what would such occasions be? I can only guess.

In order to treat human affairs properly, one must take them with a certain, qualified seriousness, for in reality they are not worthy of the greatest seriousness. As the Athenian puts it in Book 4—where he decisively revises the Protagorean dictum—god, and not human being, "is the measure of all things" (716c). It is, therefore, a fundamental mistake to absolutize anything human. Obvious instances of such erroneous thinking would be excessive love of the body, of money, and of the city itself. It is imperative, therefore, to treat human affairs and the city with only a "certain seriousness" rather than the "blessed seriousness" that the gods merit. We must keep the divine in view in order to identify properly the true status and worth of human beings. Nonetheless, one must be cautious in following the lead of the Athenian, who in a moment of inspired exuberance "looks away toward the god." For in doing so one risks becoming more like the Socrates described by Alcibiades: a man who holds fellow human beings in contempt. The Athenian and we readers must thus force ourselves to lower our gaze, but not entirely to lose sight of what is above us. It is for this reason that comedy, unlike tragedy, plays an essential role in the city. It reminds the citizens, who even though they are not allowed actually to perform in comedies are required to attend them, that they are puny, ugly, shameful, ridiculous creatures. This inoculating but superficial dose of self-ridicule, administered from the distance of the stage, is necessary to keep political affairs, which are regulated by the "truest tragedy," that is the laws, in proper perspective.

To amplify this point, I turn next to the very beginning of Book 7. Here the Athenian announces that he will discuss "nourishment" (τροφή) and "education" (παιδεία: 788a).[9] He begins with policies that apply to pregnant mothers, infants, and very young children. The general principle he assumes is that "all bodies are benefited when they are moved in an invigorating manner by all sorts of shakings and motions" (789d). This is because such motions facilitate digestion, which in turn promotes the good growth of the young. Therefore, pregnant women will be advised to walk, and infants will be carried by their mothers continually. It is, as the Athenian puts it, beneficial for the very young "to dwell as if they were always on a ship at sea" (790d). His evidence for the soundness of this proposal is the simple observation that mothers lull their restless children to sleep by rocking them continually in their arms and singing to them (790e). Motion generates rest.

Behind this simple observation, however, the Stranger offers a more general principle. He compares the rocking of a fussy baby to the Bacchic revelers who, through the therapeutic powers of disciplined and repetitive music and dance, restore equanimity to, and cure, themselves. "In both cases," the Athenian explains, "the passion being experienced is presumably terror" (δειμός: 790e), and "when someone brings a rocking motion from the outside to such passions, the motion brought from without overpowers the fear and the mad motion within and, having overpowered it, makes a calm stillness appear in the soul that replaces the harsh fluttering of the heart" (791a).[10]

The passion felt by Bacchic revelers is caused by "a poor (φαύλην) disposition (ἕξιν) of the soul" (790e). They have given themselves to the god and so have lost sight of their own humanity. By contrast, infants are too young to have been habituated to much of anything. Their terror, therefore, must be of some primal sort that lies buried deep within the human body. The therapy an infant receives is the repetitive back-and-forth rocking of a mother or a nurse. Rhythmic rocking counteracts the fierce palpitations of primal terror. If a baby is improperly raised, if it is not rocked to sleep, then this terror will be allowed to fester and grow unchecked, and the result would be cowardice. Courage, by contrast, is "triumphing over" terror (791c). Repetitive motion and sound, the singing of the mother or nurse, thus inculcates the infant with, or at least provides the bodily preconditions for, courage.

This discussion of baby-care seems both vaguely plausible and rather trivial. In fact, however, its central image, of rocking, oscillation, back and forth, back and forth, might be useful to keep in mind when reading the *Laws*. More specifically, it might be useful in accounting for the serious play, or the playful seriousness, that the Athenian Stranger, in the passage discussed above, recommends.[11] To elaborate, consider the following examples.

First, when the Athenian begins his discussion of the upbringing and education of children, he urges his companions to adopt the proper—that is, not entirely serious—attitude to such trivial matters. On the one hand, "to avoid speaking about this is completely impossible." How a child is raised will have significant consequences for the city. On the other, it would be absurd to develop precise legislation dictating how many rocks per minute a baby should receive, or how it should be swaddled. In lieu of making such laws the Athenian recommends a "middle" (μεταξύ: 822d7) way; namely, a kind of instruction (διδαχῇ) and admonition" (νουθετήσει: 788a), and the development of a set of "unwritten customs" (ἄγραφα νόμιμα: 793b). As he later puts it, as he looks back at the child-rearing practices he has recommended throughout Book 7, "we assert that these things shouldn't be left unmentioned, but that to suppose, in speaking about them, that they are being laid down as laws would be great folly" (ἀνοίας: 822d–e). It would be foolish to take human affairs so seriously that every aspect of human life, especially those concerning children, became matters of pinpoint legislation. In general, it would be "unseemly" (ἀσχήμων) for a lawgiver to speak of the "many little and frequent details regarding the management of a household" (807e).

Second, consider the at times wonderful oscillation of the topics that the Athenian treats. For example, almost immediately after discussing the teaching of astronomy, whose subject matter is the "great gods, Sun and also Moon" (821b7)—which, contrary to popular opinion, are not "wanderers" (821b7) but instead "always move in the same circular path" (822a5)—the Athenian addresses hunting. He recommends that the following "prayer" be given to the young people of the city:

> O friends, may you never be seized by a desire or an erotic love for hunting on the sea, for angling, or in general for hunting of the animals that dwell in water, or for those basket-traps that perform the toil of a lazy hunt, whether the hunters are asleep or awake! (823e)

After the righteous speech about astronomy, it is hard to read this, especially out loud—and especially in Pangle's translation—without cracking up. But immediately after this impassioned plea not to use basket-traps, the Athenian turns to a more serious subject:

> May there never come over you a longing for the catching of humans by sea, and piracy, and may you never thus be made cruel and lawless hunters! May it never enter your minds in the least to engage in theft, in the countryside or in the city!

And then, this marvelous oscillation:

> May a seductive, erotic love of bird-hunting, which is hardly a liberal pursuit, never come over any of the young! (823e)

A third example is the Athenian's treatment of leisure. After developing political arrangements so that "matters pertaining to the arts were handed over to others"—in other words, so that food, shelter, clothing and all the material requirements of life are provided without the labor of the citizens—the Athenian asks, "What then would be the way of life of human beings for whom the necessities were taken care of?" (806d). How, in other words, would citizens "who are not lacking in leisure" (ἀσχολίας: 807c7) spend their time? But this formulation is misleading, for in fact the citizens have no leisure since the Athenian recommends that "there should be a schedule (τάξιν) regulating how all the free men spend all their time, beginning almost at dawn and extending to the next dawn and rising of the sun" (807e). Free time in this city isn't all that free. Similarly, play (παίζειν: 797b2), the topic of much of Book 7, isn't all that playful since it is entirely regulated by the authorities. It is imperative, the Athenian says, that "the same persons always play at the same things" (797a).

A final example is found in the following statement made by the Athenian as he tries to determine what literature will be made available in the city.

> As I looked now to the speeches we've been going through since dawn until the present—and it appears to me that we have not been speaking without some inspiration from gods—they seemed to me to have been spoken in a way that resembles in every respect a kind of poetry. It's probably not surprising for me to have had such a feeling, to have been very pleased at the sight of my own speeches, brought together, as it were; for compared to most of the speeches that I have learned or heard, in poems, or poured out in prose like what's been said, these appeared to me to be both the most well-measured, at any rate, of all, and especially appropriate for the young to hear. I don't think I would have a better model than this to describe for the Guardian of the Laws and Educator. (811c–d)

Is this a moment of monumental self-congratulation? Is this passage meant to be the speech of a pompous and overly serious character, the sort that is regularly lampooned in comedy? It is difficult to tell from Pangle's wooden, monotonic translation. It is useful to cite the Saunders version of the same passage, the one that Pangle objects to so fervently, for comparison:[12]

> You see, when I look back now over this discussion of ours, which has lasted from dawn up till this very moment—a discussion in which I think I sense the inspiration of heaven—well, it's come to look, to my eyes, just like a literary composition. Perhaps not surprisingly, I was overcome by a feeling of immense satisfaction at the sight of my "collected works," so to speak, because, of all the addresses I have ever learned or listened to, whether in verse or in this kind of free prose style I've been using, it's *these* that have impressed me as being most eminently acceptable and the most entirely appropriate for the ears of the younger generation. So I could hardly commend a better model than this to the Guardians of the Laws in charge of education.

Saunders's "my 'collected works,' so to speak" translates λόγους οἰκείους οἷον ἀθρόους (811d1), and sounds funny. Pangle's "my own speeches, brought together, as it were" is perhaps more literal, but it is deadly serious. If the thesis of this paper is correct, then at least in this one case, Saunders should get the nod.

Notes

1. Bury 1967, vii.

2. Translations used in this essay are from Pangle 1980.

3. See Denniston 1996, 348, for a discussion of γε μήν as an adversative particle that often answers μέν.

4. See Brown 2000 for a thorough analysis of the use of ἀνάγκασαι in this passage.

5. Strauss 1975, 124.

6. Note that the word used here is the same that names the "puppets" whose shadows are cast on the wall of the cave in *Republic* 514b. Also compare *Laws* 644d, where the Athenian states that each citizen should be considered to be a divine puppet "put together either for their play (παίγνιον) or for some serious purpose (σπουδῇ)—which, we don't know."

7. Note the distinction between human and divine necessity mentioned at 818b.

8. Note that the word that Pangle here translates as "play" (παιγνία) is closely related to the one used at 803c when the Athenian says that the human race has been "devised as a plaything (παίγνιον) of the god." For this reason, Liddel, Scott, Jones 1940, citing *Laws* 816e, offer not only "toy or plaything" as the meaning of the latter, but also "comic performance, comedy." Perhaps, then, 803c should then be translated as "the comedy of the gods?"

9. Compare the discussion of play and education at 643d–e.

10. Saunders 2004, 517, explains: "*Corybantic conditions*: Frenzied pathological states accompanied by a strong desire to dance . . . The condition was cured homeopathically by the *disciplined* music and dancing of Corybantic ritual."

11. And which Russon, in his contribution to this volume, also uncovers as an implicit theme of the education proposals in *Laws* 2.

12. Pangle's harsh criticism of Saunders can be found (op. cit.) at x–xii.

11 No Country for Young Men: Eros as Outlaw in Plato's *Laws*

Francisco J. Gonzalez

The topic of this essay is a part of Book 8 consisting of little more than six pages of the Greek text (835b5–842a10) often treated by interpreters as a digression ("una digresión" [Lisi 2001, 38]) and therefore passed over without much comment.[1] Sandwiched between legislation concerning sacred festivals and a discussion of the economic organization of the state, this treatment of how the law is to impose proper measure on erotic desires is indeed technically a digression. Yet even if we did not already know that digressions in Plato are often much more important than what they digress from, an attentive reading reveals that the content of this particular digression so threatens, and in such fundamental ways, the overall project of legislation carried out in the dialogue as a whole that it resembles more a derailment than a digression. Indeed that the discussion should need to *digress* in order to address the problem of erotic desire is no accident. By the time we reach the end of this short discussion of how to master erotic desire in the citizens, the preferred law is abandoned in favor of a fatally flawed "Don't ask, don't tell" policy, persuasion gives way to force, and the founder of the new colony of Magnesia withholds his assent. Indeed throughout this text things seem just not right, out of joint, even rather absurd. My aim in this essay is simply to survey the landscape of this text and draw attention to its many odd features with the ultimate aim of showing how it leaves ἔρως outside of the law and thus leaves the law itself looking rather ineffectual. The project of legislation will of course need to continue, but now with a disturbing awareness of its limits.

The Athenian makes clear from the very start of the digression that they are about to confront a problem greater than any encountered so far and that the means they have so far relied on will fall short. Specifically, he indicates the greater difficulty the task of legislating concerning sexual relations will pose in comparison to what has come before: persuasion in these matters is indeed so difficult (πειθεῖν χαλεπόν, 835c1), we are told, that the task properly belongs to a god. The Athenian is aware, of course, that the laws cannot come directly from a god and that the legislation carried out in this dialogue is a human enterprise. Absent a god, then, we require here a bold man (ἀνθρώπου τολμηροῦ, c3) who especially values frankness (παρρησία, 835c4) and who will act alone guided by reason alone (λόγῳ ἑπόμενος μόνῳ μόνος, 835c8). This final double-qualification is striking. The insistence that the legislator must here act *alone* suggests than any consultation with others will weaken his action. The insistence on being guided by reason alone suggests that the legislation needed requires freedom from the influence of any and all desire. This man acting alone and by reason alone is evidently, if not a god in fact, as god-like as possible.

But why should legislation concerning sexual relations require, more than other legislation considered so far, such a god-like legislator? When the Athenian finally reveals the kind of law that will prove so difficult he specifies the reasons for the difficulties:

1) Indulgence in sexual desires will be especially tempting precisely in the state they have been constructing, since its citizens will be exempt from hard and menial labor and will be concerned chiefly with sacrifices, feasts, and dances (835d6–e2).

2) While the majority of desires can be mastered by the laws already established and by the watchful eye of the magistrates, while, in other words, these means can preserve the measure (μέτρον ἔχει) in these other desires (τὰς ἄλλας ἐπιθυμίας, 836a5–6), in the case of erotic desires (τῶν ἐρώτων, 836a7) it is not at all easy (πάντως οὐ ῥάδιον, 836b4) to find the φάρμακον (836b3) that could save us from danger.

3) While the examples of Crete and Lacedaemon have helped us in the case of laws on many other matters, they are of no help here, in fact contradicting what we need to establish.

One cannot overemphasize the seriousness of these difficulties. According to the first, the legislation carried out so far in constructing the colony of Magnesia does not make the task of mastering erotic desires easier but, on the contrary, *much harder.* There will be more of a problem with indulgence in sexual desire in our ideally constituted and ruled city than in any contemporary city. The second stated difficulty, i.e., that erotic desires are not to be kept in check by the means suggested earlier for imposing measure on other desires, represents a significant departure from Books 1 and 2 where the institution of the symposium was defended as a means of helping us master pleasures by partly indulging them in a controlled environment (see, e.g., 645d, 649d, 673e). There ἔρως is included among other desires and pleasures (such as anger, cowardice, etc.), given no special status, and not claimed to be especially problematic. If Book 8 is completely silent with regard to the institution of the symposium,[2] this is presumably because erotic desires are now recognized to pose a special problem that this institution will be incapable of solving. Indeed the first difficulty, with its reference to the danger posed by all of the sacrifices, feasts, and dances, suggests that the symposiums will be part of the problem rather than the solution. Finally, the third difficulty notes that in legislating about sexual relations we will have no currently existing models to follow: here even the constitutions of Crete and Lacedaemon are not part of the solution but part of the problem (see 636a–b).[3]

What kind of law, then, is needed here and what kind of case can be made for it by our god-like legislator? We learn that sexual relations between men and boys will need to be outlawed. We are then given two arguments in support of such legislation. The first is that even in the case of wild beasts male does not touch male for the purpose of sexual intercourse.[4] The second argument appeals to the principle that the laws should promote virtue and asserts that homosexual relations engender in the characters of seducer and seduced not temperance and courage but their opposites (836d–e). What, then, are we to make of these arguments?

The first argument has been seen by a number of commentators as more of a rhetorical ploy.[5] Strong evidence for this view is to be found in a passage from Book 1 in which this so-called argument is first mentioned: when the Athenian there says that one must consider that the pleasure of male mating with female for procreation is natural while that of male mating with male or female with female is contrary to nature, he prefaces his remark with the qualification: "whether it is in jesting or in seriousness that it is necessary to consider this" (636c1–2). Here the possibility is explicitly acknowledged that the "against-nature" argument is a jest rather than something having a serious claim to truth. Even if the remark does not positively deny seriousness to the argument, and even if it fits within the general playful tone of the dialogue, it at least falls short of a ringing endorsement, and understandably so, given the argument's apparent weakness.[6] Is it perhaps then simply that "drug" the Athenian suggests is necessary to counter the danger of erotic desire? But that drug was described as not at all easy to find, whereas the "against-nature" argument has been around since Book 1 and, far from being sophisticated or hard to argue, appears only to reproduce a common trope, not to say prejudice. The argument that homosexual love makes the partners cowardly and intemperate is not much more sophisticated or compelling: not only is this claim questionable, but it is directly contradicted both by what is argued in the *Symposium* and the *Phaedrus* and by a well-documented tradition of associating homosexual ἔρως with courage and military prowess (see Dover 1989, 191–192). In short, neither argument seems worthy of a god-like legislator following reason alone. Indeed we already begin to see one of the striking features of the text under consideration: the wide gap between what is said to be required for adequate legislation in the area of erotic desires and what we are actually offered. We need a god-like individual guided by reason alone, but all we get is some rather weak rhetoric that is hard to take seriously as a rationally compelling argument.

One of the problems with both so-called arguments, of course, is that they appear to treat all homosexual love as the same, without distinguishing between different forms. This is presumably why the Athenian next recognizes the need to define the terms at issue in this legislation. Strikingly, he begins by distinguishing two types not of ἔρως but of φιλία: one in which what is like is φίλον to what is like according to virtue, or even what is equal to what is equal (ἴσον ἴσῳ, 837a7);[7] and another in which what is needy is φίλον to the rich as to its contrary (ἐναντίον, 8). The first thing to note is that these two kinds of φιλία simply reproduce two traditional conceptions of φιλία that are therefore in the *Lysis* attributed to the poets and natural philosophers (213d6–216b9). If we further note that both conceptions are in the *Lysis* shown to be inadequate and refuted, we must conclude that the Athenian is here content with simply following common opinion and established tradition. In other words, while the *Lysis* seeks to arrive at the truth about φιλία through philosophical argumentation, the present discussion appeals to popular views with no greater aim than persuasion. This is confirmed by what the Athenian proceeds to tell us about the nature of ἔρως. If in the *Symposium* and the *Phaedrus* ἔρως is given extraordinary metaphysical import, here it becomes nothing more than great "intensity" (σφοδρόν, 837a9)[8] in the relations of φιλία already described. In other words, if φιλία means liking each other, whether because we are alike or unlike, ἔρως means really, really, really liking each other. Such an analysis of ἔρως is clearly not intended for the philosophically enlightened, but can only serve the purpose of persuading the ignorant to accept a law that suppresses ἔρως as much as possible.

But what in fact do the Athenian's definitions tell us about the meaning and import of the law he is defending? Since he proceeds to say that the law will prohibit the φιλία between unequals but will encourage the φιλία between equals (837d), is erotic desire countenanced when it is between equal men and does such erotic desire include physical relations or sexual intercourse? From what the Athenian says, it is clear that erotic desire in the narrower sense of physical, sexual desire is confined to the friendship between unequals and has no place in the friendship between equals.[9] Thus when he recognizes the possibility of a third kind of love that is really nothing more than a mixture of the first two (μεικτή, 837b4), he characterizes it as one in which the lover is torn between two different desires: one that craves the bloom of the beloved as if it were a ripening peach and the other that desires the soul and puts beholding *in the place of* ἔρως (837b8–d1). The law, therefore, in allowing for a pure friendship between equals who only behold each other's souls, still bans all erotic, sexual desire between men under the assumption that such desire can exist only among unequals. Furthermore, the emphasis on equality appears to rule out even *chaste* pederasty. If such a relationship is described in the text, it is as that confused, mixed form of love in which the lover is torn between sexual desire and a friendship of virtue.

Yet these superficial definitions of the terms hardly make the law more compelling or persuasive. This is made clear by what happens in the discussion at this point: while the Athenian gains the agreement of Megillus, he does not even try to gain the assent of Cleinias, for whose colony they are supposedly legislating. Instead he confesses that he must postpone the attempt to persuade Cleinias to a later time. But that is not all: even when he finally gets to persuading Cleinias, he will do so not through rationally compelling arguments, but through *charms* (ἐπάδων πείθειν, 837e6). If the Athenian cannot persuade Cleinias now and must instead resort to some unspecified charm at some later date, what chance is there that the ordinary citizens of Magnesia will be persuaded to accept this law?

Perhaps anticipating this objection, the Athenian now assures us that he knows of a special device (τέχνη, 837e9) for enacting this law. Yet if we eagerly await a clear explanation of this marvelous device, we will be disappointed. Indeed a bizarre feature of the pages that follow is the way in which the Athenian repeatedly claims to possess this τέχνη while at the same time leaving as obscure as possible what exactly it consists of. He first points out that to keep men from having sexual intercourse with beautiful people who are their brothers and sisters or sons and daughters, it has sufficed simply to say that these acts are hated by the gods (838a–c). So is the vaunted τέχνη simply a matter of asserting that homosexual love is hated by the gods and shameful? But as even the otherwise agreeable Megillus objects, what is required is an explanation of *how* the lawgiver will make all of the citizens willing to say that the prohibited loves are impious and shameful (838e2–3). The Athenian in response once again claims to possess a τέχνη (e5). Yet this second claim leads to no clarification of the exact nature of this device.

Instead we get a new description of the law that assigns it an aim not yet indicated: that of making a natural use of sexual intercourse for the sake of reproduction (τῇ τῆς παιδογονίας συνουσίᾳ, 838e6). It consequently turns out that the law is to prohibit not only intercourse between men, but also intercourse between men and women not for the purpose of child-bearing. The justification is that intercourse in both cases would be a waste of sperm (838e8) and thus against nature, making the law that prohibits such intercourse itself κατὰ φύσιν (839a6). That this is indeed a new description of the law is clear if we consider that sexual intercourse between men and women did not even figure in the classification of the different types of φιλία: given the insistence on the inferiority of women throughout the dialogue (see 781b; 917a; 944d) and the fact that we are speaking here of sexual intercourse, the relationship between men and women can clearly not be classified under that φιλία between equals approved of earlier; it also cannot be classified under that φιλία between unequals that was earlier completely prohibited. Here we have another of the many incoherencies in this text.

Yet do we not now have a new justification for the law, namely, that it accords with nature in prohibiting the waste of sperm? But now comes perhaps the strangest moment in this very strange stretch of dialogue. The Athenian imagines hearing the outcries of an aggressive young man described as "full of much sperm" (πολλοῦ σπέρματος μεστός, 839b4). This description, glossed over by prudish translations, is significant in the context: a young man full of much sperm is not going to worry about wasting sperm and therefore will find the present justification of the law completely uncompelling. But do not worry: the Athenian informs us that it was precisely in anticipation of such outcries that he claimed earlier to be armed with a τέχνη. What, then, finally, is this τέχνη? The Athenian helpfully informs us that it is both very easy and very difficult (b6–c1). It is easy to enact the law and have it obeyed if the citizens are inspired with sufficient religious dread. The difficulty is the strength of unbelief (ἀπιστίας ῥώμη, d4) that makes people refuse to recognize the possibility of such a law. Throughout these comments it still remains frustratingly unclear just what the vaunted τέχνη amounts to. It would presumably need to be a way of defeating the strength of unbelief and showing that public opinion can be made to feel dread before the law. But what is this way? What device can help us against our young man on sperm-overload?

We might finally get the answer when the Athenian next claims to have a *logos* to demonstrate that enactment of the law is not beyond human beings but possible (839d7–9): a *logos* he describes as partaking of *some persuasiveness* (ἐχόμενον πιθανότητος τινός, 839d8–9). Here it is: if athletes can abstain from sex while they are in training, then why can our citizens not do the same while in training for what they will be charmed from childhood (ᾄδοντες, 840c2) into believing is the greatest of all victories: the victory over pleasure (840c5)? Just how persuasive, then, is this *logos*? The opening comments of this section already made clear that erotic desires are going to be much harder to charm away through some drug than other desires. Our young man full of sperm might be able to control himself for a while in training for the next chariot race, but is he going to be willing to refrain always from any extra-marital sexual relations because of some charm we have said over him since childhood? In any case, the Athenian insists that this *logos* is enough: the law must go forward and with no more justification than the appeal to nature made earlier: our citizens should be no worse (perhaps also no better) than animals who pair off into heterosexual pairs when they come to the age for breeding (840d–e). Are we to hear our pacified young man now yelling, "Yea team!"?

Even if we are convinced that our virile young man could be charmed into containing his sperm, we immediately are faced with the most significant defeat (for it is hard to know what else to call it) in this discussion. Even if we could charm our own citizens from childhood, what will happen when they come into contact with the citizens of other cities and hear of the power and pleasure of lawless erotic desires? Even if everything possible has been done to isolate our city and close it off to the foreign, the Athenian must grant that the citizens could still indeed be corrupted by other Greeks and barbarians and thus, hearing of and seeing the great power of the "lawless Aphrodite" among them (τὴν λεγομένην ἄτακτον Ἀφροδίτην δυναμένην, 840e4–5), be turned against the law. What, then, is the solution to this significant problem? The response should surprise and even shock: despite having defended the possibility of this law and attempted to justify it, the Athenian now tells us that in the mentioned case of corruption through contact between our city and other cities (a situation presumably unavoidable) the law will simply have to be given up for another that is only second best (ὀρθότητα ἔχον δευτέραν, 841b6). This retreat from a law whose importance has been repeatedly stressed is no minor defeat. Erotic desires have indeed proven a special case since their victory over a law that has been defended as the best is unprecedented in the dialogue. Furthermore, just how much has been conceded here to erotic desires becomes evident when we consider the second-best law that is now introduced. If it has proven impossible to outlaw the practice of the sexual acts in question, then all that remains is to outlaw their *appearance*. The second-best law will therefore demand only that the previously prohibited sexual acts be kept *concealed* (τὸ δὴ λανθάνειν τούτων δρῶντά τι καλόν παρ' αὐτοῖς ἔστω, 841b2–3). Putting aside the lack of psychological insight shown by the Athenian when he suggests that the requirement of concealment will make these erotic desires lose their force and become rare, the idea of a law that demands and legalizes deception is in itself deeply troubling. The virile young man must be rejoicing at the trouble he is causing his elders.

If possible, however, matters get even stranger. Apparently fearing that those with corrupted natures (τοὺς τὰς φύσεις διεφθαρμένους, 841b7) will fail to obey even the second-best law, the Athenian asserts that they will be *forced* (βιάζοιτ'ἄν, 841c1–2) to obey by three things: fear of god, love of honor, and desire for the beautiful forms of the soul rather than of the body (c4–6). The unavoidable question here is why the Athenian has switched from talk of "charming" to talk of "forcing." The answer presumably is to be found in the very incoherence of what the Athenian is suggesting here: those with corrupted natures are clearly not going to be naturally motivated by a fear of god or a love of honor or a desire for beautiful psychic forms.[10] Some sort of force will necessarily need to intervene. But if even the second-best law commanding universal hypocrisy can be upheld only through some sort of force, the Athenian's proposal appears increasingly implausible. This is presumably why he suddenly grants at this point that the things he has said are perhaps like the wishful thinking (εὐχαί) one finds in a story (ἐν μύθῳ, c6–7). It is indeed the case that as this section of the dialogue progresses the Athenian sounds more and more like an idle dreamer.

Undeterred nevertheless, the Athenian once again appeals to force in asserting that we will *force* (βιασαίμεθα, 841d1) one of two things regarding erotic matters: either that no one will touch anyone but his spouse or that any man who has extramarital affairs will keep this hidden from everyone (μὴ λανθάνων ἄνδρας τε καὶ γυναῖκας πάσας, 841e1–2) on pain of being disqualified from any kind of civic honor. But now we are suddenly and abruptly informed of a qualification: the laxity of the second-best law will not apply to love between men; *that* will not be tolerated even if kept hidden! (841d5). So the law we are apparently left with is as follows: do not engage in extramarital sex unless you have to, in which case restrict it to the opposite sex and keep it hidden from everyone else. Our virile young man might now be scratching his head and wondering why he would obey the law regarding the sex of his partner when he is at the same time commanded to keep the whole relationship under cover; behind the veil of deception and false reputation, why would he not deposit his excess sperm wherever he pleases?

Perhaps this problem prepares us for the very strange conclusion of this utterly strange discussion: while Megillus claims to be happy with what has been said and enthusiastically accepts the law,[11] Cleinias, when asked for his opinion, postpones giving it until the right occasion (καιρός, 842a8). As we have seen, up to now the Athenian has not even sought Cleinias's agreement, clearly fearing that he would not receive it. Now Cleinias explicitly refuses his assent and offers to give his opinion only later when the occasion is right. We are given no indication of what would count as the right occasion, and we can assume that there is no way of specifying or defining in advance what would constitute the right occasion; certainly no law could determine it. There is therefore not even any guarantee that the right occasion will ever come. Furthermore, since Cleinias is the one whose job it is to found the colony of Magnesia, his deferral of opinion leaves the Athenian's proposal for dealing with erotic desires in suspense, not only here in Book 8, but for the remainder of the dialogue. Not only has the law judged best given way to a second-best law, but even the latter is left hanging.

This analysis of the "digression" in Book 8 has highlighted the tensions, incoherencies, failures, abrupt shifts, and just plain oddities that characterize it. What I wish to do in conclusion is to argue, on the basis of this analysis, that erotic desires have compromised, if not even derailed, the project of legislation as described in other books of the *Laws*. Most of the following problems threatening this project have been present just below the surface throughout the dialogue, but the problem of regulating ἔρως brings them fully to the fore and in an unprecedented way:

1) For the first and only time in the *Laws*, a law judged to be correct must be abandoned in favor of a law that is less correct.[12] This is not to deny that there are other examples of compromise in the *Laws*. The use of the lot is a concession to the inability to realize perfectly the more divine equality of giving due measure to things unequal (757d–e). The laws regulating who gets married to whom are acknowledged to occasion anger and resentment, so that they require the support of persuasion (773c–d). Regulations concerning the upbringing of children must be left unwritten out of fear that written laws would incur ridicule (790a), though this does not prevent the Athenian from proceeding to regulate children's games. The laws concerning inheritance, given that they require kin to marry kin with no consideration given to the qualities of the two parties, are acknowledged to be burdensome and likely to be resisted in some cases (925d–e). Therefore, provision is made for one of the parties to make the case, before either the law-wardens or the judges, that the lawgiver, if he were present, would not have enforced the law in this particular case (926c). However, all of these instances of recognizing resistance to the laws and

making concessions are quite different from the case in Book 8 for the simple reason that they do not go so far as to revoke a law in favor of some inferior law. The closest parallel[13] is the recommendation of common meals for women: while the Athenian considers this arrangement something good and practically indispensable (780c), he does allow for the possibility of its being rejected after closer examination (783b). However, this arrangement does not encounter the kind of problems we have seen the law regarding ἔρως face, and the Athenian therefore does not go so far as to propose an alternative, second-best arrangement.

The Athenian does indeed express uncertainty at 841e45 about whether we should speak here of two laws or of one, and this might tempt one to conclude that what is proposed in Book 8 is not so radical after all, i.e., simply a revision or qualification rather than an abandonment of one law for another. However, the reason for the Athenian's uncertainty is presumably that what the second law commands is simply the *appearance* of what the first law commands in fact. The second-best arrangement is therefore not so much a second law or a different conception of what is just, but rather a license to obey the first law in appearance while violating it in deed. This substitution of a law for its fraudulent appearance only makes Book 8 all the more anomalous. Even if the Athenian is willing to compromise on common meals for women, he never suggests as a solution putting up a sign outside the dining halls that reads "Women Admitted" while in fact barring them from entering.

2) For the first and only time in the *Laws*, not only is a significant part of the moral lives of the citizens left outside the purview of the laws, but the law must explicitly demand that the citizens keep their behavior *hidden* from all. Though even the size of their utensils is determined by law (746d–747b), the citizens are to keep their sexual behavior to themselves! Earlier at 785a1, the Athenian does indeed say that sexual conduct shall be passed over in silence by the law unless it becomes a problem, but presumably the words in Book 8 cited above represent a recognition that sexual conduct *will* become a problem and unavoidably so. That the laws should not only pass over in silence a major and clearly problematic aspect of the private lives of the citizens but should actually command secrecy and deception with regard to it is an idea truly unique to Book 8. Pradeau does not appear to recognize this exception when he claims the following to be true of the project in the *Laws* as a whole: "What Plato thereby rules out from the outset is that an activity could be authorized in silence or out of the reach of the law."[14] What makes the proposal in Book 8 so shocking is

precisely that Pradeau is absolutely right with regard to the *rest* of the dialogue.

In Book 7 (788a–c) we are told that while it might seem improper and undignified to legislate about small and trivial things, allowing the citizens to get into the habit of going against the law (παρανομεῖν) even in these small and trivial matters will *destroy* (διαφείρει) the laws (788b6–c1). Book 5 (738e) speaks of the need for everyone in the city to know everyone else so that no one's character can remain in the dark. At one point in Book 8 itself (838c8–d2) public opinion (φήμη) is praised for its power of preventing people from even breathing (ἀναπνεῖν) against the law. Against this background, a law that legislates the concealment of an important part of the lives of the citizens and thereby undermines its own power to shape their characters represents a shocking aberration.[15]

J.-M. Bertrand, who has seen well the magnitude of what is proposed and conceded here, writes of the second-best law that it "institutes dissimulation as a formal obligation"[16] and then expresses as follows the evident contradiction: "In this way is formed within the city, where nothing should nevertheless remain hidden, a world in which no one is required to confess his perversity."[17] The problem of ἔρως, in short, has not only defeated a particular law, but has undermined the very foundation of the project of legislation carried out in the *Laws*. In doing so, it perhaps only exposes an inescapable hypocrisy built into the city as proposed. In an extraordinary passage later in the dialogue, the Athenian proposes the abolition of oaths sworn in court on the grounds that "almost half" of the citizens would otherwise certainly perjure themselves (948d–e).[18] This argument appears to acknowledge significant *de facto* dissimulation and dishonesty within the city. And since the adulterers are expected and even required to lie, they least of all, presumably, should be made to swear an oath!

3) The ideal of combining persuasion with force that constitutes one of the other central pillars to the project of the *Laws* (see the end of Book 4) must here be abandoned. When persuasion becomes nothing but wishful thinking and telling stories, one must have recourse to force and force alone. Stories or *mythoi* of course play a part in the prelude to other laws: at 870d and 872d–e, for example, a prelude is supplemented by a μῦθος according to which the avenger of kindred blood ordains that the doer must in time suffer what he has done (see also 713a). But here in Book 8 we do not have such a specific mythos with a serious point, but only general wishful thinking. There is a parallel to such wishful thinking in Book 5 when the objection is raised that the legislator is simply assuming the

citizens will comply, as if he were dreaming or making a city and citizens out of wax (746a7–8). The response made there is that the legislator must make the pattern as perfect as possible and then be willing to modify details in its realization (746b–c). But what makes the parallel far from exact is that in Book 8, as we have seen, the problems with both the preferred law and the second-best law amount to much more than a mere modification of details. A better parallel is perhaps the recourse in Book 10 to an argument against the atheists that not only is too long for a prelude (887a3) but that also oversteps the bounds of legislation (νομοθεσίας ἐκτός, 891d7–8). The Athenian is even indignant at having to provide an argument when songs and stories should suffice (887c–888a) and admits that his arguments are spoken somewhat excessively (σφοδρότερον, 907b10) in the desire for victory over wicked men (907b–c).[19] Another similarity is that the argument in Book 10 is directed against a young man (900c) and in general people corrupted in mind (τὴν διάνοιαν διεφθαρμένοις, 888a5) and suffering from a sickness (νόσος) (888b8). The argument is furthermore described as rather too much for old men like Megillus and Cleinias, so that the Athenian must present it by himself (892d–893a). But these parallels only emphasize the difference: that in Book 8 there is in the end *no adequate argument* and therefore no recourse but force.[20] The argument about doing what is natural in imitating animals, if we do not take it as a jest, has at least been shown to have little power of persuasion, and the special τέχνη repeatedly claimed by the Athenian has been seen to be so vague and so ill-defined as to prove rather its absence.

4) For the first and only time in the *Laws,* a major law fails to win the consent of Cleinias *who is the one in charge of founding the new colony of Magnesia* (702b–d).[21] Even if his consent were eventually to be won, the difficulty of procuring it does not bode well for the effectiveness of the law in question. Indeed not even the compromise or second-best law wins Cleinias's consent. In contrast, when the Athenian encounters the young atheists in Book 10, he has Cleinias immediately and completely on his side.[22]

5) Persuading Cleinias, and presumably therefore also the citizens, is made to depend on the "opportune moment." But this καιρός is the one thing the law cannot control. When and if the opportune moment should arise for its acceptance is not in the law's power. Thus the project of legislation is here made dependent on something beyond the scope of law and thereby rendered uncertain and precarious. This dependence of the law on the καιρός along with chance (τύχη) is indeed a theme present throughout the dialogue. At 709b7 the Athenian tells us that all human matters are

steered by God "along with the opportune moment and chance [καὶ μετὰ θεοῦ τύχη καὶ καιρός]."²³ If the Athenian proceeds to allow τέχνη a place here, it is only in the name of being "less harsh" (ἡμερώτερον). Significantly, one event in which both τύχη and καιρός are said to play an essential role is Cleinias's encounter with the Athenian and Megillus at the very time that he has been assigned the task of producing a legal code for a new colony (702b5, b7). Thus one can conclude that if τύχη and καιρός are at the origin of the present conversation and thus the present project of legislation, the problem of ἔρως shows the ability of both to derail and indefinitely postpone this project. This conversation found the opportune moment to begin, but now it must await the opportune moment for dealing with ἔρως.

It is incredible, to say the least, that such a short stretch of text should so profoundly undermine in these five related ways the project of legislation carried out in the dialogue as a whole. It is as if everything that has been kept under covers in the rest of the dialogue rears its head here in the guise of ἔρως. It is as if our hot-headed "seminal" youth embodied everything opposed to the legislative "play" of our sober old men (685a7–8; see also 712b1–2 and 769a1). And when erotic desires are thus granted their brief say, the result is a perversion of the law, a division among our legislators in the dialogue, an abandonment of persuasion for force, and a deferral of the universality of law to the opportune moment. The project of legislation will of course continue. The old men will pursue their sober play. But we are left wondering where their city will be founded and become a reality if it is no city for young men.

Notes

1. Thomas Pangle's interpretative essay, for example, skips it entirely, concluding his discussion of *Laws* 8 at 835b (Pangle 1980, 495–496).

2. Holger Thesleff and Debra Nails have seen here a sign of the dialogue's composition by different hands (2003, 26). But it seems to me that the silence could be intentional.

3. For general discussion of the scanty and conflicting evidence for the acceptance of homosexuality in Sparta and Crete, see Dover 1989, 185–196. Dover also considers, with a healthy dose of skepticism, the view that homosexuality originated with the Dorians. In a postscript, however, he grants that the earliest extant depiction of homosexual courting comes from Crete, 650–625 BCE (205).

4. According to the manuscripts, this argument would perhaps be persuasive (πιθανῷ λόγῳ), but Bury's translation follows Badham's emendation of ἀπιθάνῳ, which does not seem to make sense in the context. The argument based on nature is certainly presented

as a persuasive one elsewhere in the dialogue. Pangle, however, can adopt Badham's reading and make sense of it by offering a translation that limits the "unpersuasiveness" to the cities of Crete and Sparta: "his argument would probably be unpersuasive, and not at all in consonance with your cities."

5. Sandra Boehringer characterizes this argument from nature as only a rhetorical strategy (and therefore the Athenian's reference to a τέχνη) and one that relies on anthropomorphic depictions of animals that makes them like ideal humans (2007, 63–64). The argument, she claims, is not rational, but rests on a falsification (63). And such paralogisms are justified by the end of producing future offspring for the city.

6. Dover characterizes it as "weak, if only because Plato knew virtually nothing about animals . . ." (1989, 167)!

7. See 693c and 701d for the claim that friendship and wisdom are the same goal. Friendship with the gods is also based on similarity (716d). But how is the above compatible with the claim at 776a that longing and distance are essential to the bond of φιλία?

8. The same word is used to characterize excessive love of self (731e) and is there said to result in blindness with regard to the object of one's love (731e–732a).

9. See Follon 2003. Though granting that the distinction initially made between φιλία and ἔρως appears to be only one of intensity (188), Follon argues that the suggestion of violence and vehemence in this intensity "seems to suggest" that "in a strict sense" ἔρως should be confined to the second and third forms of φιλία (i.e., not applied to the ideal form between equals) (188). Yet he must acknowledge that immediately at 837d the Athenian speaks of the three types of ἔρως. Follon concludes that what we have here is a stricter sense and a looser one. This suggestion appears to be supported by the rest of the dialogue where we find talk of ἔρως for virtue (e.g., 643d2, 688b2–4, 711d6–7, 734a1–2), and even for hunting and angling (823d–e)! On the other hand, we are told at 783a3–4 that the ἔρως of sexual intercourse is the sharpest or most intense (ὀξύτατος), which presumably allows it in certain contexts to be identified with ἔρως in the strictest sense.

10. We are indeed told later that even in the wicked there is something divine that enables them to distinguish right from wrong (950b), but what the Athenian appears to need here is something stronger.

11. Is this because Sparta practiced secrecy with regard to sexual relations, as suggested by Plutarch (Lyc. 15.8)? Dover's own conclusion is that "an alliance between ignorance and partisanship [vis-à-vis Sparta] is a poor foundation" for the hypothesis of Spartan hypocrisy (194). In any case, what is unique about the proposal in the Laws is that secrecy and hypocrisy are legislated and thus made a matter of public policy. If Megillus thinks he is agreeing to something familiar, he has at the very least failed to grasp the full import of what the Athenian is proposing.

12. Thus Jean-François Pradeau, speaking of the Athenian's introduction of a second law, comments: "Cette capitulation de la loi, qui cède devant des moeurs pourtant défaillantes et invite en quelque sorte à sa propre transgression, est un cas d'espèce parfaitement exceptionnel dans les Lois" (Pradeau 2008, 14).

13. Noted by Schöpsdau 2003, 256.

14. "Ce qu'écarte ainsi d'emblée Platon, c'est qu'une activité puisse être autorisée dans le silence ou à l'écart de la loi" (Pradeau 2008, 107).

15. Later in *Laws* 8 itself we are told that there is no shame in taking in stealth pears, apples, and pomegranates (845b–c). But this parallel only emphasizes how much more serious it is to enjoy in stealth illicit sexual pleasures.

16. "institue la dissimulation comme une obligation formelle"

17. "Se construit de cette façon dans une cité, où rien pourtant ne doit demeurer caché, un monde dont nul n'est censé avouer la perversité" (Bertrand 1998, 429). And Bertrand sees this as leading to a fundamental hypocrisy in the city: "La dissimulation devient une règle de droit dans une société qui se content ainsi d'apparaître vertueuse mais se soucie peu de l'être véritablement" (429). And in the end Bertand sees here an irreconcilable tension between the demands of theory and the demands of power: "On a l'impression donc que la construction politique, quelque parfaite que soit prétendue la constitution d'une cité, induit nécessairement l'obscurité et la distorsion des image que le théoricien croit devoir récuser, mais que le pouvoir utilise à son profit" (430).

18. I thank Mitchell Miller for drawing my attention to this passage.

19. Pradeau writes of the preludes: "Il ne s'agit pas pour le législateur d'exposer rationnellement l'opportunité de telle ou telle conduite, et encore moins d'enseigner à ses concitoyens un savoir de type scientifique sur les différents objets dont la loi est susceptible de traiter, mais bien de les persuader que telle conduite est louable quand telle autre ne l'est pas, en leur délivrant pour ce faire une forme d'admonestation parentale" (Pradeau 2008, 118–119). But if this is true in general, does not *Laws* 10 stand out all the more as an exception?

20. On the debate concerning whether or not the preludes in general constitute attempts at rational persuasion, see Bobonich 2002, 109–119. Bobonich recognizes a diversity of types of preludes varying significantly in sophistication. In this case, the wishful thinking of *Laws* 8 not only must be placed rather low in the scale, but also stands out through its explicit appeal to force.

21. The reason for Cleinias's reluctance is perhaps the tradition of an institutionalized form of pederasty in ancient Crete, given mythical expression in the story of Zeus and Ganymede. See Aristotle, *Politics* 1272a23–26. But if a certain type of pederasty was accepted even in Sparta, as the Athenian appears to suggest earlier in mentioning that he is here departing from the customs of both Crete and Sparta, why is Megillus so much more persuadable than Cleinias? See note 11 above for one possible but not fully convincing reason.

22. Even if Cleinias has "grave ethical shortcomings," as Bobonich insists (122), he is still one of the best products of one of the best current constitutions and repeatedly shows himself capable of altering his views in response to argument and persuasion; so if he cannot be persuaded of the goodness of the proposed legislation concerning ἔρως, it is highly unlikely that a significant number of citizens, much less the majority, could be.

23. Saunders translates "by the secondary influences of 'chance' and 'opportunity'," a translation that appears to take the μετά to mean "after."

12 On the Implications of Human Mortality: Legislation, Education, and Philosophy in Book 9 of Plato's *Laws*

Catherine Zuckert

Plato's *Laws* has often been treated as a "late" work in which the philosopher sets out a plan for a city that, unlike the city-in-speech described in the *Republic,* could actually be put into practice.[1] I have argued elsewhere that the interpretation of the *Laws* as a "late" work not only rests on weak evidence but also ignores the indications of an early dramatic date.[2] In this essay I propose to show that reading the *Laws* as literally putting forth a legislative proposal ignores the inquiring, if not, strictly speaking, philosophical character of the content as well as the implications of the dialogical form of the work.[3]

For example, in his well-known account of *Plato's Penal Code,* Trevor J. Saunders complains that "Plato was not a tidy legal draftsman."[4] But in making such an observation Saunders misconstrues the character of the discussion of penal legislation in Book 9 of the *Laws* in two important respects. First, neither "Plato" nor, to be more precise, his Athenian Stranger claims to be drafting laws. Both are inquiring what the best and most necessary laws would be. At the beginning of Book 9 the Athenian explicitly states, "it is fortunate for us that there is no necessity for us to legislate, but that by inquiring about every regime, we try to discern how the best and most necessary would come into being. . . . For we are becoming lawgivers, but we are not lawgivers yet" (857e–858a, 859c). Second, in the *Laws* Plato is not legislating for a citizen body or even writing directly to readers. He is relating the conversation an anonymous Athenian has with two old Dorians, one of whom has responsibility along with nine other Knossians to legislate for a new colony. In describing the Athenian's attempt to show the Dorians what they need to know in order to draft better laws, Plato is showing how the Athenian tried to educate them. By treating the contents of the last four books of the *Laws* as a "penal code," Saunders obscures not only the quasi-philosophical character of the inquiry but also the complicated relation of philosophy to law and education dramatized in the dialogue.[5]

The Athenian makes the quasi-philosophical character of the dialogue explicit relatively early in Book 9 when he comments:

> We didn't make a bad image [in *Laws* 4, 720a–e], when we compared all those living under legislation that exists now, to slaves being doctored by slaves. For it is necessary to know something like the following: if one of those doctors who practices medicine on the basis of experiences without reason (ἄνευ λόγου) were to encounter a free doctor carrying on a dialogue with a free man who was sick—using arguments like a philosopher—fastening upon the disease from its beginning and going back to the entire nature of bodies, he would laugh and say . . . : "You fool! You are not doctoring the sick man, but seeking to educate him, as if he needed to become a doctor rather than well!" (857c–e)[6]

Cleinias thinks the so-called doctor would be speaking correctly, and the Athenian affirms that a "man who goes through laws the way we are now is educating the citizens, but not legislating." In conversing with the old Dorians, readers are thus reminded, the Athenian is not legislating; he is teaching his interlocutors how to become legislators. In teaching them how to become legislators, he is using arguments like a philosopher, but he is not philosophizing, strictly speaking. Legislation, education, and philosophy are shown to be related, but distinct activities that should be distinguished from one another.

The comparison of a legislator to a free doctor, in contrast to a slave doctor, shows how legislation is similar to, but not the same as philosophy. The free doctor (or legislator) seeks to educate his patient (as well as, perhaps, learn himself) by asking the sick man (citizen or subject) questions in an attempt to determine the source as well as the nature of the disease.[7] The doctor or legislator's ability to cure or improve his patient presupposes knowledge of the goal: health or virtue. The analogy may be also limited; it is strange to treat virtue as merely a recovery from, if not the absence of vice.[8] But the analogy between the legislator and the doctor nevertheless points to the fact that neither of them seeks knowledge for its own sake; they both seek and then use what knowledge they have to cure the patient (or to make citizens virtuous). Their knowledge is, in other words, both instrumental and remedial. Like the slave doctor (or all past legislators), the free doctor (or legislator) warns his patients (or people) that there will be an undesirable, often painful result, if the patient does not follow his prescriptions. Rather than merely threaten patients (or people) with harm if they do not obey the doctor's (or legislator's) orders, the free doctor (or legislator) attempts to persuade his patients (or people) to follow his orders willingly—partly by leading them to see the reasons why he has prescribed the medicine (or other measures) he has, but also partly by threatening them with dire results, if they do not obey. The first time the Athenian introduced the comparison of the legislator to a doctor, free or slave, he had uncharacteristically boasted that the recognition of the need for such persuasive "preludes" or prefaces to the laws, which remained commands backed up by threats of punishment, was his great innovation (722b–c). He also characterized their own conversation up to that point (722d–e), as well as his subsequent restatement and improvement of his recommendations (723e), as such a prelude.

Imagining himself, Cleinias, and his Spartan companion Megillus addressing the other Knossian legislators for the colony, the Athenian had suggested that education for virtue was *the* goal of the laws when he asked their "pupils" to agree that

> no one will give precedence to anything that impedes the effort to enable every member of the community, whether his nature be male or female, young or old, to become a good man [ἀνήρ], possessing the virtue of soul that befits a human being . . . even if the alternative is destruction of the city itself. (770c–e)[9]

But, turning from a description of the offices and laws he is proposing for their city-in-speech to the punishments that should be inflicted upon those who do not obey the laws, the Athenian admits that laws can never entirely form or educate human beings.

It might appear to be shameful, the Athenian concedes, to propose penalties for breaking the law in a city which devotes as much effort to educating its citizens as the city he has described. (We might observe in passing that Socrates does not prescribe any such punishments or penalties for the "city-in-speech" he describes in the *Republic*.) "But," the Athenian points out, "we are not legislating, like the legislators of old, for heroes and sons of gods, when both the legislators and those for whom they gave laws were of divine descent; we are human beings legislating for human beings" (853c).

Acting like the "free doctor" he has described, the Athenian traces the problem—both the need for laws and the limited power of laws—back to its origin in mortal human nature. "It is necessary for human beings to establish laws and live under them, or they will differ in no way from the most savage beasts"

(874e–875a). As he pointed out earlier in arguing for the necessity of education (653a–e), human beings are not orderly by nature. We not only have to learn to become orderly, moreover, we also have to learn what order should be inculcated and how.[10]

Legislation is required in order to remedy a natural defect; but the Athenian also shows that the same natural defect limits the power of law to remedy it in two distinct ways. First, and most obviously, because human beings are not orderly by nature, they naturally resist attempts to impose order on them. The Athenian thus argues that those who refuse or prove themselves unable to become orderly have to be killed or banished from the city, if the other members of the community are to live together in peace. Even those who learn to accept a certain amount of order in their lives are apt to resist it, however. That is why the Athenian suggests that it is better to persuade people to obey laws by providing them with the reasons the laws are needed rather than simply ordering them to do what they are not naturally inclined to do and threatening them with painful punishments if they do not comply. The sort of education he is providing to his interlocutors in this dialogue and that he urges them to provide for their citizens in "preludes" consists in a kind of persuasion, not in knowledge per se.

The second, more serious and fundamental difficulty concerns the legislators themselves: "There is no human being with a nature sufficient both to know everything needed to care for human beings in a regime and to be able and willing always to do what is best." The problem with regard to the legislator is thus twofold. First, it is hard for human beings to learn what the true goal of political associations is, because they are attached, by nature, first and foremost to themselves. Like Cleinias and Megillus at the beginning of the dialogue, most human beings believe that the purpose of political association is, first, to protect the lives and property of its citizens from attacks by other "wild beasts" and, then, when they and their goods are secure, to acquire the goods of others by attacking them. Human beings have to learn, as the Athenian is trying to persuade his old Dorian interlocutors, that the goal of political association is not, first and foremost, preservation of themselves or their city and, secondarily, the accumulation of wealth; the goal is, rather, to make every citizen as virtuous as possible. Because human beings are naturally attached to themselves more than they are to others, it is hard for them to recognize "that the true art of politics must not care for the private (individual), but for the common—for the common binds cities together, while the private separates—and that it is more profitable for both the individual and the community that the common be established" (875a). But, second, the Athenian warns that even if someone were to advance sufficiently in the art to know that this is the way things are by nature, and ruled a city as an autocrat without an audit, he "would not be able to adhere to this conviction and continually nourish the common before the private," because "his mortal nature would always urge him to prefer the private to the common, to get more than his share, irrationally fleeing pain and pursuing pleasure, and putting both before what is more just and better" (875b).[11]

By emphasizing the "mortal" character of human nature, the Athenian reminds his interlocutors (and Plato his readers), it is our perception of our inevitable death that leads us to cling, irrationally, to our own lives and goods. And it is this attachment we feel by nature to ourselves and our own that makes it difficult for us not only to learn that it is better for us as individuals as well as for the community to subordinate the good of the individual to the good of the community but also to act on the basis of that knowledge.[12]

The rule of law is necessary for human beings with their faulty natures, for the same reason it is necessary that the rule of law will always be inferior to the rule of reason or intelligence per se. "If, by divine dispensation, some human being was born with a nature adequate to attain these things," the Athenian concludes, "he wouldn't need any laws ruling over him. For no law or order is stronger than knowledge, nor is it right for intelligence to be subordinate or slave to anyone, but it should rule over everything, according to nature, truly and freely" (875c).[13] At the beginning of his description of the laws for his city-in-speech, the Athenian had thus stated that νόμος (law) should have its source or origin in νοῦς (714a) and that not "man," as Protagoras had claimed, but the god should be the "measure" of all things (716c).[14]

In emphasizing the necessarily "second-best" status of the rule of law in contrast to the rule of intelligence or knowledge, the Athenian Stranger sounds very much like Plato's Eleatic Stranger in the *Statesman* (294a). But the differences in the reasons Plato's two "strangers" give for both the necessity and the inferiority of the rule of law to the rule of intelligence are as enlightening as the common conclusion.

The first reason both "strangers" suggest that the rule of intelligence is virtually impossible is the difficulty any human being will experience in acquiring the requisite knowledge. But the knowledge the two strangers suggest is required is quite different. As we have seen, the difficulty the Athenian sees is, first, for human beings to learn to prefer the common to the individual and, then, to act consistently on the basis of that knowledge. We would characterize the knowledge the Athenian regards as most important as "moral." The difficulty the Eleatic expounds upon at great length is how to separate the statesman's "god-like" knowledge (*Statesman* 303b) of how to coordinate all the arts necessary to care for the people of the city (305d) from all those other arts. In particular, he explains, a statesman must have the ability to purge human beings who prove themselves not to be capable "of sharing in a manly and moderate character and everything else that pertains to virtue" (308e–309a) and to bind the others together at the bodily, animal, or "human" level of generation as well as psychically with the "divine" bonds of "true opinion" (309b–c) so that they will be able to preserve the city.[15] The knowledge the Eleatic thinks a statesman (as opposed, perhaps, to a legislator) needs to possess is thus instrumental, not "moral" so much as "technical." According to the Eleatic, a statesman knows how to order the lives of others, not his own.[16] In striking contrast to the Athenian, the Eleatic Stranger does not manifest any concern about the way in which human beings acquire the knowledge required to rule. He and his interlocutors seek merely to determine what that knowledge is (in contrast to other forms of τέχνη and ἐπιστήμη). Neither he nor they show any desire to obtain the requisite knowledge themselves or to put it into practice. On the contrary, the Eleatic suggests, they have sought to define the statesman not for its own sake, but "for the sake of becoming more skilled in dialectics." By practicing how "to give and receive an account (λόγος) of each thing" (286a), they may thus be learning how to philosophize (*Sophist* 253c–e), but they are not learning how to legislate or rule.[17]

Like the Athenian, the Eleatic argues that even if a human being acquires the requisite knowledge, he will probably not be able to rule on the basis of that knowledge. But the reasons the Eleatic provides to support that conclusion are again very different from those of the Athenian. First, the Eleatic points out that even a person who knows what is best for any particular individual to do in any specific set of circumstances will have to employ general rules, because that person will not be able to be with every single individual all the time to make a precise determination of what he or she should do, even though general rules per se will not perfectly fit every person or situation. Second, and more decisively, the Eleatic argues, people who lack the knowledge of a statesman will not be able recognize anyone who actually possesses it. "Since there is no king who comes to be in cities . . . like those who naturally arise in hives— one who is obviously exceptional in body and soul—once people have come together in cities, they have to write down laws in running after the traces of the truest regime" (301e). Again, the problem is two-sided. On the one hand, people who lack knowledge cannot perceive it in others. On the other hand, having been persuaded by some unscrupulous individuals to let them rule without legal checks or audits after they leave office, people will have learned from experience to fear those rulers (who, unchecked by law, may use their power to kill, imprison, or expropriate the property of other citizens). As a result of the combination of their ignorance and experience, such people can at most be persuaded by certain advisors to set down as law what has been learned from much trial and error and to insist that all office-holders obey the law, unless these officials can convince the people as a whole that it would be better to modify or, in exceptional circumstances, evade the legally mandated restrictions. The fundamental problem, according to the Eleatic, is that lacking the knowledge needed to rule, most people cannot recognize that knowledge in another exceptional human being. On the other hand, according to the Athenian, even such an exceptional human being, because he is human, would not be able to act on the basis of his knowledge all the time.

Does Plato think people have to settle for the "second-best" rule of law instead of the best, the rule of reason, because most, if not all people do not know what to do under all circumstances and so have to rely on the wisdom accumulated from past experience and written down in the form of general rules? Or, does Plato think that human beings have to insist on the rule of law, because our natures are such that no one can ever learn always to prefer the common good to his own particular desires?

The arguments Plato attributes to the Eleatic Stranger suggest that the second rationale, articulated by the Athenian, is the rationale certain advisers have used to convince people to write down the experience they have accumulated over time in the form of laws and insist that all rulers obey them. It is, in other words, a popular, persuasive argument.[18] That is, moreover, exactly the way in which the Athenian characterizes his own statement of the necessity for the rule of law, even though he recognizes that it is only "second best." He presents this notion as a "prelude" to the laws he will propose concerning the punishments of those who wound others. He has already explained why he thinks such persuasive preludes should be added to some laws to convince people to obey them. Indeed the Athenian announced earlier (722d–723b) that he thought that their entire conversation, at least up to the point at which they pronounced actual legal commands, constituted such a prelude. It should be called a "prelude" (προοίμιον) rather than an "argument" (λόγος), because it was designed to put its listeners into a frame of mind more favorably disposed to receive the law and thus apt to learn something.

In considering what the penal law should be, we see that the Athenian first makes suggestions, then expands upon his suggestions in response to the objections or questions raised by his interlocutors. Proceeding "like a philosopher" (or "free doctor") he leads his interlocutors gradually from the understanding of punishment as retribution, with which most people begin, to a much more complex and nuanced view.

Observing both that citizens of their city will have received an education that should have prevented them from engaging in criminal activity and that they must nevertheless take precautions against the general weakness of human nature, especially in foreigners and slaves, the Athenian begins his account of the penal law with the crime of temple robbing. He does not explain why he begins with this particular crime. At the very beginning of his description of the city-in-speech, we might recall, he urged his interlocutors to look to the "god" or νοῦς. But in his discussion of crime and punishment he does not take up the question of why the regime needs to insist upon its citizens holding certain beliefs or what those beliefs must be until he has discussed the nature of penal legislation more generally. He begins instead with a concrete manifestation of one of the passions that leads human beings to break the law against the highest authorities (not men, but gods). Presumably his interlocutors are more comfortable with the concrete and specific than with the abstract and general. But the Athenian nevertheless treats the punishment of temple-robbing in very general terms. He urges his interlocutors to adopt a brief prelude to persuade people goaded by an evil desire to despoil sacred things not to give way to it and then adds an account of the penalty that will be inflicted on those who do not obey. He suggests that the punishment of citizens, who have been educated by the city, should be different from that of foreigners and slaves. However, he insists in all cases that "no judicial punishment under law would make anyone bad; it aims at making the one receiving the punishment better or less wicked" (854d). He then states a series of general propositions that appear to follow from this general claim (although the Athenian does not supply the reasoning). 1) If a citizen is convicted of a grave injustice against the gods, his parents, or the city, he will have proven himself to be incurable and should be killed, the least of evils. Having been killed, the citizen will not become worse and his example will benefit others. 2) The relatives of a criminal should not be dishonored or share in the punishment of the criminal, because they did not commit the crime. 3) The relatives of a criminal can, however, help him pay a monetary fine. Such a criminal is presumably curable. But, since the land allotments all belong to the city, an individual or his family should pay a monetary fine only from what they own in addition to the land. If he and his friends cannot cover the fine, the criminal is to be shamefully imprisoned and otherwise humiliated. There will be no cure if there is no punishment. 4) No one is ever to be completely dishonored for a single fault. The hope is always to cure criminals so that they can re-enter society. The purpose of punishment is to make criminals better—or, when that proves to be impossible—to make them less bad and unable to corrupt others by eliminating them.

Having set down the general principles to be used, the Athenian briefly describes the composition of the courts and the procedures that should be used for making judgments, including cross-examinations that would be repeated a second day to make sure that the judgment rests on the deliberation and not the passionate reactions of the judges to the crime.[19] He ends his initial description of the penal law first by briefly applying the general principles he has stated to the capital crimes of instigating civil war and treason, where, as in the case of temple robbery, the penalty is banishment or death. Finally, he applies these principles very generally to stealing, where the retribution is to be a fine or imprisonment for those unable to pay the fine.

The Athenian might not have said any more about the penal law had Cleinias not asked, if indirectly, whether the Athenian had not contradicted himself by treating temple robbery as a capital crime, punishable by exile or death, but then proposing a general punishment for stealing of twice the value of the object stolen, without regard to the greater or lesser value of the object or from whom it was taken.[20] It is in response to this question that the Athenian reminds his interlocutors of the similarity between what they are doing and the "free doctor," i.e., that they are not legislating, but learning how to legislate. He had initially proposed a sketch of the penal law. Cleinias's question leads him to investigate the reasons for that law.

Rather than specifying what the law is or even should be, the Athenian and his interlocutors agree that they should make a survey of the laws that have been proposed by others so that, like house-builders, having collected various materials they could use, they can select the best. In order to determine what is best, the Athenian indicates, although he does not say so explicitly, they need a standard of judgment. That standard would presumably be what is noble and just. But here, the Athenian observes, there seems to be a contradiction in widely held opinions. On the one hand, people claim that the just and the noble are the same. On the other hand, they regard just punishments as shameful (or ignoble) for the person punished.[21] Even in his initial, brief sketch of the penal law, the Athenian had suggested that part of the appropriate punishment for stealing, at least in some circumstances, should include shame and humiliation.

As with the "second-best" status of the law, so concerning the relation of the just to the noble, the distinctive character of the Athenian's treatment of the issue comes out, if we compare it to the way another Platonic philosopher treats the same issue in another dialogue. In this case, that other philosopher is Socrates.

The Athenian begins his attempt to harmonize popular conceptions of the relation between the just and the noble by stating a principle often attributed to Socrates. If, as Socrates explicitly maintains (e.g., *Republic* 505d), everyone wants what is truly good for himself, then, as the Athenian states here, "the bad are all bad involuntarily." Since "the unjust man is presumably bad, but the bad man is involuntarily so," moreover, "the man who does injustice appears [to be] involuntarily unjust" (860d).

To show how that understanding would apply to the formulation and application of penal law, the Athenian suggests that instead of distinguishing between involuntary and voluntary injustice (since the latter does not really exist), the way most penal legislation does, one should distinguish between injury, i.e., harm unintentionally done to another, for which the law should require compensation to the injured, and "injustice," from which the law seeks to cure the perpetrator. He defines unjust actions, in general, as those performed under the influence of a variety of passions, in opposition to the individual's opinions about what is just. And he then defines just deeds as those done according to "the opinion about what is best (whatever a city or certain private individuals may believe this to be) that holds sway in souls and brings order to every man, even if it is in someway mistaken" (864a).[22] He explicitly recognizes that many other people consider injuries done on the basis of a false understanding of justice "involuntary." But, he points out, the justice or injustice of a deed does not depend on whether it hurts another. It is just as possible to benefit an undeserving person unjustly as it is to harm an innocent person. The law mandates compensation for injuries, because, the Athenian has already pointed out, it never aims at harming anyone. The law may require unpleasant punishments, even the death of the criminal, but these punishments are all designed to prevent further wrongdoing, if not to improve the soul of the criminal.

Understanding injustice to consist in acting on the basis of one's passion rather than one's opinion about what is right, the Athenian distinguishes among the passions by asking which of them lead to more or less deliberate and thus more or less "voluntary" unjust actions. People who act immediately on the basis of fear or anger are less unjust than those who deliberate and plan their responses and should be less severely punished. Those who harm others in order to amass money in order to maximize their pleasures and minimize their pains or those who act out of envy for the honors attained by others are the worst—indeed, to be regarded as incurable—because their passions dominate their opinions about what is right, not merely for an "insane" moment, but after they have had a chance to think about what they are going to do.

The psychology of criminality the Athenian proposes is more complicated than the famous three-part description of the soul Socrates gives in the *Republic*. Whereas Socrates suggests that unjust behavior results from the domination of the reasoning part of the soul (λογισμός) by the desires (ἐπιθυμία), with or without the cooperation of spiritedness (θύμος), the Athenian suggests that opinions about what is just may be violated on the basis of θύμος or fear (φόβος), the desire to maximize pleasures or pains, envy (φθόνος) or honor-loving (φιλοτιμία), and two kinds of ignorance (ἄνοια)—plain ignorance of what is just and the worse kind, thinking that one knows what is just when one does not.[23] Rather than suggest that θύμος can and should form an alliance with reason to control desire, as Socrates does, the Athenian presents θύμος as the first cause of "involuntary" injustice. The purpose of punishment, according to the Athenian (880e), is to restore friendship among the citizens. Compensating for losses or "injuries" and curing or removing criminals, temporarily or permanently, are the primary means. Punishments inflicted on the basis of anger are apt to be matters of revenge which prompt retaliation, not friendship. Because they arise from anger rather than an opinion about what is right, they also tend to be unjust.

Like Socrates in Book 4 of the *Republic*, the Athenian presents justice—at least in politics and in practice—as a matter of opinion, not of knowledge. As all readers of the *Republic* also know, however, the discussion there continues. Socrates is pressed to explain the three radical changes he suggests would be necessary to make a city truly just: 1) that, having the same natural talents or proclivities, male and female guardians should receive the same education so that they can perform the same civic functions; 2) that guardians not be allowed to have any property (of their own or as private families), so that they will not give way to the temptation to prefer the private to the public; and 3) that "kings" become philosophers or philosophers, "kings." The Athenian does not suggest that the old Cretans institute any of these radical innovations in Magnesia. He urges them to give male and female citizens a more similar education than they receive in any other extant regime, including Sparta; but the education he sketches out is not identical for members of the two sexes. Women are not to hold office in Magnesia during their child-bearing years, i.e., until they are forty years of age. Introducing the laws, he states:

> That city and that regime are first, and the laws are best, where . . . as the old proverb holds . . . the things of friends really are common. . . . if women are common, and children are common, and every sort of property is common; . . . . if, insofar as possible, a way has been devised to make common somehow the things that are by nature private, such as the eyes and the ears and the hands, so that they seem to see and hear and act in common; if, again, everyone praises and blames in union, as much as pos-

sible delighting in the same things and feeling pain at the same things, if with all their might they delight in laws that aim at making the city come as close as possible to unity, then no one will ever set down a more correct or better definition than this of what constitutes the extreme as regards virtue. (739c–d)

But, the Athenian immediately adds, "such a city is presumably inhabited by gods or children of gods" (739d–e).[24] He and his interlocutors should take this regime as their model, but they should not try to make everything common. The most they will be able to do is to minimize conflict over property by having all land belong to the city and allocating equal shares to citizens to use. He does not say anything about the need for philosophers to rule if the evils in cities are to cease.

The Athenian does not even mention the word "philosophy" until, in response to Cleinias's question about the difference between the punishment he suggested for temple-robbery and the punishment he suggested for stealing more generally, he recalls the comparison he had drawn earlier between a legislator and free doctor and says that the free doctor proceeds "like a philosopher," seeking knowledge by asking his patient questions. The only other occurrence of the word "philosophy" occurs at the very end of the dialogue when the Athenian explains (967b–d) that "poets took to reviling those who philosophize as dogs vainly howling," because even those (e.g., Anaxagoras) who suggested that the heavenly bodies which move with such wonderful precision must have been ordered by mind (νοῦς) continued to err about soul, insisting that everything is originally and fundamentally bodily. The Athenian provides his interlocutors with reasons to believe that soul (or motion) is more fundamental than body in the long rationale or prelude he gives for the law concerning piety in Book 10. But, he explicitly recognizes, his interlocutors are not familiar with the "writings" that claim that the sun, moon, stars, and earth are not gods or divine things, but are rather merely earth and stones, incapable of thinking about human affairs.

The basic reason the Athenian does not talk about philosophy, much less suggest that philosophers should become kings, is that his interlocutors do not know what philosophy is. The character of his interlocutors thus sets limits to the content and validity of the arguments presented in the dialogue.[25]

By contrasting the Athenian's brief description of the best regime he urges his interlocutors to use as a paradigm in legislating with Socrates' description of the same, readers of the *Laws* nevertheless see that the Athenian's explanation of the reason that the rule of law will always be second-best is inaccurate and incomplete. In tracing the problems experienced with the rule of law to the limitations of mortal human nature the Athenian does not take account of an admittedly very rare and exceptional kind of human being. In responding to the skeptical reaction of Plato's brothers to his suggestion that evils in cities will not cease until philosophers become kings, Socrates shows (*Republic* 485a–486e) that people with philosophical natures possess all the virtues. Such people will not be wise, strictly speaking; but, since they love and thus seek the truth above all else, they will come as close to being wise as a human being can. Likewise, because their love of truth is so strong, they do not care about material goods or fame. They will, therefore, be moderate and just, because they will not try to deprive others of fame or fortune. Regarding human life as a transient good of less value than the eternal truth, they will also be courageous, because they do not fear death. They also must have the intellectual skills and capacities necessary to learn.

At first it looks as if philosophers should rule, because they alone possess knowledge of the things that truly are. By looking at the ideas, Socrates suggests (*Republic* 500c–d) philosophers cannot only imitate the virtues themselves but also impress them on the souls of their fellow citizens, as if they were blank slates. Philosophers and only philosophers deserve to rule, in other words, because they and they alone possess knowledge of the true goal of any regime. They do not, like the Athenian and the legislators for Magnesia, have to rely merely on opinions about what is just.

Nor does Socrates think, like the Eleatic Stranger, that ordinary people will never allow a philosopher to rule, because they will not be able to distinguish him from unjust imposters who claim to have the knowledge that would entitle them to rule without legal limitations or audits. On the contrary, Socrates claims, the reason why people laugh at the suggestion that philosophers should become kings is that they have never encountered a true philosopher. Should a person with a philosophical nature arise among them, his relatives, friends, and fellow citizens are apt to contribute to his corruption by urging him to pursue the goods of the body, rather than the goods of the soul, truth, and prudence the way Socrates urged his fellow Athenians (*Apology* 29d–30b). All human beings seek what is truly good, Socrates observes, but few, if any know what the good-in-itself is. Not merely acting, but thinking under the influence of their most immediate desires, most people have false, unjust opinions about what is truly noble and good.

Following his famous image of human nature with regard to education as a cave from which a few individuals may be forced to ascend, Socrates observes that the "virtues" inculcated in the city he described earlier as opinions are like bodily habits, "whereas the virtue of prudence is somehow more divine" (*Republic* 518e). But the effects of the exercise of prudence also vary, depending on whether it is directed to good or bad goals. Like both the Athenian and the Eleatic Strangers, Socrates advocates the rule of intelligence (be it in the form of φρόνησις rather than νοῦς). Recognizing that the rule of pure intelligence is impossible to achieve, strictly speaking, because human beings have bodies, Socrates nevertheless suggests that "if you discover a life better than ruling for those who are going to rule, it is possible that the well-governed city will come into being" (*Republic* 520e–521a). Only those who recognize that they cannot obtain what they most want by means of ruling (that is, only philosophers), who do not seek material goods or fame (which they understand to consist merely in opinion and thus to have much less value than the eternally unchanging truth), will rule solely for the common good and not in their own self-interest.[26] People generally can understand the reasons for this suggestion, even if they themselves do not possess or recognize the kind of intelligence required for someone to rule justly. For many years in many places people have understood, if only as a "rule of thumb" that it is bad to nominate oneself for office. People who seek rule or power are suspect. Only those who do not put themselves forward should be selected, because they do not seem to have anything to gain for themselves.

Like both Plato's Athenian and Eleatic Strangers, Socrates concludes that it is highly unlikely, if not simply impossible that a human being with the requisite "divine" intelligence will ever rule. All three of Plato's philosophers agree that the rule of intelligence is unlikely, because the natural capacity required is very rare and the education required not merely to preserve but to develop that capacity even rarer. But the reason that Socrates suggests that the rule of intelligence will not occur in any city is not, as the Athenian states, the inability of mortal human nature per se to overcome its attachment to itself. Nor is the reason, as the Eleatic suggests, the inability of others to recognize the intelligence or requisite knowledge in any human being who might come to possess it. The reason, according to Socrates, is that the overwhelming love of truth that makes philosophers the only kind of human beings who cannot acquire what they want by means of rule also makes them completely uninterested in ruling.[27] Since they do not wish to rule, they would have to be forced to do so. But only those philosophers who owe their education as philosophers to the city could justly be compelled to rule. They could not literally be forced, physically, to pay attention to the needs of the city, of course; but they could be "compelled" to do so by their own sense of justice. However, the incurring of such a debt by later philosophers obviously presupposes the previous rule of some philosopher who instituted the means of educating others. An individual might by some rare chance be born both a prince and a philosopher, but it would take more than that chance to protect an individual born with such a rare nature from corruption by his friends and family or to interest him in the affairs of the city once he had begun to appreciate the joys of philosophizing.

Neither the Athenian nor the Eleatic Stranger explicitly makes the Socratic claim that evils will not cease in cities until philosophers become kings; and neither espouses the reason Socrates gives for why philosophers are not apt to rule. But Plato dramatizes the difficulty Socrates articulates in both the *Laws* and the *Statesman*. As I have already noted, neither the Eleatic Stranger nor the mathematically trained gymnasts to whom he speaks shows any interest in acquiring, much less exercising the knowledge they identify as that belonging to a statesman. In the *Laws* thoughtful readers are gradually provoked to ask why the Athenian has come to Crete. At the beginning of the dialogue he looks as if he is seeking to learn about their laws from the old Dorians; but after they ask him to propose a city-in-speech at the end of the third book, it is clearly the Athenian who is instructing or educating them. At the end of the dialogue (969c), we are left wondering whether Cleinias and Megillus will be able to prevent the Athenian from leaving by using every contrivance to make him share in founding the city he has described in speech. They have, implicitly if not explicitly, been shown that a philosophical education is necessary for instituting the best possible regime, even if they have not actually learned what it is to philosophize.

Many modern American readers are apt to take the Athenian's statement of the reasons why human beings can, at most, institute the "second-best" rule of law and never experience the direct rule of undiluted intelligence as "Plato's" recognition of the plain (because familiar) truth. The Athenian's statement sounds very much like James Madison's famous observation in *Federalist* 51 concerning the need to institute a system of checks and balances in which the interest of the man is attached to the constitutional rights of the place:

> It may be a reflection on human nature, that such devices should be necessary to control the abuses of government. But what is government itself, but the greatest of all reflections on human nature? If men were angels, no government would be necessary. If angels were to govern men, neither external nor internal controls on government would be necessary.

Madison not only insists that "enlightened statesmen will not always be at the helm." He also argues that any attempt to give all the citizens of a regime the same opinions would result in a tyrannical destruction of individual liberty:

"As long as the reason of man continues fallible, and he is at liberty to exercise it, different opinions will be formed. As long as the connection subsists between his reason and his self-love, his opinions and his passions will have a reciprocal influence on each other." Indeed, Madison proceeds to argue that "the diversity in the faculties of men, from which the rights of property originate, is not less an insuperable obstacle to a uniformity of interests." Echoing the philosophy of John Locke, Madison concludes, "the protection of these faculties is the first object of government."

Plato's philosophers do not agree that the first object of government is the protection of the diversity in the faculties of men to amass property." On the contrary, they insist that the goal is making human beings as good or virtuous as they can be. The attachment most people show to their own lives, liberties, and property is the source of injustice.

Plato's philosophers recognize the difficulty of ensuring that all citizens of a regime hold the same opinions. That is one of the reasons the Athenian urged his interlocutors to add preludes to the laws—to persuade people who would not be inclined to obey otherwise to do so. Although he proposes both an intensive and extensive education for all citizens, moreover, he recognizes at the beginning of his consideration of the penal code that they will not all be persuaded to obey. That is the reason punishments become necessary.[28] The Athenian explains that it is not the use of power per se but only the use of power in one's own private interest at the expense of the common that makes a ruler unjust. Since the natural tendency to prefer one's own good to that of the community is the source of most injustice, Plato's philosophers do not agree with Madison in thinking that "the first object of government is the protection of the diversity in the faculties of men to amass property." On the contrary, they insist that the goal is making human beings as good or virtuous as they can be. Plato's philosophers recognize that attempts to see that all citizens hold the same opinions will not make those citizens truly virtuous. His philosophers also recognize that human nature is such that most people will resist such attempts, covertly if not overtly. That is the reason laws have to be enforced.

In contrast especially to the Athenian, whose dramatic situation makes it impossible for him to include the rare philosophical exception, Socrates insists that the pessimistic view of human nature underlying the insistence of the need for the rule of law in place of the rule of intelligence is too general to be accurate and too negative to be true. Granting that philosophers are not apt ever to become rulers, Socrates insists that private individuals can live, justly, as philosophers. And Plato shows in his dialogues that non-philosophical individuals can be persuaded that philosophy is not necessarily a threat to political order (or the related maintenance of religious faith). Indeed non-philosophers can be persuaded that educating potential rulers philosophically can have positive political results. Philosophical education which proceeds voluntarily on the basis of question and answer is different from legislation, which can and should be based on such inquiries, but which also includes the threat or use of force. Philosophers may not literally go into the assembly and propose laws. (The Athenian may appear to be doing so, but he is actually just talking, in private, to two other old men who may later propose some of the things the Athenian has suggested.)

In his three dialogues that deal most directly and fully with the question of the best political order Plato nevertheless shows that philosophers can and should be concerned about political matters. Most importantly of all, however, particularly in his Socratic dialogues, Plato demonstrates that the negative view of human nature most people tend to acquire on the basis of their own experience is too narrow. The capacities and potential of some rare individuals are much greater. For reasons that have not been made clear in this essay, Plato also shows that these rare individuals care about the lives of the less talented. We need not despair as much as we often do about the character of our race—or, perhaps, the world in which we find ourselves. To take the arguments of the Athenian Stranger as Plato's own last words is to miss the most important point made in his dialogues.

Notes

1. See Morrow 1960; Saunders 1992, 469; Stalley 1983; Bobonich 2002. Mark Munn, in his contribution to this volume, seeks to locate the dialogue in its specific historical context, the mid-fourth century, i.e., toward the end of Plato's life. David Roochnick also begins his essay by quoting R. G. Bury's judgment in the introduction to his translation of the *Laws*, 1984, vii, that the "pedantry, tautology and discursive garrulity" of the dialogue shows that the aged Plato's powers were failing.

2. C. Zuckert 2004; 2009, 3–5, 51–58. In the *Politics* (1264b26–27) Aristotle says that the *Laws* was written after the *Republic*, and Diogenes Laertius (3.3) reports that "some say that Philip of Opus transcribed the *Laws*, which were in wax." But Aristotle's remark does not give us any guidance about the order of the rest of the dialogues, and an inference from a centuries-old rumor that Plato must have left the text of the *Laws* unfinished does not provide a firm basis for determining the order or dates at which the dialogues were written. See Dorter 1994, 1–17; Howland 1991; Cooper 1997, xiv, on the problematic character and basis of the "chronology of composition." Munn, in his contribution to this volume, takes the references to the subjugations of Locri and Ceos in Book 1 (638b) to show that Plato was referring to events during his own life, even though Pangle 1980, 517n45, argues on the basis of Post 1929, and his review of des Places's edi-

tion (Post 1954), that in neither case is the Athenian Stranger referring to any particular event.

3. As John Sallis has pointed out, the noun φιλοσοφία does not appear in the *Laws*. As Pangle notes in the index to his translation of *The Laws of Plato*, 557, verbal forms of the word appear only twice, at 857d and 967c. I take that fact to indicate that the Athenian understands philosophy to be a kind of activity and that it is implicitly present in the *Laws*. It is not explicitly present most of the time, because the Athenian and his interlocutors are discussing legislation, which has some similarities to, but is fundamentally not the same as philosophizing.

4. Saunders 1991, 216.

5. Although I disagree with Saunders about the character of the "penalties" (δίκαι) proposed in the last four books of the *Laws*, I agree with him about the structure of organization of the dialogue into three parts: the "prologue" the Athenian announces has come to an end at the conclusion of *Laws* 4, his legislative proposals, including the design and allocation of offices, in *Laws* 5–8, and the penalties or, more generally, consequences of the limitations of the laws in *Laws* 9–12, in opposition to the organization proposed by Mitchell Miller in his contribution to this volume, who also suggests that the dialogue was left unfinished. As Miller himself would no doubt recognize, such a suggestion is always problematic with regard to Plato's dialogues, because the dialogues always, more or less explicitly, leave something further to be discussed.

6. Quotations of the *Laws* are taken from Pangle 1980, but occasionally modified on the basis of my own reading of the Greek text in Bury 1926.

7. See Michael Zuckert's contribution to this volume, 13–16, 29–30.

8. However, in the *Gorgias* Socrates also insists that his refutations (ἔλεγχοι) are corrections (κολάσματα) and thus presumably part of the remedial art of treating the soul, or justice. That seems, indeed, to be the basis of his claim (521d) to be the only person in Athens at his time even trying to practice the true political art (See Arends 2007, 55). It is probably no accident that the only two mentions of the word "philosophy" in the *Laws* occur, first, in the context of punishment and, second, in castigating the error of previous philosophers that the Athenian has corrected.

9. By asking the legislators to agree, the Athenian not only shows that legislation depends ultimately upon some such agreement concerning the goal of the laws and the city they regulate, but also that such an agreement on virtue as the goal does not necessarily mean that legislators know what virtue is. As he shows from the beginning to the end of his conversation with the old Dorians (cf. *Laws* 631b–638b and 962a–968b), they do not.

10. See John Russon's discussion of both the attractive and the problematic compulsory aspects of the education the Athenian proposes in his essay in this volume.

11. As Robert Metcalf points out in his contribution to this volume, the long prelude with which the Athenian's delineation of his proposed laws begins with an affirmation that "there can be no rest from evils and toils for those cities in which some mortal rules rather than a god" (713e).

12. Eric Sanday states the problem more generally at the beginning of his essay on *Laws* 11 and 12. Because human beings are not like gods, eternally the same and unchanging, but are, on the contrary, not merely generated, but constantly becoming, the process of "persuasion" must be continuous, i.e., must necessarily always begin again

from the beginning. Benardete 2000a shows how the tension between the need for unchanging laws and the unending change associated with generation or becoming permeates the dialogue.

13. Gregory Recco in this volume discusses one of the fundamental compromises of the rule of reason per se made necessary by the not entirely reasonable or virtuous character of the people to be ruled—in order to bind everyone "equally" to the community.

14. Miller, in his contribution to this volume, emphasizes the references to the god as measure from the beginning to the end of the dialogue. But M. Zuckert, 17–26, and Sara Brill, in their essays bring out problems in the political theology on which the regime of the *Laws* is purportedly to be based.

15. Quotations taken from Benardete 1984b, modified occasionally on the basis of the Greek text in Plato 1995.

16. The contrast between the knowledge the Eleatic attributes to the statesman also stands in marked contrast to the use Socrates finally urges his interlocutors to make of the "city in speech" he has described in the *Republic*, as "a paradigm for the man who wants to found a city within himself. . . . It doesn't make any difference whether it is or will be somewhere else. For he would mind the things of this city alone" (592b). (Bloom 1968).

17. Benardete 1984a, checked with the Greek text in Plato 1995.

18. Görgemanns 1960, emphasizes the popular character of the entire dialogue.

19. In the *Apology* (37a–b) Socrates claims that he would have convinced the judges to dismiss the charges against him rather than to convict him, if Athens had a law that prohibited them from hearing and deciding in the case of a capital crime in a single day.

20. Cf. Benardete 2000a, 251. The question remains, even if one takes account of the difference in Greek law between robbery from the temple sanctuary and the theft of sacred funds or from places outside the sanctuary, noted by Pangle 1980, 533n7, relying on Gernet 1917, 66, 88–89.

21. In the *Gorgias* 473a–480d Socrates points out the same contradiction in public opinion in attempting to show Polus that people should not seek to escape punishment but that, on the contrary, they should accuse themselves, their family, and their friends of wrongdoing, so that they can be corrected. Like the Athenian, Socrates also compares justice to medicine (*Gorgias* 464b–465d) and thus points to its remedial character.

22. I follow Pangle 1980, 257; Strauss 1975; Saunders 1968; and Stallbaum 1859–60, in taking κἂν σφάλληταί τι as "even if it be somewhat mistaken" rather than "even if some damage be done," in contrast to Weiss 2006; England 1921, 403; O'Brien 1957, 85; Bury 1926, 235; and Taylor 1934, because the Athenian's distinction between injustice and injury is a distinction between the intention to do what is just (even if it is mistaken) and the result (injury), whether intended or not.

23. Socrates explicitly states that the psychology he presents in *Republic* 4 is imprecise (435d), but many commentators have failed to note it.

24. This statement is the primary reason most readers have taken the *Laws* to represent both a later and a more "realistic" description of the best possible regime than that given in the *Republic*. As noted above, Aristotle says in the *Politics* that the *Laws* was written later. However, the date at which Plato composed the dialogue, which is unknown, would not necessarily coincide with the dramatic date, i.e., the time at which readers are to imagine that the conversation took place. In all the thirty-three other

dialogues in which Socrates appears, it is fairly clear that the dialogue was written by Plato after Socrates was dead. The fact that the Athenian mentions only two of the three radical reforms Socrates proposes in the *Republic* is significant. In *Laws* 10 the Athenian reminds both his interlocutors (and Plato's readers) that the old Dorians do not know anything about philosophy. The character of his interlocutors thus puts important limitations on what he can argue.

25. For a fuller account of the way in which the character of the interlocutors affects the character of the argument of the entire dialogue, see Eric Salem's discussion of *Laws* 1 and Michael Zuckert, 86–93, in this volume.

26. For these and other reasons Strauss 1983, 17, 27, 61, says that the discourse in the *Laws* is "sub-Socratic."

27. As both Munn, 2, 19–21, and Francisco Gonzalez, in this volume point out, in the *Laws* ἔρως is a passion to be restrained and attached to political goals, not to philosophical endeavors. Neither Socrates nor his erotic search for knowledge of the good-in-itself and the beautiful-in-itself is present, although toward the end of the dialogue (*Laws* 961a–966d) the Athenian indicates that members of the Nocturnal Council will need to undertake such an investigation if they are to obtain knowledge of the end or goal of the laws.

28. Likewise in the *Republic* 414d–417b Socrates states that he does not know how anyone could persuade people to believe the "noble lie" he nevertheless suggests all citizens must believe to deem their city entirely just. He also admits that persuasion alone will not suffice; the founders or legislators of the just city will also have to deprive guardians of any privacy in order to make sure that they devote their entire attention to what is common. Like the Athenian, Socrates suggests that human nature (the body) makes it difficult for most human beings consistently to put what is common before what is private. But in the singular case of the philosopher, Socrates points out, what he or she most desires for himself or herself, the truth, is and can be held simultaneously in common and in private.

13 "A Soul Superlatively Natural": Psychic Excess in *Laws* 10

Sara Brill

Early on in the lengthy prelude that is to be delivered to the would-be atheist, the Athenian makes a statement about soul whose ambiguity and profundity beg comparison with that fateful description of the good from *Republic* 6 as ἐπέκεινα τῆς οὐσίας (509b). If, observes the Athenian, soul can be shown to be generated prior to things like fire and air, then "it would be most correct to say it to be διαφερόντως φύσει" (892c).[1] As the adverbial form of διαφέρω, διαφερόντως means primarily "differently from;" when used in conjunction with a genitive it can indicate "above," and this specification to its kind of "difference from" recommends the adverb's use to indicate "especially," "pre-eminently" or as Bury renders it, "superlatively."[2] To claim that ψυχή is διαφερόντως φύσει is to suggest that ψυχή exists as both surpassingly and superlatively natural, which is to attribute to soul a deeply ambiguous relationship to nature.

This is a fruitful ambiguity, and one that is in keeping with the general tenor of the discussion of soul in Book 10. The Athenian's characterization of the soul as exceedingly natural is contingent upon both a conception of φύσις and a demonstration of soul's generation, a showing of its priority with respect to genesis. This approach implies a relation between φύσις and genesis made explicit in the Athenian's summary of the atheist's conception of φύσις as γένεσιν τὴν περὶ τὰ πρῶτα [generation or coming-to-be of things primary] (892c). As the prelude continues, the Athenian does not expressly challenge this general formulation of φύσις; instead, he attempts to reconfigure the atheist's conception of the relationship between φύσις and ψυχή by asserting that soul is the primary cause of all motion. In doing so, the Athenian attributes to soul generative capacities whose magnitude and scope blur the distinction between psychology and cosmology.

The shape the Athenian's contention with impiety takes in Book 10, namely the development of an account of soul that will be delivered to the impious as an antidote to their impiety, attests to the political efficacy of "psychology." At the same time, the particular account of soul the Athenian presents, with the excesses it attributes to ψυχή and their cosmic significance, offers a commentary on the cosmological status of the laws under which the polis itself operates, and by which its citizens are to be treated. Thus the account of soul in Book 10 has significant implications for the *Laws'* overarching conception of the role of the polis in the lives of its citizens and the cosmos in which it stands. This essay explores the relationship between the psychology the Athenian promotes in the preludes against impiety and the legislative project undertaken in the *Laws*. More specifically, in drawing out the account of soul embedded in the preludes against impiety and the cosmology they promote, we will explore the source of the curative function that is claimed for legislation throughout the *Laws*. Section 1 sketches the theological and legislative context out of which the preludes against impiety arise. Section 2 analyzes who the impious are and identifies the therapeutic work the preludes are to do on their souls. Section 3 focuses on the relationship between soul and mind that is promoted by the preludes in order to explicate both the vision of health that grants the preludes their efficacy and the role the polis plays in this vision.

* * *

The legislative project undertaken by the Athenian and his interlocutors in designing laws for Magnesia is predicated upon an intimate association between law and divine nous. Given the structure of the *Laws*, the means of contending with the impiety of the young cannot but have an impact on the legislative project undertaken in the dialogue. Indeed because this "second-best city" is imagined as having value only insofar as it imitates, to the extent possible, the mind of the divine and because its laws are a principle means of its doing so (713e–714a), impiety is a crime against the very foundation of the city itself. As Cleinias observes, the legislation against impiety which the three men have been discussing serves as a defense of law as such (890d) and of the particular laws they have been creating (887c). In contending with those flirting with impiety, the Athenian engages in a radical if understated revaluation of the divine, transforming archaic theogony (against which the atheist reacts in formulating his cosmology) into a noetic theology (which does not need to operate independently of a noetic cosmology).

There is not space here to investigate the full measure of the significance of impiety to the *Laws* (Eric Sanday's chapter in this volume makes some compelling claims about this significance); I will limit myself to a sketch of what I take to be the essential features of the dialogue's treatment of impiety. The Athenian Stranger's concession in Book 5 that the eradication of private property is possible only amongst gods or children of gods (739c–e) signals a difference between the *Laws'* city-in-speech and that of the *Republic*.[3] The production of the greatest possible civic unity in Magnesia will proceed not by eradicating private property, but by refiguring the citizen's relationship to property, that is to say, refiguring the way in which the citizen thinks of, behaves toward, and refers to his or her own.[4]

Because the ownership of property marks the city as distanced from the gods and their children, Magnesia in its very founding is already flirting with a kind of impiety, namely the impiety of calling one's own that which ultimately belongs to the gods. And indeed this appropriating gesture is explicitly conceived as the source of many great evils by the Athenian.[5] Shaping how Magnesia's citizens conceive of and behave toward their own can thus be presented as combating this general, diffuse impiety. More specifically, while property will be permitted the citizen, the citizen in turn will be asked to consider his identity and life as belonging to the gods and to the city and to behave accordingly.[6] That this project will involve a relatively elaborate psychology is signaled at the start of Book 5 with the Athenian's observation that the most divine possession [κτημάτων] a citizen has is his soul because it is most his own (726a). This description of ψυχή as a possession signals the dialogue's reformulation of what constitutes property, as does the enigmatic elision between what is θειότατον and what is οἰκειότατον, between what is divine and what is most one's own.[7] That one's ownership by the gods extends to ownership by the city (to the extent that the city imitates divine nous) is strongly suggested in the conclusion to Book 6, wherein the beginning and end of life are determined by a civic gesture—the writing and erasing of names in one's ancestral temple (785a–b).

The various pathologies outlined in the *Laws* can be treated as manifestations of the failure of this effort to refigure how citizens relate to property. Indeed the general and diffuse impiety that accompanies a failure to properly conceive of and relate to what is one's own takes many more specific forms depending upon the extent to which this project fails. For instance, the excessive self-love identified in Book 5 as a cause of all ἁμαρτίαι (731e), the condition of πλεονεξία called injustice (906c), the innate inability to avoid self-gain and do what is best for the community (875a–c), and the unexpiated hamartia of the past that the would-be temple robber is told is the cause of his desire (854a–b) can all be read as conditions in which the manner in which one relates to what is one's own and to what is for others is flawed and in need of treatment. The specific impiety to which we shall turn presently, the impiety of the young, finds its source in three beliefs, and it is in the treatment of these beliefs that the Athenian feels compelled to present the psychology that will occupy much of the book. Before we look more closely at this treatment, I would like to outline the legislative context in which they occur.

Granted the position of this psychology within preludes addressing the impious—that is, within a legislative project that takes itself to be therapeutic in nature and that maintains the practice of appending preludes to laws as intimately related to its curative capacity—we will need to identify the alleviative function it is supposed to fulfill; that is, we will need to identify the conditions of soul these preludes are to treat. In light of the above comments, the therapeutic thrust of the preludes delivered to the impious in Book 10 is found in their attempt to correct how three types of the impious think about what belongs to them. The preludes do so by offering a cosmology in which what is most one's own is presented as an offshoot of a much larger and potent cosmic force. In these preludes individual psychology is to be transformed by means of an account of cosmic psychology (or of the psychology of the cosmos). But in order to understand how such a prelude could be successful we must notice one crucial feature about the preludes in general.

If it is the case, as it is suggested in Book 9, that the preludes supplement the laws' blindness to particularity (875d) by speaking to the legislated herself and attempting to make her an ally of the law through both argument and threat (intimacy of address should not be taken for nonviolence),[8] then our understanding of the preludes must be informed by a grasp of the person to whom the preludes are addressed. This is to say that the preludes, like the Platonic dialogues in general, are decisively shaped by the perspectives of a variety of characters. No matter how far these preludes may stray from the kinds of conversations Plato depicts Socrates as having, I agree with André Laks's conclusion that, "the Socratic model of a dialectical conversation constitutes the horizon within which the theory of legislative preamble must be situated."[9] I do so even as I am persuaded by Catherine Zuckert's argument in this volume that the *Laws* occurs at a far remove from Socratic philosophizing and even as I will highlight the manner in which the preludes, in mutating and pushing against this horizon, strain the limits of interlocution. This horizon requires us to identify the variety of perspectives presented in this dialogue, perspectives that are often adopted, given the interlocutionary limitations of Cleinias and Megillus, by the Athenian himself. The extent to which the *Laws'* dramatic frame is also dialogic is certainly grounds for discussion, but that the *Laws* has a dramatic frame is important to keep in mind. Attention to the *Laws'* curious dramatic structure forces us to recognize that, in asking ourselves, "What do the preludes say?" we must also ask, "To whom are the preludes addressed?"[10]

* * *

Near the end of Book 10 the Athenian identifies six classes of impiety necessary for the legislator to distinguish because they require penalties that are "neither equal nor similar" (908b). In discerning who falls into these classes, we may take as a preliminary answer to this question those whom the Athenian identifies at the start of the book as prone to particularly grave offences, namely, the young. Further valuable information about these young people and those by whom they are influenced is given in the Athenian's early admonition [παραμύθιον] of the impious, wherein he offers a general diagnosis of impiety: "No one who believes [ἡγούμενος], as the laws prescribe, in the existence of the gods, has ever yet done an impious deed voluntarily, or uttered a lawless word: he that acts so is in one of these three conditions of mind—either he does not believe in what I have said; or, secondly, he believes that the gods exist, but have no care for men; or thirdly, he believes that they are easy to win over when bribed by offerings and prayers" (885b). The Athenian's response to Cleinias's question of how one is to contend with these beliefs is to define a certain posture one must adopt toward the people who possess them. Like the good doctor described in Book 4 (720c–e), one must listen to them (885c).[11] But here we can note a discursive disruption, as this posture is made possible only by a kind of speaking, the speaking for the legislated. In order to listen to the legislated, the Athenian must address "himself"; that is, he must address the persona he has adopted as the legislator, by taking on the persona of the legislated, who are addressing the legislators. The Athenian must both give and receive the demand of the legislated. Thus it is by merit of a certain discursive gymnastics and ventriloquism that this scene of address is created.

The image that the Athenian assigns to the impious is hardly flattering. The tone which he attributes to them is mocking and demanding; he answers it by addressing them as children and telling them that their views are neither novel nor radical (888a–c). However, the impious are not without talents in rhetoric and public debate; the demand they make upon the Athenian both appeals to the model of legislation he has adopted and attempts to translate this model into the idiom of the court. The legislated charge the legislators with deceiving people by using groundless arguments for the sake of manipulating citizens (886e), and demand that they prove the existence of the gods (885e).[12] When Cleinias suggests that proving the existence of the gods is as simple as pointing to the heavens, and attributes impiety to a simple inability to master one's desire for pleasure (886a–b), the Athenian finds it necessary to complicate this diagnosis of impiety by calling attention to a broader cultural and political landscape in which impiety is allowed to flourish, a landscape beset, according to the Athenian, with "a very grievous unwisdom [ἀμαθία] which is reputed to be the height of wisdom" (886b). In elaborating upon this "unwisdom," the Athenian outlines a political landscape in which the theologies produced by ancient poets have not only failed to provide a check to the pursuit of pleasure, they have also created a class of individuals who, in rebelling against them, propound a cosmology that fosters ἀκρασία by asserting there are no gods.[13] Thus the stance of the atheists must be viewed in its reactive connection to a particular kind of theology.

This is a shrewd strategy on the part of the Athenian. By locating the position of the atheist within a particular cultural and intellectual framework, and specifically as a reaction to (and thus dependent upon) a particular theological context, the Athenian sets the stage for the putting-in-place of the atheist that will be continued in the prelude delivered directly to him. Moreover, he also signals to the reader that any attempt to contend with the beliefs that produce impiety must not only replace akratic cosmology with some other form of cosmology, it must also replace archaic theology with some other theology. This is to say that akratic cosmology will be replaced by noetic cosmology; noetic cosmology in turn will provide a theology that depicts the gods as bearers of mind.

The Athenian's preliminary exchange with the impious tells us that the impious are the inheritors of this cultural landscape, of this constellation of beliefs in which a particular vision of the gods provokes a conception of nature that purports to refute any such vision and to resent its advocacy as a manipulative deception expressed in specious argumentation. This exchange leaves the reader with the sense that many of the impious are predisposed to argument (even if this manifests itself as a love for eristic) and thus that the preludes to these people can take the shape of something like dialectic.[14] However, I want to focus less on the dialectical or argumentative character (or lack thereof) of these preludes and more on the manner in which their substance is fitted to the psychic condition of the person they are addressing. Given this general introduction to the impious, we can now inquire into the specific conditions of soul attributed to the atheist, the deist, and the traditional theist (to follow Robert Mayhew's designations).[15] Because the prelude delivered to the atheist is the longest and that upon which the other two preludes are based, my focus will be on this prelude, followed by a sketch of the other two characters and their preludes.

Prelude for the Atheist

What does the atheist believe? Or rather what portrait of the atheist does the Athenian deliver to the atheist? The belief that engenders the condition of soul of the atheist turns out to be a misconception of what constitutes the "first cause of becoming and perishing in all things" (891e). The atheist falls prey to a widespread misunderstanding about ψυχή that attributes to ψυχή a generation later than that of the body (892a). The cosmology to which the atheist is victim is one in which things come into being primarily by the interaction between φύσις, whose most primary manifestations are soulless bodies of earth and fire, etc. (889b), τύχη, which governs the mingling of these natural forces (889b–c), and τέχνη, which provides a secondary and lesser source of things, secondary because later and lesser because it receives what is good about it from nature (889a). Legislation, especially that which asserts the existence of gods, acts counter to the "natural" tendency to dominate: "as to things just, they do not exist at all by nature, but men are constantly in dispute about them and continually altering them, and whatever alteration they make is authoritative, though it owes its existence to art and the laws, and not in any way to nature" (889e–890a). Thus the atheist is persuaded by sophists who align law with τέχνη against nature, and who, on the basis of this antagonism, chart out a politics that valorizes injustice under the rubric of living a natural life.

Because the atheist's beliefs lead to impiety, the "cure" or treatment for this psychic condition must involve a set of counter-beliefs, an alternative to the akratic cosmology. In his response to this cosmology and the politics it suggests, and thus in his antidote to the condition of soul fostered by such a cosmology, the Athenian tacitly accepts the atheist's general vision of φύσις, namely that φύσις is the "production of things primary" (892c). The atheist's error lies in what he considers such primary things to be: "That which is the first cause of becoming and perishing in all things, this is declared by the arguments which have produced the soul of the impious to be not first, but generated later, and that which is the later to be the earlier; and because of this they have fallen into error regarding the real nature of the divine existence" (891e). This is to say, the Athenian will assert that it is the soul (what the atheist had aligned with τέχνη and with later and secondary creation) that is responsible for the first productions and thus it is the soul that should be called by the atheists most natural (892c). The therapeutic move to be found in the *logos* that follows is expressed in its radically reconfiguring the relationship between φύσις, τύχη, and τέχνη such that the motions of soul—phenomena like joy, sorrow, hatred, love, reflections, memories, opinions true and false[16]—manifest in φύσις and τέχνη alike, are the primary workings of the cosmos and are responsible for the generation and dissolution of all things. In this alternate cosmology, the operation of τύχη, namely the combination of elements into things, is replaced by the presence and absence of mind; law, like soul itself, will indicate the inadequacy of the presentation of the relationship between φύσις and τέχνη as antagonistic.

But this antidote to atheism only functions by asserting some extremely provocative claims about the origin and nature of soul. The cosmic priority which this account grants to ψυχή is such that it is by merit of psychology, or, better, psychogony, that the existence of gods can and must be gleaned from the motion of the heavens. It is this psychogony that is to defeat the incredulity of the atheist by providing an alternate cosmology. Given its significance for the success of the prelude, it is necessary for us to gain a stronger grasp of just what conception of soul, what psychogony and psychology, the Athenian maintains as capable of combating the atheist's cosmology. What is it necessary to believe about soul in order to excise atheism from one's soul?

In this prelude, the fecundity of soul is a function of soul's alignment with a kind of motion, an alignment accomplished by appeal to the phenomenon of living being itself. The Athenian presents the kinetics at the heart of this prelude by identifying ten kinds of motion and ordering them according to a hierarchy in which the motion capable of moving itself is granted the highest honor and conceded to be the motion that causes all others. The Athenian then connects this "self-movement" with ψυχή by attaining agreement from his interlocutors that the condition of things capable of moving themselves is that of being alive and that presence of soul as also associated with creating in things the condition of being alive (895c).[17]

Armed with the agreed definition of soul as "self-movement" the Athenian draws out several of its implications: soul is the cause of motion and change in all things (896b), soul is the oldest [πρεσβυτάτη] of all things generated (896b),[18] soul is prior to body (896b), the "things" of soul are also prior to body (896c–d), soul is the cause of all things, including opposites like good and bad (896d), and the soul controls heaven (896e). As the Athenian elaborates upon how soul causes motion, he and his interlocutors agree that there must be at least two kinds of soul, good soul (soul in conjunction with [προσλαβοῦσα] mind) and bad soul (soul consorting with [συγγενομένη] ἄνοια) (896e–897b). In attempting to determine which kind of soul governs heaven they investigate which motion is proper to mind, an investigation which requires the use of an image. On the grounds of its tendency toward self-sameness, revolution is recommended as the best image for the motion of mind (898a–b);[19] as this motion is also most indicative of the motion of the heavens they conclude that it is good soul or several good souls that govern the heavens. This conclusion is further illustrated by a consideration of how "good soul" might move, in which the movement of the sun is taken as caused by soul (which implies that the sun and other heavenly bodies are not soulless) and is indicative of the movement of the cosmos as a whole. The Athenian and his interlocutors conclude their discussion of the sun's motion with the agreement that the sun, like the cosmos itself, is moved by a good soul and further agree that this soul is a god (899a–b). They then end their prelude to the atheist by setting down "limiting conditions": either the atheist must show that soul is not older than body or he must believe in and honor the gods (899c).

Prelude for the Deist

The preludes to the deist and the traditional theist explicitly build upon this picture of ψυχή and cosmos by drawing out the implications for human life of an ordered and mindful cosmos overseen by rational gods. However, the condition of soul of the one who believes the gods neglect human affairs is a bit different than that of the young atheist. This potentially impious person is driven not by a denial of the gods, but by a certain bind, a certain incapacity to square his belief in the gods with his perception of the apparent flourishing of unjust people. Here is the portrait the Athenian paints of this person: "My good sir [ὦ ἄριστε],"[20] let us say, "the fact that you believe in gods is due probably to a divine kinship drawing you to what is of like nature, to honor it and recognize its existence; but the fortunes of evil and unjust men, both privately and in public—which, though not really happy, are excessively and improperly lauded as happy by public opinion—drive you to impiety by the wrong way in which they are celebrated, not only in poetry, but in tales of every kind" (899d–e). While the atheist has fallen victim to a vision of the cosmos handed to him by certain sophists, the person who fears neglect from the gods is a victim of his own observations and the many stories told and songs sung that valorize an unjust life. There is a powerful resonance here between the Athenian's description of the soul of this young person and Plato's depiction of Glaucon and Adeimantus in *Republic* 2.[21] Here as in the *Republic*, the truly enigmatic human phenomenon is the person who seems to have a natural love of justice, a passional predisposition toward measure and harmony.[22] The existence, against all tendency toward πλεονεξία and excessive self-love, of such a human is the phenomenon that most begs philosophical attention and inquiry. And here, as in the *Republic*, attempting such an account will require the employment of a vast conceptual apparatus. For now, however, let us simply observe that the prelude must contend with the impression that injustice pays, and I take the necessity of the discursive supplement of the charm to the prelude to signal Plato's acknowledgement of the power and traumatizing force of this experience. According to the Athenian, what the deist lacks, and what both the prelude and its supplementary charm are intended to provide, is a vision of the expiation of unjust deeds. They do so by means of an elaborate spatial metaphor in which theodicy is figured as the movement of souls to appropriate places and is governed by the cosmic law of "like to like." Throughout this prelude and charm, the tropes of ownership and kinship play a decisive role: as both the property of the gods and as kin to the gods by merit of their possession of soul (902b),[23] humans should be assured of the care and attention of the gods who, in their solicitude of what is their own, are exemplars of ownership.

Prelude for the Traditional Theist

The traditional theist is also one who has fallen prey to stories about the gods from both poets and prose writers. Like the deists, these impious people are misled by their own conception of divinity. However, the conception of the gods formulated by such people so far surpasses in depravity the claim that the gods neglect humans as to make Cleinias describe the people holding this opinion as the worst and most impious people (907b). The opinion about the gods that sparks in Cleinias this ardent, zealous condemnation is presented by the Athenian as likening gods to guardians and those who bribe them to wolves: "it is just as if wolves were to give small bits of their prey to watch-dogs, and they being mollified by the gifts were to allow them to go ravening among the flocks" (906d). Such a person takes the gods to be more corrupt than those human practitioners of τέχναι who manage to fulfill their duties without succumbing to corruption. Their discussion of the people who hold such views of the gods also has a maddening effect on the Athenian and his interlocutors themselves, driving them to a passionate and contentious denunciation of such people that violates their earlier agreement to tame their θυμός (887c–888a) and argue against the impious dispassionately, a failure to which the Athenian calls their attention (907b–d). Beyond the preludes already delivered to the atheist and the deist, there does not seem to be much hope held out for convincing this person otherwise; however, the law prohibiting the possession of private shrines (909d–e) which concludes Book 10 seems designed with this particular form of impiety in mind, suggesting that with this type of person the limits of persuasive argument have been reached.

Frank and Ironic Impiety

There remains one more criterion relevant to the legislator's discernment and treatment of impiety, the (infamous and fraught) distinction between the "frank" [παρρησίας, 908c][24] and the ironic [τὸ εἰρωνικὸν, 908e] impious person, a distinction perhaps most clearly illustrated in its demarcation of two kinds of atheist:

> "For while those who, though they utterly disbelieve in the existence of the gods, possess by nature a just character, both hate the evil and, because of their dislike of injustice, are incapable of being induced to commit unjust actions, and flee from unjust men and love [στέργουσιν] the just; on the other hand, those who, besides holding that the world is empty of gods, are afflicted by incontinence in respect of pleasures and pains, and possess also powerful memories and sharp wits—though both these classes share alike in the disease of atheism, yet in respect of the amount of ruin they bring on other people, the latter class would work more and the former less of evil." (908b–c)

It is from out of the class of the ironic impious that one finds diviners and jugglers, tyrants, demagogues, and generals, "those who plot by means of peculiar mystic rights of their own, and the devices of those who are called sophists" (908d). With respect to both the deist and the one who believes the gods can be bribed, the ironic or acute forms of their impiety turn their victims into "ravening beasts" who, "besides holding that the gods are negligent or open to bribes, despise men, charming the souls of many of the living, and claiming that they charm the souls of the dead, and promising to persuade the gods by bewitching them, as it were with sacrifices, prayers, and incantations, and who try this to wreck utterly not only individuals, but whole families and states for the sake of money" (909a–b). This passage draws together again both those who believe in the gods' neglect and those who believe the gods can be bribed, a sobering reminder of the depths to which even those who possess some "natural" kinship with the gods (899d) can fall if their corruption is not checked.

Indeed this distinction between frank and ironic impious people would not be possible if the only cause of impiety was ἀκρασία, which is why the Athenian corrects Cleinias's claim that it is only a weakness with respect to pleasure and pain that causes impiety; by pointing to the persuasive power of the sophistic position on the cosmos, the Athenian sets the stage for the corruption of those who, while they naturally love justice (and perhaps *because* they do), are traumatized by the apparent flourishing of unjust people and so are predisposed to be persuaded by the arguments of the sophists about what is natural and about the falsehood of justice. What Cleinias's somewhat naive diagnosis fails to consider is the more dangerous possibility that even people predisposed to love justice and the gods can be turned away from justice and the gods; what Cleinias fails to discern is the *array* of impious people (the jarring connection between the sophist, the charlatan, and the people persuaded by each) and the work of a variety of cultural and political factors in producing this array.

Consequently, the preludes must be constructed with an eye to both individual psychology and social institution. Much of the work done by the preludes in addressing the impious consists in pointing out their psychic condition and locating them within a larger framework that requires of them certain metaphysical, theological, and cosmological commitments that they themselves can attest to. In locating the impious within a cosmic structure of which they are part, in presenting their psychic conditions and the inclinations that arise from them as part of a larger psychic structure that exceeds them, the prelude attempts to put the impious in their place, as it were, a gesture that grants, on the one hand, the security of theodicy the deist desires[25] and, on the other hand, a kind of self-knowledge and humility that the atheist and those who believe the gods can be bribed are taken to lack.[26]

For the frank impious person, the antidote lies in pointing to the existence of people, like themselves, who do have a natural love for justice and order, and to play up the metaphysical and cosmological implications of such a love. The strategy the prelude employs is to show frank impious people that they are not at home in the very cosmology they espouse; their predisposition toward justice and order cannot be explained by the beliefs they have claimed as their own. This is especially true for the frank deist, whose attention is to be turned from the apparent flourishing of unjust people (the phenomenon that causes this person so much torment) to the remarkable occurrence of those naturally predisposed to love justice.[27] The Athenian presents the prelude's cosmology as able to account for *both* πλεονεξία and a natural predisposition toward justice; the atheist's cosmology, on the other hand, can only account for πλεονεξία and cannot explain an innate love of justice and related phenomena like the eruptions of order exhibited by children in play and by all humans in dance. The only explanation offered is chance, and the Athenian is gambling that once the impious have been recognized as having a place in an orderly cosmos, for many of them this recourse will appear symptomatic of an impoverished perspective.

That not all impious people will be persuaded by these preludes is implied by the penalties the Athenian goes on to assign to impiety, penalties which are supposed to reflect the taxonomy of impiety the Athenian has produced. According to the Athenian, as there are three causes of impiety (the three beliefs just discussed) and two kinds of impiety that result from each (frank and ironic), there are six classes [γένη] "which require to be distinguished, as needing penalties that are neither equal nor similar [οὐκ ἴσης οὐδ᾽ ὁμοίας]" (908b). Since imprisonment is imposed in all cases of conviction for impiety, the differences between these classes will be a function of the location and conditions of their imprisonment. This in turn is possible because there are three kinds of prisons in Magnesia: the public prison near the agora where most convicts are housed, the reformatory [σωφρονιστήριον] located near the assembly room of the Nocturnal Council, and the third, called "retribution" [τιμωρίας], located in the wildest and most isolated part of the country (908a). The "frank" impious people, people who are suffering from "folly being devoid of evil disposition and character [ἀνοίας ἄνευ κάκης ὀργῆς τε καὶ ἤθους, 908e]," and who require "admonishment and imprisonment" [τὸ δὲ νουθετήσεως ἅμα καὶ δεσμῶν δεόμενον (908e)], are to receive a penalty of no less than five years in the reformatory where they will be visited only by members of the council charged with visiting them in order to "minister to their soul's salvation by admonition" (909a).[28] Those who, after the period of their incarceration, appear to be reformed are allowed back into Magnesian society; those who are convicted a second time are put to death (909a). The "ironic" impious people, those who are "like ravening beasts" (θηριώδεις, 909a) and for whom, according to the Athenian, even two deaths is not enough (908e), are to be imprisoned in the countryside and refused any visitors whatsoever, receiving only a food ration determined by the law wardens. That they are to be imprisoned until death is not explicitly stated in this passage, but is strongly suggested both by the absence of any specification as to a means for or result of their rehabilitation and by the legislative detail that should such a person have children, those children are to be received by the guardian of orphans from the day of their parent's conviction (909d). Upon death, these impious are denied burial; their bodies are to be thrown outside the borders of Magnesia, with a penalty of impiety for anyone who dares to bury them, enforceable by anyone who chooses to prosecute (909c). Thus two deaths are indeed allotted to these people: the symbolic death of imprisonment in the most isolated place and under the most isolating of conditions, marked by the appropriation of the convict's offspring and reiterated in the denial of burial, and physical death.

The Athenian's delivery of the penalties to the impious, his "interpretation" of the law regarding impiety (907d) is incomplete, since it specifies not six but two main kinds of punishments, those for the frank and those for the ironic. Perhaps we are to infer that, for the classes of frank impious, distinctions will be drawn in terms of the length of time incarcerated; nevertheless, the Athenian fails to follow through with the demand to produce six separate penalties (908b). This apparent lapse, along with the admission that repeat offenses are possible and the suggested impossibility of rehabilitating three of these classes (not to mention the limitation placed on oath taking in Book 12 (948d–e), which bodes poorly for efforts to stem the tide of impiety) serve to remind the reader that all of this legislation occurs under the specter of its failure. As we return to discuss in more detail the psychology that is hoped to render these punishments super-fluous, we should have in mind already the admission of the possibility (and even the likelihood) of its failure.

* * *

The clinical context of Book 10's account of soul (its occurrence as a prelude and thus as a form of treatment) advises against assuming that it represents what Plato takes to be true about the soul. Rather, the safer assessment to make about the preludes, in my opinion, is that they tell us quite a bit about what Plato suspects it is necessary for citizens to believe about the soul, given the politi-cal and cultural landscape that has produced the particular condition of soul and set of beliefs the Athenian describes. This is not to say that Plato is "lying" or is not concerned with the truth;[29] in fact, given the resemblance of some of these potentially impious people to some of the young men he depicts as par-ticularly philosophically-leaning elsewhere in the dialogues, there is reason to believe Plato intentionally presented the Athenian as being particularly careful and thoughtful in his "answers" to the impious. Nevertheless, the curious clini-cal operation granted to the preludes ties their claims to a particular constel-lation of concerns in such a manner as to assert their immersion within a po-litical environment, not their transcendence of it, and we should be mindful of this stance. Granted the strong political inflection of the preludes in general, it is necessary to ask where we might locate the role of the polis in the relationship between ψυχή and κόσμος that is asserted by the preludes against impiety. In-vestigating this question will give us a sharper sense of the vision of health that informs the very legislative structure that recommends the use of therapeutic preludes.

One particularly striking element of the psychology developed in these pre-ludes is its emphasis on the excesses that attend to ψυχή and their cosmic ef-fects. The pervasive ignorance about the soul and its origin (892a–b), the Athe-nian's characterization of their discourse about the soul as alien and unfamiliar (see 891d ἀηθεστέρων . . . λόγων and 891e: a *logos* that is οὐκ εἰωθότα) as well as violent (892e–893a),[30] and the "definition" of soul as self-movement (896a) all attest to a certain limitlessness of soul. Indeed to describe soul as self-motion is to attribute to soul an ecstatic character that, for Aristotle,[31] renders such an account nearly nonsensical, but that I hope to show is in fact in keeping with the general portrait of the soul the Athenian has been drawing. A psychology predicated upon self-motion is a psychology of ekstasis. This ecstatic quality of soul, in turn, gives us some indispensable information about the relationship between soul and mind in the *Laws*.

The ensuing discussion of soul's motion also contains numerous illustrations of its character. Soul's motion, for instance, is described as infinitely malleable (894c), infinitely excellent (894d), exceedingly effective (894d),[32] and as graspable by mind alone (898e). What the mind can grasp is that there are three ways in which soul might move the body of the sun: psychic infusion, psychic occupation, or some other wondrous capacity: "either it exists everywhere inside of this apparent globular body and directs it, such as it is, just as the soul in us moves us about in all ways; or, having procured itself a body of fire or air (as some argue), it in the form of the body pushes forcibly on the body from outside; or, thirdly, being itself void of body, but endowed with other surpassingly marvelous potencies [ἔχουσα δὲ δυνάμεις ἄλλας τινὰς ὑπερβαλλούσας θαύματι], it conducts the body" (898e–899a). Both the plurality of possibilities and the assertion of surpassingly wondrous capacities emphasize the limitless character of the soul. The very mind by means of which the speakers have recourse to describe these possibilities is itself a source of excess, as is illustrated in the impossibility of describing the movement of reason without an image: "In making our answer let us not bring on night, as it were, at midday, by looking right in the eye of the sun, as though with mortal eyes we could ever behold reason and know it fully; the safer way to behold the object with which our question is concerned is by looking at an image of it" (897d).[33]

Perhaps the most telling illustration of psychic excess, however, is found in the Athenian's account of the kind of motion for which soul is responsible—namely, all motion.[34] Indeed the prodigious operation of soul is such as to shatter it: in order to describe the kind of motion that the heavenly bodies conduct the Athenian finds it necessary to split soul into *at least* two kinds, good soul and bad soul (896d–897b). This is to say that the motions the soul can cause threaten its unity to the point where, in this dialogue, Plato ceases to contemplate this unity and instead, for the sake of the preludes, splits soul into two. Thus the soul's excesses comprise also a deficiency, insofar as they require the supplement of mind in order to produce the motion that is observable in the heavens (897b).

However, what I find most remarkable about this need for supplement is that soul receives mind as something that is fitting to it, that discloses something about it, that brings to light its capacities, and that augments those capacities. I take soul's reception of mind to shed some light on the characterization of soul as διαφερόντως φύσει, and to suggest that the ambiguity of the phrase is fully intended. To say that soul exceeds as well as exemplifies nature is to say that soul exceeds certain boundaries and horizons,[35] which is also to suggest that in order to operate within those boundaries and horizons some kind of limit needs to be imposed on soul. At the same time, such a limit would do nothing but enable soul to take on the variety of forms of motions to which it subjects itself, and thus this limit is somehow both "external" to it and intimately related to it, intimately its own.[36] Such an enhancing and augmenting limit would act not merely as an *addition* to soul, but as a *prosthetic* to soul. Because of its ambiguous suggestion of replacement, augmentation, and generation, of filling in, enhancing, and innovating, and because it is reducible neither to the natural nor to the artificial but answerable to the living, prosthesis is an idiom uniquely suited to describe the relationship between soul and mind as it is presented in the *Laws*. Soul, endlessly malleable, endlessly plastic, endlessly transforming, tends toward prosthesis. Or, to speak more precisely, we could say that soul tends toward prosthetic limits. Mind and its closely related phenomenon, law,[37] provide precisely such enhancing, augmenting, and enabling limits.

To contextualize this claim a bit, recall that the Athenian has described a cosmos for which an assertion of antagonism between φύσις and τέχνη, an assertion made by the atheist, is ill-suited because it denies the generative force of soul and its effects. He has also given an account of soul as having been separated into at least two by the excessive and prodigious generation of which it is the cause. Mind emerges as that entity both separable from soul (soul can receive mind or operate without mind, consorting with mindlessness)[38] and capable of providing soul with those limits that allow soul to render its motions in an orderly fashion. I have suggested prosthesis as a conceptual apparatus capable of capturing the nature and effects of soul's reception of mind. Further illustration of this prosthetic function can be seen if we turn our attention from the life of the cosmos to the character of human life itself.

The ecstatic character of cosmic soul belongs to living beings as well, insofar as their living is aligned with self-motion, and has bearing on the very nature of legislation as well as the structure of discourse of the dialogue itself. Indeed it is νόμος that helps to indicate the insufficiency of the rigid and antagonistic distinction between φύσις and τέχνη, and that operates with the limiting function granted to mind.[39] The clinical function that is reserved for both law and prelude, and that is emphasized whenever the curative capacity of voicing the law and prelude is observed, attests to the law's prosthetic character.[40] What is it that grounds the therapeutic operation of the prelude, what vision of health, if it is a health of the soul and thus a health of that which cannot be circumscribed by φύσις alone? From what the Athenian has said thus far, what grounds such a conception of psychic health is a vision of human flourishing that must somehow be imposed upon soul in the form of prosthetic limits like mind and law.[41] After all, there is at least one important difference among the disease, plague, and injustice which the Athenian presents as all instances of πλεονεξία (906b–c):[42] diseases and plagues operate within the limits imposed upon them by their "bodily" nature, even if those limits are conceived simply as a function of mortality itself. Injustice does not operate within the same limits, as is evinced by the fact that people who "catch" injustice do not necessarily die from it, and may even appear to flourish from it, to return to the experience that so traumatizes the one who believes the gods neglect human affairs. If injustice, unlike disease, is a corruption that does not carry its own limitation, then the human soul is in need of prosthetic limits in order to assure some end to human corruption. Laws are such prosthetic limits. At the same time, the Athenian's cosmology presents such a vision of human flourishing as not simply imposed on soul but invited by soul, just as mind is both external to but also somehow intimately related to soul. The *Laws'* construction of soul's relation to mind, then, bears a striking resemblance to its construction of the citizen's relation to the city. Both the cosmic and individual soul must actively take mind as an ally; for human beings, doing so requires or at least is greatly facilitated by a good city.

Further traces of soul's tendency toward prosthesis and of the varieties of psychic prostheses that exist, are found in the Athenian's discussion of divine law in the prelude to the deist. So powerful and traumatizing is the experience of the flourishing of unjust people that a *logos* about the nature of the Whole and the All, about the gods' care for the All and thus their care for its parts (an argument made by the comparison between the gods and practitioners of τέχνη; see 902d–e, for instance), proves insufficient, and a discursive supplement becomes necessary. Or, as the Athenian puts it, such a person still needs "some words of counsel to act as a charm upon him" (903a–b). It is in the course of delivering this charm that the Athenian characterizes theodicy as the creation of places that are appropriate to the conditions of souls and the allocation of souls to those places, and presents this theodicy as automatic, as a veritable physics that operates by means of a psychic attraction whereby souls exert a gravitational pull upon one another, settling into communities in places that are somehow appropriate to them. Granted the curious presentation of this gravitational pull—curious because the condition of one's soul is presented as a function of one's will and yet also as subject to transformations "according to the law and order of destiny" (904c)—all that remains for the god to do in this system "is to shift the character that grows better to a superior place, and the worse to a worse, according to what best suits each of them, so that each may be allotted its appropriate destiny" (903d). What the god imposes then is this gravitational pull of souls upon one another and toward regions appropriate to them. Indeed the Athenian concludes this charm, this supplement, by speaking in the voice of the Olympian gods themselves, stating: "O thou child and stripling who thinkest thou art neglected by the gods—the decree that as thou becomest worse, thou goest to the company of the worse souls, and as thou becomest better to better souls; and that, alike in life and every shape of death, thou both doest and sufferest what it is befitting that like should do toward like" (905a). Thus this discursive supplement includes a legislative prosthesis, that is, a certain order of movement is imposed upon the soul in the form of the law "like to like," but imposed by those entities who are themselves one manifestation of soul's reception of mind.[43]

This law of "like to like" and the ambiguity attendant upon it—that it is presented as both a function of the gods' activity and of the character of soul itself—illustrates the manner in which νόμος fluctuates between φύσις and τέχνη and thus exhibits soul's excessive character and its need for/invitation of prosthesis. Several other formulations of the "like-to-like" law in the dialogue help to measure the full significance of this prosthetic. For instance, what is described in Book 10 as the action of a god needs to be measured with the characterization of the same state of affairs as automatic earlier in the dialogue. In Book 5 the Athenian observes that few people notice the greatest judgment against wrongdoing [κακουργίας]: "to grow like unto men that are wicked, and, in so growing, to shun good men and good counsel and cut oneself off from them, but to cleave to the company of the wicked and follow after them; and he that is joined to such men inevitably [ἀνάγκη] acts and is acted upon in the way that such men bid one another to act" (728b). Here the law of "like to like" ensures the inevitability of these souls' entropy, such that corrupt souls gravitate toward other corrupt souls, eschew the better, cleave to the worse, and act according to the community with which they have surrounded themselves. This gravitational pull of like to like, the propensity of character or soul to flock to those like itself, is treated in this passage as automatic, as a fact of the behavior of soul.

In the prelude delivered to the one contemplating the murder of a parent in Book 9, the Athenian employs an ancient "account" in which expiation for the murder of a parent is only attained when "the soul which committed the act pays back murder for murder, like for like" (873a). Here, as with Book 10, the law of "like to like" is presented as a formulation of divine justice. Another version of this law occurs in Book 8, wherein the Athenian asserts that like is "friends" with like (837a–b). However, the addition of the notion of friendship (φιλία) in this passage, as distinct from the simple association asserted in Books 9 and 10, creates a crucial difference between these two versions of the ancient rule, a difference to which the Athenian attests when he notes in Book 4 that like is attracted to like only amongst those who are measured [μετρίῳ]; for those who lack measure no amity, no friendship, is possible (716c). This statement should be weighed against the Athenian's assertion in Book 5 that the greatest penalty to wrongdoing is that it makes the wrongdoer more like bad men and puts him in their company (728b–c). If such a movement belongs to soul as such, then why must the gods impose it upon human souls?[44] My contention is that this ambiguity points to what the *Laws* presents as the specific domain of the polis. While the association between those who are similar is treated as inevitable, and will in Book 10 function as an effect that attends upon the commission of deeds and acts as an automatic penalty for wrongdoers (they must suffer one another's company), that the company so forged would be one of friendship is possible only in the absence of wrongdoing (or the presence of measure); thus the community of souls may be amicable or acrimonious, but necessary nevertheless.

This point is extremely helpful in navigating the description of theodicy in Book 10 in which a discussion of physical space mutates into an emphasis on psychic conglomerates. Insofar as the charm conflates the places appropriate to souls with the community of like souls, "Hades" emerges as particularly close to the city itself, and the city emerges as the scene of the soul's reception of its prosthetic limitation/augmentation. And indeed the ultimate result of the legislation against impiety is the formation of "places," prisons, and the allocation of different kinds of impious people to them. In this sense, the penalty performs in deed what the charm asserts in speech, and creates a this-worldly Hades, a Hades on earth, which would be in keeping with the chilling call in Book 9 to create laws on earth that fall in no way short of those in Hades (881b) and with Seth Benardete's provocative claim that Hades, "is nothing but another name for the city."[45]

It is, however, important to keep in mind that, given the conception of soul promoted here, a Hades on earth is deemed necessary because of the particular conception of soul that is at work in the dialogue, a conception in which soul's excesses are not *necessarily* limited by any mandate to promote human flourishing. The locus for such a mandate is the city itself, and thus the city is the place in which soul receives prosthetic limits. In this sense there is no grounding for psychic prosthesis, for psychic health, outside of the particular political and cultural constellations of particular cities. Human dwelling and flourishing are radically contingent. At the same time, however, that such a mandate can be more or less amenable to the soul, there are better and worse prostheses, and the limitless malleability of soul seems also to be precisely that which invites prosthesis. What seems to be emerging here is an outline of politics not as the effort to approximate an ideal, but as the effort to devise ever more subtle psychic prostheses, an effort that would involve critical engagement with particular laws and with the practice of legislating itself.[46] This is to say that the scene of psychic phenomena is not simply cosmic put also deeply political. Both a cosmology and a politics are outlined in the psychology the Athenian produces in order to make the point that there are gods who care for humans and cannot be bribed.

Such a cosmology and politics involves a particular vision of the relationship between ψυχή and polis. The psychology at work here provides an image of the city as that arena of human striving wherein human action and psychic condition reciprocally affect one another and coalesce into the character not only of the individual but of the city itself. It provides a panoptic view of the city as the living medium of action. This psychology is thus an instrument of the *Laws*' legislative effort to make citizens identify with the city itself, to see themselves as the sum of the community their actions help to foster. What such a vision of the city offers the impious in particular is the "assurance" (which the Athenians suggests will seem assuring or threatening depending on the kind of impious person one is, but is therapeutic in either instance) of a this-worldly automaticity of punishment by providing the place wherein collectives of human souls form communities of better and worse, thereby providing the environment in which the soul gravitates toward that which it most resembles. Thus the "like-to-like" law, treated at once as a function of the gods' mindful intercession in the world of human affairs and as an attestation to the tendency toward mind within the human soul, is taken to be an impulse toward that revolving, self-same motion of the heavens that is itself the best likeness of the movement of mind.

Notes

Portions of this essay have appeared in my "Psychology and Legislation in Plato's *Laws*," *Proceedings of the Boston Area Colloquium in Ancient Philosophy*, v. 26 (2010), 211–242.

1. My translation. Bury 1967: "it would most truly be described as a superlatively natural existence"; Saunders 1975: "it will be quite correct to say that soul is pre-eminently natural"; Pangle 1980: "it would be most correct, almost, to say that it is especially by nature." Unless otherwise noted, citations will be from Bury's translation.

2. LSJ sv.

3. The Athenian's formulation of civic unity also includes an interesting shift from the *Republic* with respect to the status of the body—in the *Republic* it is the only private "property" permitted; in the *Laws* even the body is to be communized to the extent possible (see 739c–d.)

4. Indeed, as Glenn Morrow notes, "Plato asserts that the establishment of a right attitude toward property is the foundation (krēpis) of all legislation, the security of the state" (Morrow 1993, 101). Morrow cites 736a, but we also find this proper attitude encapsulated in the justification for prohibiting the taking of lost, abandoned, or buried property in Book 11: "For never should I gain so much pecuniary profit by its removal, as I should win increase in virtue of soul and in justice by not removing it; and by preferring to gain justice in my soul rather than money in my purse, I should be winning a greater in place of a lesser gain, and that too in a better part of me" (913a).

5. See the opening of *Laws* 10 (884a) as well as the general discussion of the evils of πλεονεξία toward its end (906c).

6. See, for instance, 902b; see also 906a–b: the gods and daemons are our allies [σύμμαχοι] while we are their possessions [κτῆμα]; and of course the very early and famous presentation of human beings as playthings of the gods (644d–e); and the later characterization of human things as lacking in seriousness (even though they must be treated as such; see 803b–c and David Roochnik's essay in this volume). We can also see in this general project some further motive for the dialogue's privileging of old age. The divinity of soul grounds the dialogue's sanctification of age; the elderly are to be honored because their sheer endurance through time is treated as a testament to the excellence of the gods' property.

7. The suggestion that what is most one's own really belongs to the divine is borne out throughout the rest of the dialogue. It can be seen, for instance, in the claim in *Laws* 11 that one's parents are to be honored because the elderly are living statues to the gods (931d–e), and in the description, as part of the funerary law outlined in *Laws* 12, of the soul as that which makes a person who they are and of corpses as soulless altars to the gods (959 b–d), and in the law concerning the burial of suicides in *Laws* 9 (875b–d).

8. Throughout this essay I will take for granted the violence of the law, the Athenian's frequent assertion of the inadequacy of law, and his various critiques of law, as well as the more subtle and in some ways more troubling violence that attends even to the "persuasive" preludes such that while gentleness emerges as desirable, its legislative instantiation is enigmatic and perpetually incomplete. On the violence of the law, see especially André Laks's masterful account in Laks 2000, 277–278, 286–290.

9. Laks 2000, 289.

10. I take this question to be a bit different than the question of who is speaking, even as I recognize that it may be neither possible nor desirable to systematically distinguish between these two questions. At least three possible answers to this question present themselves. First, the Athenian is speaking with and to Cleinias and Megillus, who, amongst other things, are identified as Cretan and Spartan respectively, are middle-aged, are not particularly well-versed in dialectic, and who have adopted, for the sake of conversation as well as for Cleinias's Cretan colony, the personae of legislators. Thus the Athenian is speaking as a nascent legislator and also with nascent legislators. Moreover, he and his interlocutors do so by adopting the voices of both the legislator and the

legislated. In fact, given Cleinias's and Megillus's lack of experience with conversations of this sort (an inexperience to which our attention is called explicitly in this book) and the Athenian's strategy for dealing with this inexperience, namely, to speak for them (892d–893a), a second answer to the question "who is speaking?" must be: the Athenian is speaking to himself. Thirdly, of course, we cannot ignore the perspective that no one is speaking here, not even the Athenian. Plato is the writer (and therefore can be viewed as the speaker), and his Cleinias emphasizes and celebrates the written character of the law in a passage (890e–891a) whose relationship to a position espoused by Socrates in the *Phaedrus* merits much further consideration than I can give it now.

11. Before we get swept up in the possibilities afforded by this call to listen, we must remind ourselves that the voice to which the Athenian claims they must listen is his own. The stance he will adopt throughout the legislating of impiety, the stance that enables this entire discussion to resemble a dialogue, given the limitations of Cleinias and Megillus (892e–893a), is that of giving voice to the impious, answering and asking as the impious as well as the legislator. In order to have a substantive dialogue, the Athenian must bifurcate. And what his assertion that they listen to the words of the impious signals to us is that he is now going to adopt the posture of the one who knows the impious better than they know themselves, or, in the words of the Athenian, he and his interlocutors should consider "what it is that people in their camp really intend" (888e–889a).

12. This is to say, the legislated accuse the legislators of corruption. The Athenian and his interlocutors initially accept this context. The Athenian asks: "Are we to make our defense as it were before a court of impious men, where someone had accused us of doing something dreadful by assuming in our legislation the existence of gods" (889e–887a) and receives a reply in the affirmative. Eventually, the Athenian counters this move on the part of the legislated by inverting the charge. He will present the position of the legislated in such a manner as to make them answerable to the charge of corrupting the youth, a reversal made most explicit by Cleinias's response to it: "What a horrible statement you have described, Stranger! And what widespread corruption of the young in private families as well as publicly in the states!" (890b). This exchange, and the courtroom scene it presents, evokes Socrates' trial and then inverts it.

13. In doing so, the Athenian draws together two figures, those ancient poets who have produced stories about the gods, and contemporary investigators of nature, sophists. While the Athenian will exercise some restraint in critiquing the ancient stories of the gods, and will state that it is rather the views of the sophist that must be held responsible for the beliefs that lead to impiety, the significance of his mention of the ancient composers of theogonies in this context should not be lost. The theologies of the ancient poets, suggests the Athenian, actually leads to sophistic, akratic cosmology.

14. The Athenian's description at 891c–d of the atheist's views as not only harmful but erroneous suggests that the prelude is intended to be, to the atheist, both therapeutic (correcting with respect to health) and also the case (correct with respect to the truth); that these two need not always accompany one another is implied in the *Republic* by the therapeutic function attributed to the lie in speech (382c–d). For a recent treatment of the argumentative status of these preludes, see, Bobonich 2002, along with the critical discussions of this work by Kahn 2004, Brisson 2005, and Gerson 2003.

15. Mayhew 2008.

16. 892b, 896d, 897a.

17. As though to acknowledge that the conclusion the Athenian is to draw from this correlation—namely, that soul is self-motion—is in need of further argumentation, the Athenian then briefly segues into a discussion of the three things that can be attributed to any thing: substance, definition, and name. That being alive entails a certain divine solicitude is repeated in the preludes to both the deist (902b) and the one who maintains the gods can be bribed (906b).

18. I take the claim that soul is πρεσβυτάτη to be strongly honorific; ψυχή is oldest and first in the sense of best and greatest (ordinal, nor cardinal numbering). At the same time, given the "definition" of soul as self-moving motion, and thus as generated but undying (904a), we must conceive of something like psychic time. As the actions of soul are the workings of love and hatred, sorrow and joy, wish, memory, opinion, etc. this would be a time of psychic deeds and effects, a time of perpetual psychic generation. Psychic time is pathic and ergonic time; it is the working through of passion and action. As such it has intimations for the working through of deeds and suggests a temporality to ethics. While there is not space to develop this line of thought here, I submit that doing so would shed further light on Plato's use of afterlife myths in general, in which the working through or expiation of unjust deeds is a frequent topic, and in the Laws in particular. The fate of individual souls outlined in the charm to the deist, the time it takes a soul to migrate to the community of souls appropriate to it, offers an image of the time and space of violence and its expiation.

19. See E. N. Lee's provocative discussion of rotation and nous (Lee 1976).

20. Note the difference between the address to this atheist "O, child" and the address to this person: "my good man."

21. At 365d–e Adeimantus identifies precisely the three beliefs that the Athenian considers the source of impiety, as Stephen Menn also observes (Menn 2005). Note Socrates' expression of surprise and admiration that Glaucon and Adeimantus have not been simply swept up by the cultural forces valorizing tyranny that surround them (368a–b).

22. Laks's discussion of the "human prodigy" and the significance of dance in the Laws (Laks 2000, 277–278) is quite helpful on this point; see also John Russon's essay in this volume.

23. See also 906b: human beings are to be saved by the justice, temperance, and wisdom "which dwell in the animate [ἐμψύχοις] powers of the gods, and of which some small trace may be clearly seen here also residing in us." I take the manifestations of order in play and dance and the love of justice to be evidence of this "trace" of divinity.

24. The Athenian context of the cultural milieu the Stranger has been outlining is made apparent in this distinction. For a recent study of the significance of παρρησία in Athens, see Monoson 2000 and Glenn Morrow's concluding comments on Plato and Athens in his commentary on the Laws (Morrow 1993, 591–593).

25. The deist simply needs a vision, a scale by means of which to locate the expiation of unjust deeds; what this prelude and its charm offers him is the equivalent of a wide-angle lens.

26. Insofar as this lack can be seen to stem from, or be a manifestation of, excessive self-love [τὴν σφόδρα ἑαυτοῦ φιλίαν], whose warping effect on judgment the Athenian has previously emphasized (731e), the Athenian's comment that such preludes will make

the impious more disposed to hate themselves [τοὺς ἄνδρας ἑαυτοὺς μὲν μισῆσαι, 907c] is particularly revelatory of the intended therapeutic thrust of these preludes and the specific psychological and cultural context in which they are operating.

27. As with Socrates in the *Republic*, it is the enigmatic character of the good to which the Athenian would call attention.

28. This period of incarceration, in which those who naturally love justice are instructed by members of the Nocturnal Council, may be the closest thing Magnesia sees to the practice of philosophy, a Magnesian version of Socratic dialogue, an idea pointed out to me by David Roochnik.

29. Recall the function allocated to the lie in speech in the *Republic*—as a treatment for the mad, as a cure available to the politician and as a means of approximating the truth about matters that remain deeply obscure (382c–d).

30. "The argument now in front of us is too violent [σφοδρότερος], and probably impassable, for such strength as you possess; so, lest it make you faint and dizzy as it rushes past and poses you with questions you are unused [ἀήθεις] to answering, and thus causes an unpleasing lack of shapeliness and seemliness, I think that I ought now to act in the way described—question myself first, while you remain listening in safety, and then return answer to myself, and in this way proceed through the whole argument until it has discussed in full the subject of soul and demonstrated that soul is prior to body."

31. "But surely even if the soul itself moves itself, then at any rate it would be moved, so that, if every motion is a stepping outside itself of the thing moved insofar as it is moved, the soul would step outside its own thinghood, if it moves itself not incidentally, but motion belongs to its thinghood in its own right" (*De Anima*, 406b13ff.). Joseph Sachs offers a sobering cautionary warning about two possible effects of attributing to soul such a character: "To avoid this consequence, one would have to say that the soul is that which, by its very nature, moves or alters itself in ways that do not belong to its nature. Finding the nature of the soul in self-motion may sound impressive, but it seems to be either contradictory or empty" (Sachs 2002, 60). I am hoping to put a lot of weight on Sachs's "seems" here.

32. In both references from 894c a form of διαφέρω is used.

33. This passage and the image proposed, the motion of the sun, has powerful resonances with *Republic* 6.

34. The attribution of all motion (good and bad) to soul does suggest a difference between the Laws and Timaeus; however, the weight of this difference may not be as substantial as it appears, see Parry 2002, 289–302.

35. Again, Aristotle is helpful here: "But though [fire] is in some way jointly [of nutrition and growth] it is surely not simply the cause, but rather the soul is, for the growth of fire goes on without limit, so long as there is something burnable, but all things put together by nature have a limit and a proportion of size and growth, and this belongs to soul, not to fire, and to the articulation of the meaning more than the material" (416a14ff.). Insofar as nature is the site of limit, were soul to exceed nature it would also exceed limit. Of course for Aristotle it is the manifestation of limit as a manifestation of soul that, in part, recommends the inquiry of soul as contributing to the inquiry into nature, while it is the character of fire to go on without limit, and I am claiming that Plato's account of viciousness suggests that body operates under certain limits which soul does not.

36. With limit understood in this sense, the presentation of soul's reception of mind in the *Laws* resonates with the *Philebus*'s presentation of the fecund and generative work accomplished by number, law, and order in bringing limit to the unlimited (*Philebus* 23d, 25d, 26b, 27b).

37. On the relationship between νόμος and nous see 713e–714a and 957c; the qualification in this latter passage, namely that the learning pertaining to the laws is sovereign with respect to human betterment if they are set up correctly is important, but maintains the relationship between νόμος and nous by shifting the burden from the laws themselves to their instantiation by the legislators. See also the correlation between logismos and nous at 967b. That enslavement to the laws is enslavement to the gods, see 762e. At 741b the lot distributing property is itself called divine. At 902b it is agreed that all mortal things are possessions of the gods.

38. The controversy surrounding the question of whether Plato conceives of nous as separable from ψυχή is longstanding; I am persuaded by Menn's (1995) argument for separability, and would only add that in the *Laws* Plato is as concerned to indicate their intimacy as their separability. Mind has a unique relationship to soul, and I have tried to capture the nature of this relationship with the notion of the prosthetic function (as enabling limit) mind supplies to soul. Menn takes the separability of ψυχή and nous as evidence that Plato has a theology distinct from his metaphysics and physics; I view this separability as Plato also intimating that psychology cannot be reduced to theology, metaphysics, or even physics. In this, I diverge from Pangle's claim that "psychology and theology are in the end the same" (Pangle 1976, 1059–1077). At the very least, it is necessary to draw a distinction between, on the one hand, observations about the theological effects of psychology and the psychological effects of theology, and, on the other hand, observations about the nature of philosophic investigations of the soul and the gods. The final chapter of Friedrich Solmsen's *Plato's Theology* illustrates well the importance of maintaining such a distinction (Solmsen 1942, 177–193).

39. It should also be noted that νόμος is not the only limiting or correcting entity in the dialogue. For instance, amongst the arsenal of techniques and instruments needed by the legislator in order to counteract the desires for food, drink, and sex that can lead to hamartia, law is listed as only one of three greatest [μεγίστοις] forces (783a); the other two, fear and true account, mingle with some frequency in the preludes themselves, as well as in the Platonic corpus as a whole, and we can note throughout the *Laws* Plato's concerns about the efficacy of human legislators to properly instantiate the laws. For this reason I remain, with others, unconvinced by Chris Bobonich's claims about the rationality of the procedures for legislating in the *Laws*. See Bobonich 2002 and the critical comments by Kahn 2004, 337–362, Brisson 2005, 93–121, and Gerson 2003, 149–154.

40. This character is also consistent with figurations of legislation in other dialogues. I have in mind here in particular the Protagoras myth, in which δίκη is presented as a gift from Zeus meant to correct Epimethean shortsightedness in denying humans any means to defend themselves (322c–d).

41. It would be hasty to assume that Plato is necessarily concerned with human flourishing as such. However, the Athenian's comments in *Laws* 1 about war and peace do imply a preoccupation with human happiness in this dialogue. See also 718a.

42. "But there are certain souls that dwell on the earth and have acquired unjust gain which, being plainly bestial, beseech the souls of the guardians—whether they

be watch-dogs or herdsmen or the most exalted masters—trying to convince them by fawning words and prayerful incantations that (as the tales of evil men relate) they can profiteer among men on earth without any severe penalty: but we assert that the sin now mentioned, of profiteering or 'overgaining,' is what is called in the case of fleshly bodies 'disease,' in that of seasons and years 'pestilence,' and in that of states and politics, by a verbal change, this same sin is called 'injustice'" (906b–c).

43. See 897b–c, 899b: the soul with mind is wise and good, the soul or souls that rule heaven are souls with mind (and thus wise and good), and these souls are gods.

44. I find Gabriela Carone's distinction between the account of ψυχή as such and the account of human ψυχή in particular a compelling response to this question, and would add only that the question itself becomes less important if the mindful intercession of the gods in the form of the law is seen as an enhancement or augmentation (a prosthesis) that is invited by human soul (Carone 1994).

45. Benardete 2000b, 35, cited in Burger 2004, 58.

46. This assertion requires far more development than I can give it here, and would have to contend with the image of legislating as painting at 769a–e, a brief discussion of which appears in my "Psychology and Legislation in Plato's Laws." See also R. F. Stalley's brief address of the checks and balances in the Laws as a rebuttal to Popper (Stalley 1983, 184–185).

14 Property and Impiety in Plato's *Laws:* Books 11 and 12

Eric Sanday

At the end of the project traced out in Plato's *Laws,* the Athenian Stranger asks what it would take to arrive at an end of the lawgiving.[1] In this essay I focus on the way in which the problem of ending relates to the ongoing incompleteness of political community in the so-called "second-best" city that is the subject of the dialogue. I propose in this chapter that the character of the city as second best implies that its very incompleteness is necessarily constitutive of its health, and that the success of the lawgiver will hinge on the city's ability to live with and allow for the ongoing breakdown of its project. It is my contention that the problem of incompleteness governs the concluding books of the *Laws,* and that interpreting these books in light of this problem allows us to understand the function of the Assembly (σύλλογος) introduced in Book 12, which the Athenian refers to as the "perfect and permanent safeguard" of the city they have generated. Key to the reading I will offer is the recognition that impiety extends beyond the limits of personal belief, as identified in the Book 10 reference to the young, and is rooted in the material foundations of life in the city, especially in property, contracts (συμβόλαια), and other institutions first introduced in Book 11.

In Book 10 the Athenian defines impiety as a very serious type of ignorance that is received by many as great wisdom, that body is older than soul. In this essay I interpret this serious ignorance as the forgetfulness of the sources of one's being, which would include forgetfulness of the gods but also the city as a whole, the families and groups of which it consists, and the weight of tradition in which those groups are rooted. I will focus on the way the institutionalized foundations of daily life in the city, especially those clustered around ownership and the transfer and inheritance of property, are causes of the forgetfulness of the sources of one's being, ultimately calling for the institution of the above mentioned Assembly. This chapter will show that the problem of impiety extends beyond the narrowly defined scope it is normally granted in interpretations of the *Laws,* and that in spite of posing real danger to the health of the city and its citizens, impiety is necessary to the city's flourishing.

Mapping Books 11 and 12

It is hard to deny that Books 11 and 12 of the *Laws* seem unedited.[2] Much of the content appears to be presented without any of the connective tissue that appears throughout the rest of the books, and there is less thematic unity to the points that are in these books than one finds in other parts of the dialogue. Book 11 breaks unceremoniously with the Book 10 discussion of piety, turning to an analysis of business transactions (συμβόλαια), which is itself a loose collection of topics including property (913a–922a), family matters (922a–932d), various bodily harms (932d–934c), and a grab-bag of such things as insanity, slander, beggary, and oratory (934c–941a). However, if there were an organizing principle to the themes addressed in the book, it would seem to be property. The first section of Book 11 deals with property laws pertaining to individual citizens, e.g. the principles of equitable distribution of property, the power of money, laws governing retail trade; the second section of the book deals with property laws pertaining to families, e.g. inheritance, marriage laws, father-son disputes, husband-wife disputes, and parentage.

Book 12 offers even more evidence of being unedited than we find in Book 11. It lacks an introduction, and the ensuing discussion ranges widely from abuse of office (941a–942a), military organization (942a–945b), audits of magistrates (945b–948b), travel abroad (949e–953e), property law (954a–956b), organization of courts (956c–958c), and funerals (958c–961a). The dialogue does not regain its polish until the discussion turns to the Assembly that gives the laws their finishing touch of irreversibility (960b–968b). The discussion of the Assembly does not contradict what precedes it, but neither does this discussion obviously respond to any of those other concerns. Thus the safest conclusion is that Books 11 and 12 consist of material left over from the *Laws* proper—appendices—and as such they may not deserve to be treated as books at all.

In this chapter it will be maintained that Books 11 and 12 are a vital and necessary part of the development of the *Laws,* and the topics covered in these books are placed here for important reasons, even if they are incompletely edited. I treat the dialogue to be a response to the problem of impiety within a political context, i.e. inevitable forgetfulness of the source of being within the polis, and these books as responses to important unresolved questions from Book

10. They address the impiety within the civic and economic practices on which the city is founded, material conditions without which the city cannot survive. Treated this way, the discussion of the Assembly at the end of the dialogue offers a partial solution to problems of incompletion related to Magnesia's status as a second-best city.

According to references in the extant text, the organizing principle tying together disparate elements of Books 11 and 12 is contracts (συμβόλαια), which is introduced at the outset of Book 11 (913a) and not brought to a conclusion until midway through Book 12 (956b). The Athenian explicitly ties the discussion of contracts to the structural level of the project:[3]

> Once the parts of the whole city have been fully discussed, how many and which ones must come to be, and laws have been said concerning all the greatest contracts to the extent of our ability, the remaining thing would have to be the δίκαι.[4] (956b)

Taken together, these passages suggest that the Athenian Stranger is identifying everything from Book 11 up to the middle of Book 12 as contracts, or agreements. Of course it might be objected that the placement of these passages is contingent.[5] But even if we were to exercise healthy doubt as to the placement and, therefore, centrality of the theme of contracts, the Athenian makes it clear that he intends to partner contracts with the discussion of the δίκαι, and these paired topics are to be coordinate with the dialogue's other governing divisions.[6] I take the return to the δίκαι mentioned here in conjunction with the conclusion of the section on contracts to fulfill the promise made in Book 6 for "a precise division of the δίκαι and composition of the laws would most correctly occur at length toward the end of the lawgiving (νομοθεσία)" (768c). Although pursued only briefly in Book 12, I take the discussion of contracts to be coordinate with the δίκαι that follows and therefore to be central to the structure of the whole dialogue.[7]

From the other direction, the discussion of contracts is central to the whole as part of the more complex and far-reaching theme of impiety. Book 10 begins by looking back over what has been accomplished in Book 9 and ahead toward material in Books 11 and 12:

> After acts of outrage let some one legal custom of the following kind be stated for all acts of violence: that no one carry off or lead away any of the things that belong to other people, nor to use one of his neighbor's things, if he does not persuade the owner, for *on such a [cause] indeed have depended, do depend, and will depend all the bad things discussed*. The great-

est of the remaining things are the unrestrained and unprovoked acts of violence of the young, which are greatest of all when [these acts] occur against the sacred things, and especially great whenever they take place against the things belonging to the city and its people as a whole and hallowed things, or the things shared in parts [of the city], either one of the tribes or some other such share-group. Second and secondly is whenever someone commits violence against the private shrines and tombs, and [whenever] someone does violence against parents, third, with the exception of those spoken of earlier. A fourth kind of outrage is whenever someone being heedless of authorities leads or carries away or uses something of theirs without persuading them. And fifth would be the civic [status] of each of the citizens being violated, demanding judicial penalty (δίκη). (*Laws* 10, 884a–885a, emphasis added)

In Book 10 the Athenian is concerned with impiety explicitly directed toward the gods, and in Book 11 he is concerned with the material and institutional foundations upon which daily life depends and on which foundation all identity rests, including individual, group, family, and city identity. Thus from textual references to the δίκαι that are to follow contracts and the preceding discussion of impiety it is *prima facie* apparent that a discussion of contracts should fall where it does in Books 11 and 12 and that this discussion is intended to have significant structural importance.

In what follows I first show that the subject of contracts is substantively related to the other more obviously philosophical concerns that frame it, and that in particular "contracts" refers to a type of impiety rooted in the material institutions of the city, especially property. The structural impiety rooted in practices of exchange and material conditions arise within the broader context of bringing the lawgiving to an end, so we will be particularly interested in understanding the specific type of closure the Athenian gives to the lawgiving and how the end of the lawgiving relates to the city's constitutive incompleteness.

Contracts

Overarching themes of incompleteness and reversibility integrate the diverse topics the Athenian discusses in Books 11 and 12 and tie them into the dialogue's larger structural concern with impiety. Key to these connections is the capacity of reversibility contained in the city's material foundations, which pointedly contrasts with the power of irreversibility embodied by the Assembly. As we will soon see, the destabilizing and uprooting power of reversibility is essential to the material foundation of the city, e.g., contracts, retail trade, and money, but this selfsame power is simultaneously a valuable resource for the city's virtue and health.

According to the Athenian, there are two importantly contrasting types of end. On the one hand there is the natural end of a human life (958c–d); on the other there is an end that preserves, specifically an end that will preserve the political entity to which human beings have given rise (960b). After the execution of verdicts, the Athenian turns to discuss the end of a human life:

> Next after this, for a man having been born and raised and having borne and raised children, and having engaged with measure in contracts, and paying penalty if he wronged someone and receiving payment from another, growing old with the laws, as is the share (μοῖρα) of people, there would come an end according to nature (τελευτὴ γίγνοιτ᾿ ἂν κατὰ φύσιν). (958c–d)

This leads into a discussion of funerals: location of the graves, size of the burial mounds, size of the grave-marking stone, procedure for carrying out the funeral, the appropriate beliefs regarding the soul and the body, and the laws governing funerary rites, violations of which are judged by the Guardians of the Laws and punished by all. The Athenian concludes those passages by saying:

> But in each instance an end (τέλος) is not quite the doing (δρᾶσαί) nor the acquiring (κτήσασθαι) nor the founding (κατοικίσαι); having discovered the ever-perfect preservation for what has been generated, now then [it is right] to think that all that needs to be accomplished has been accomplished, but before that [it is right] to think the whole is incomplete (ἀτελές). (960b–c)

The complicated relation between the incompleteness of the city and its perfection is especially important to see here. The Athenian introduces the idea of completeness with reference to "the designations (πρόσρημα) given to the Fates" (960c),[8] prefacing his comments by invoking the names of Lachesis, Clotho, and Atropos, and announcing that he and his companions have yet to "naturally implant" (ἐγγίγνεσθαι κατὰ φύσιν) the "power of irreversibility" (τὴν ἀμετάστροφον . . . δύναμιν) in the laws. It is in clarifying and drawing out the philosophical implications of the "perfect and permanent safeguard for what has been begotten" that a discussion of property becomes not only instructive, but indispensible.

In light of the attempt to bring the lawgiving to a proper end by implanting within the laws a power of irreversibility, it is telling that property represents a constant threat of reversibility. Let us recall that property first emerges in Book 10 as a root cause of violence in the city. The same theme is repeated in Book 11, which begins:

> To the extent possible one should not touch my things, nor in turn move them not even the shortest distance without persuading me at all at any time: according to the same [reasons] I should do (δρᾶν) the same concerning the things of others, having a sound mind (νοῦν ἔχων ἔμφρονα). (913a)

The severity of the problem posed by theft relates directly to the schism between the imagined best city and the city rooted in material foundations. In the best city there is no gap between property and identity, the soul animates everything on which it depends and incorporates it seamlessly into its identity. By contrast, in the second-best city the material foundations in which identity is vested and nourished are detachable appendages.[9] The Athenian addresses the specific case in which a treasure (θησαυρός) is set in store for a people but discovered by someone not related by descent to the one who originally set down the treasure. The Athenian provides manifold support through sayings, myths, and direct praise for divine ordinance he says was originally set down by a sort of founding father: "what you didn't set down (κατατίθημι), don't take up (ἀναιρέω)."[10] The Athenian asks us to let unattended property appear as presided over by gods, even in the absence of the owner to whom the property rightly belongs. The Athenian proposes the following:

> If someone leaves behind one of his things somewhere, whether willingly or unwillingly, let the one who happens across let it lie, considering that the δαίμονα guards these sorts of things [which have been] made sacred to the goddess by the law. (914b)

The sheer emphasis the Athenian places on protecting the bond between groups and their material foundations draws attention to the reversibility of the relationship the city has to its material foundations. In his remarks the Athenian asks us to believe that things are presided over by δαίμονα, but he makes no attempt to deny that property appears simply as present, uninflected by its past and uncommitted to the future. This is just how property appears: as something to be taken up and disposed of as anyone sees fit. The Athenian insists that we subordinate the appearance of orphan property to the appearance of belonging-to or being-invested-with communal identity, laden with a past, a context, and a meaning that has already in a sense been laid down for it. When we see property, the lawgiver wants us to see the person, the family, the posterity, and ultimately the gods to which it belongs and of which it speaks. But this insistence cannot correct the fact of property—that it presents itself without parentage, without connection to person or community, and it addresses any passerby as a person in general.

The orphan appearance of property points to a more serious problem. Property never really takes us on as the particular persons we are, i.e. with our own particular past and future, and that of our family, community, history, gods. Just as much as I can take over property from someone else in general, as an orphan, so too can property be taken from me. In relation to this kind of property, I never become more than a person in general. In simply appearing fungible, transferable, belonging to anyone in general, property constitutes us as abstract persons. Property is a tacit incitement to forget the sources of being.

A person free to take up any identity, not only the one she has set down or that has been set down for her, has adopted the abstract relation to place and time that is the root of impiety. The Athenian has made every possible effort to combat this abstract identity in the citizens by situating the city in the most appropriate type of terrain, dividing its places, apportioning the times of the year according to specific purposes, and rigidly prescribing individual identities.[11] In light of this extraordinary attempt to solidify the relationship of the city to its places and times, the abstract and reversible character of property poses a tacitly corrosive incitement that should be read as an institutionalized form of impiety. Living in the best city would demand one to automatically and unproblematically see property as being sourced in an individual, group, or family, which belongs primarily to the city, to ancestors, and ultimately to the gods. Living in the second-best city demands that we live "as if" this were the case, even though appearances infallibly suggest otherwise. These points regarding the threat of reversibility rooted in the simple presence and therefore transferability of property are borne out in the discussions of money and retail trade.

The Athenian's instructions to the lawgiver and the Guardians of the Laws regarding money and retail trade (918b–920b) confirm the view that the power of property is both a resource and a threat. The power of money, according to the Athenian, is to render "even and symmetrical property consisting of any sort of thing that is asymmetrical and uneven" (918b). Money is the tool used by the merchant, the hireling, the innkeeper, etc., "fully to provide for all [human beings] resource for needs and evenness in properties" (918c). Unfortunately these practices contain an implicit promise of gain, which solicits a desire for unlimited increase (918d). The best human beings are able to remain unmoved by the solicitations of abstract and reversible wealth. If the best individuals were to become innkeepers and retail traders, the reciprocal gift-giving relationship between guest and host would be maintained. The average person however does not offer the gift of hospitality but holds their guests prisoner and charges them a ransom (919a). Three laws are written to protect the city against the corrosive promise of wealth and threat of poverty implicit within retail trade: (1) no one of the 5,040 hearths is ever to become a retail trader, wholesale trader, or render service to private persons who do not *"return an equal service"* (except to family members). The point here is that no service is to be exchanged for money (919d–e).[12] (2) Those who do engage in retail trade must be resident aliens or strangers (920a), presumably because these people are already uprooted from the land and the past. Most importantly for my purposes, (3) the Guardians of the Laws are to understand themselves to be guards not only of those whom they can easily guard against becoming outlaws, having been well educated and nurtured, but all the more "the ones not of that sort pursuing pursuits that have some strong impulse toward encouraging those who pursue them to turn out bad" (920b). The Athenian explicitly acknowledges that certain practices prompt human beings to become bad. The promptings of the retail trade and similar promptings implicit in the nature of property all point to institutionalized impiety woven into the material foundations of the city, which cannot be eliminated but which also have been given no strong positive reason for being preserved.

The corrosive effect of money is found in its power to detach a thing or a service from the person, the family, the land, and past from which that thing or service emerges. It is on this basis that money allows for the even distribution of goods and services, by providing an abstract basis for exchange and distribution. It is possible to live with abstract exchange and property without becoming corrupt, and as we see the laws against retail trade are only properly directed at the average citizen, for whom this trade is prohibited.[13] To be required to uphold the best city through the strength of imagination, or by actively ignoring real possibilities etched in one's surroundings, is just what it means to live in the second-best city.[14] However, and this is the important qualification that allows us to understand the Athenian's political philosophy, the destructive possibilities continuously enjoined by property, money, and retail trade, are also resources for virtue and the transformation from habit to understanding, as the institution of the Assembly will soon show.

Before turning to the Assembly, however, it should be clarified what relation the material foundations of the city have to the other sources of impiety explicitly identified in the text, which include human nature, the terrain, custom, poor birth, and bad upbringing. Each of these is given as a reason to explain the human tendency to take up property, money, and retail trade in a way that is destructive to the community. I want to turn our attention to places in the *Laws* in which the other sources of impiety are identified in order to argue that, far from superseding the sources of institutional impiety, these contending explanatory principles all presuppose and confirm the problem of material foundations. Once we see how central this problem is to the constitution of the city, we will be in a position to appreciate fully the implications of the point that the dangers posed are simultaneously a resource for virtue.

The impious view that body is older than soul hinges on the assumption that particular experiences, pleasures, meanings, and possessions are the most basic stuff of which happiness consists. In Book 10, impiety is described as the view that the material foundations of things are the origin and ongoing source for the life of the soul. In the text of the *Laws* more broadly there are at least three other causes cited as explanations for the perversion of the relationship between soul and body: (1) the nature of human beings, (2) human history, and (3) human education/culture (including the terrain in which the polis is situated and the tacit educational effects this terrain has on the virtue of citizens).[15] Book 9 is especially helpful for identifying the various causes of impiety; it names history, culture, and nature in particular. However, these texts do not all carry the same explanatory power, and some specifically seem intended to cure a problem rather than explain it.

According to 854a–b of Book 9, human history is cited as the cause of impiety. In this passage the Athenian suggests that the ἱερόσυλος (sacrilegious person) be told by the laws that there is an "evil that moves you, urging you to go toward sacrilege," and that this evil has neither a human nor divine origin but is "some goad engendered in human beings from ancient and unpurified injustices (παλαιῶν καὶ ἀκαθάρτων)" (854b). Given that this passage occurs within a prelude meant to invoke the proper orientation in the citizen, and given that it is offered as something to tell the sacrilegious person, it seems that the gadfly of natural injustice stemming from ancient unpurified injustices is meant as a curative directed at a soul with a very specific illness. It is unclear that the Athenian wishes or needs to inform the citizens of the cause of their impiety except for the sake of correcting certain damaging views.

Later, roughly halfway through Book 9, in the midst of describing the penalties for murder and considering the conditions of the soul that mitigate or exacerbate the severity of a crime, the Athenian says, "money has the power to engender tens of thousands of erotic desires for its insatiable and limitless acquisition" (870a). This claim points to money itself as an institutional cause of a certain kind of impiety, but the hold money has on the soul is attributed to impiety stemming from "nature" (φύσις) and a "lack of education" (ἀπαιδευσία). The "lack of education" is in turn attributed to the rumor (φῆμις) spread around by Greeks and Barbarians that celebrates wealth as if it were an independent value (870b). Thus the governing causes seem to be in a general sense nature and culture rather than the institutions of money and property.[16] This reading is reinforced when we consider the remedy proposed for this impiety: the noblest and best thing the Athenian says is to tell the truth about wealth. The truth told is that "[wealth] is for the sake of the body," and "the body is for the sake of the soul," and the happy desire is to be wealthy justly and moderately (870c). Thus it seems it is not wealth that corrupts the soul but the cultural understanding of wealth more broadly that gives wealth its power to corrupt.

Expanding on this theme, the perversion of the relationship between soul and body is attributed at the end of Book 9 not to human cultural attitudes toward wealth but to mortal nature itself. There the Athenian is describing someone who is good in soul but who rules autocratically, i.e. without being audited.[17] The point made there is that even someone with virtuous attitudes and convictions can be corrupted because, it seems, there is an aspect of mortal nature that remains uneducated by virtue. The Athenian says the cause of the virtuous person's corruption is mortal nature, which (1) *always* strives to get more than its fair share, and (2) *naturally* prefers the private before the common (875b). This discussion feeds into the consideration of the acts of outrage against elders with which Book 10 begins.

All of these claims strongly suggest that property may serve as the occasion for impiety, but that culture, and mortal nature itself, are the more fundamental causes of ruin in the soul. In what follows, I argue that it is not human nature per se that the Athenian has in mind but a certain unavoidable and healthy stage of human education, brought to the fore in Book 10, in which one must presuppose an indeterminate relationship to place and time and open oneself to the rudderless abstraction implicit in life's material foundations. This posture of the soul has the potential to be crippling to virtue, but it equally has the potential to be taken up as a resource.

The impiety of the young in Book 10 is attributed more than anything to a refusal of inherited or received authority. Specifically, the cause of impiety is tied to the young who, for reasons relating to youth, take special interest in challenging the existence of gods. The Athenian tells Cleinias that the source of the problem is "some very serious ignorance (ἀμαθία τις μάλα χαλεπή), appearing to be great wisdom" (886b). This very serious ignorance is in part attributed to ancient written accounts that describe the genesis of heaven, the gods, and their mingling (886c); the Athenian claims these accounts are destructive of the "services and honors" (θεραπείας καὶ τιμάς) toward parents (886d). It is also attributed to the impiety of the new and wise men who claim that the heavenly bodies are earth and stones, unthinking, and that in spite of being raised properly, these people still say "that [of] all matters that are becoming, having become, and being about to become, some [are] by nature, some by artifice, and some through chance" (888e), and that "the right thing is whatever someone wins using force" (890a). The Athenian boils down this latter source of impiety to a certain mistaken use of *logos*: "the one saying these things is likely to consider fire and water and earth and air to be first of all things" and believe they are oldest (891c). These four are named "nature," and soul emerges or is generated from them. The Athenian responds to these two types of serious ignorance with arguments (1) for the existence of the gods, (2) that the gods care about human affairs, and (3) that the gods are impassive; these arguments span the text from 891e to 907b.[18] The problem with these young people and their insolence is, in a word, that they do not understand that soul is prior to body.

Looking over the various ways in which the sources of impiety have been articulated in Books 9 and 10, from the introduction of the δίκαι in Book 9 to the arguments for the impassivity of the gods in Book 10, the Athenian's frustration with impiety exposes an absurd parallel, almost identity, between nature and virtue. The Athenian becomes exasperated by being forced to address the problem of injustice at all. In Book 9 the Athenian says it is in a certain way shameful to assume that in a city such as theirs, best equipped for the practice of virtue, someone will grow up who shares in the evils of other places. He says it shameful even to anticipate and protect against wickedness, as if it were inevitably part of the polis. The Athenian is forced to acknowledge that he and his fellow citizens are not gods legislating for gods, as much as he might wish this were the case, and he thinks he knows what that would mean. We are, he says, the children of men legislating for the seeds men, and there is no blame in anticipating the "seed that cannot be cooked" (853b–d). But there is an absurd assumption at play here: that the process of becoming virtuous is analogous to boiling seeds, and that a person would naturally become virtuous once exposed for sufficient time to the appropriate influences. Even in the best possible human world it will always be necessary to make room for freedom, i.e. to make room for the young to break with the principles in which the city is rooted in order that the city may be renewed as a place for the divine in nature. From this point of view it is absolutely inevitable that there will be problems with impiety and impious attitudes in the city, for impiety is a necessary aspect of the city's process of regenerating itself. The city re-emerges with each generation affirming the possibility that things could be radically otherwise.

At a certain inevitable stage of educational development one adopts the stance of a person in general, breaking with the familiar, in order to begin to see for oneself and to establish oneself as one's own. This is the wellspring from which philosophy flows. The impious view that soul is younger than body is implied by this period of adolescence, which has its constant and abiding institutional correlative in money and property. Money and property should not be thought of only as the unfortunate occasions for impiety but as the supporting and necessary constituent parts of the environment in which the person in general, i.e. the citizen, can emerge and hold herself in tension with the given context of her emergence.

With property we are dealing with aspects of the city that remain steadfastly "outside the law," constantly undermining and challenging the efficacy the law, and yet it is an aspect of the city that is inexorably part of everyday life. Books 11 and 12 offer sustained reflections on structural and institutional insolence that are irreducible and necessary to the birth of virtue in the city. Customary, daily, and necessary practices contain a degree of institutional impiety that is simply necessary not just for the bodily functioning of the polis but for its health as a distinctively human city. It seems that the *Laws* directs the lawgiver neither to expel nor to purify the practices that stand outside the law but to accommodate them and manage them, so that they may be used as resources to the extent possible. This is the nature of the ending that will serve as "the perfect and permanent safeguard of what has been begotten," that the laws be able to accommodate and even draw on their own undoing. This work of accommodation is the explicit purpose of the Assembly, and the discussion of the Assembly occurs at the end of the *Laws* after the Athenian has been able to clarify the ambiguous power of the city's material foundations.

The Assembly [958d–968b]

Turning now to the end of the *Laws* in Book 12, we will examine the way in which the Assembly (σύλλογος) instituted there responds to the problem of completion. The value of this final section will be to demonstrate that the Assembly has the primary function of transforming an unavoidable weakness of the city into a resource for education in virtue.

The various types of ending that introduce the Assembly in Book 12 constructively recall discussions of reaching completion from earlier in the *Laws*, specifically the analogies to works of art, e.g. the Book 6, 769–772d discussion of the Guardians. There the Athenian refers to painters who keep touching things up and never reach an end (οὐδὲν πέρας ἔχειν). He draws analogy to someone who gets it in his mind to paint something as beautiful as possible and requires of his work "that this never get worse but always better" (τε ὡς κάλλιστον ζῷον καὶ τοῦτ᾽ αὖ μηδέποτε ἐπὶ φαυλότερον ἀλλ᾽ ἐπὶ τὸ βέλτιον) (769c). This painter, being mortal, would leave someone behind to constantly touch up and improve the painting, guarding the figure against time.[19] Similarly, the lawgiver will want to write the laws with complete precision (πρὸς τὴν ἀκρίβειαν κατὰ δύναμιν ἱκανῶς), but like the painter will discover "very many necessarily left incomplete" (πάμπολλα ἀνάγκη παραλείπεσθαι) (769d). The work of lawgiving is thus never finished. The noticeable point is that a proper ending will entail coming to terms with a constitutive incapacity to reach an end. The work of establishing the laws will therefore be ongoing, and this work will be done by the Assembly outlined precisely in its composition and purpose in the final ten pages of the dialogue.[20]

Our study of the Assembly begins with the three different modes of engaging the laws. The first mode of engagement with the laws comes up in the ordinances governing Travel Abroad [949e–953e], where travel is regulated in service of receiving and defending the laws through understanding rather than habit. The second mode of engagement is discussed under ordinances governing the process of becoming a judge [956b–958d]. And the third is the description of the Assembly itself [958d–968b]. This comparison will help us to see more precisely what is at stake in the work of the Assembly.

The laws governing "Travel Abroad" (949e–953e) are partially for the sake of confirming the correctness of the laws as established and partially for testing and strengthening the truth of these laws. The first type of observation mission will be sent abroad because Magnesia must mix with other cities in order to have a good reputation and to be looked upon by "the Sun and the other gods" as having good laws (950d); these missions are called "political trips." The observers must not be younger than forty, and they must not travel in private capacity. Upon return, they are tasked with teaching the young that the legal customs pertaining to other regimes are inferior. The higher level observation mission consists of members no less than fifty years old, no more than sixty, who spend as many as ten years (as they choose) abroad under the aegis of the Guardians of the Laws (νομοφύλακα), and they must report to the Guardians when they return. These missions (1) observe the legal customs among the rest of humanity, and (2) seek out divine human beings with whom it is altogether worthwhile to keep company (συγγίγνεσθαι), and who will (3) explain "some utterance" concerning the laying down of laws (θέσεως νόμων), or education (παιδεία), or upbringing (τροφή) (952b).

On the surface of things, it is not clear at first why Magnesia engages the outside world at all. These two modes of engagement only expose the city to the corruption and sickness of innovation (949e), where innovation is the very thing the Nocturnal Council (6.758a) protects against. As we look a little further, however, it becomes clear that Magnesia does stand under compulsion to own itself and its customs, which means to possess itself in some way superior to mere momentum of habit. At 951b the Athenian says that laws governing the sending and receiving of strangers do honor to Zeus (953e) by bringing the city into contact with others and preventing the city from becoming isolated. An isolated city could not be "tame" (ἥμερος) and "perfect" (τέλειος), he says, because it would be "unsociable" (ἀνομίλητος). A city would not be able to defend laws if it had accepted these laws merely out of habit (951b) and not knowledge (γνώμη). The ability to defend its laws well is the condition for entering into friendship and doing honor to Zeus, the god of friendship.

The value of observation missions, then, is to help the city transform its laws from habit into knowledge. The mechanism by which this happens is that the members of the observation missions must take on and endure the reversibility of their inherited practices by exposing themselves (and their souls) to the danger and sickness of detachment from inherited customs. The observers become uprooted, like ships at sea, and to an extent they allow themselves to become detached from the city's inherited ways. The law students play host to the powers of reversibility, corruption, and innovation, but do not become sick, or at least not crippled in the process. To the contrary, they become more intelligent and more virtuous. From this point of view, the concrete work of the ambassadors who travel abroad might not involve changing much, just details of the laws, but they would do so having plumbed the depths of the laws and exposed them to the light of critical scrutiny.

The openness to the contingency and reversibility of inherited practices that one sees in the observation missions sent abroad is also an important resource in the process of becoming a judge (956b–958d). The Athenian says that of all the studies, the study of established laws is the most powerful way to make oneself "better" (βελτίω) (if the laws are "correctly established"), which the Athenian says confirms the truth of the etymological connection between the name for intelligence (νόος) and the name for "our divine and wondrous law" (θεῖος ἡμῖν καὶ θαυμαστὸς νόμος). The education of a judge consists in the study of the "written things" (γράμματα) broadly construed concerning what is just, noble, and good. The juror (δικαστής)[21] in training must use the writings of the law-giver as an internalized (κεκτημένον ἐν αὑτῷ) "antidote" (ἀλεξιφάρμακον)

> ... to guide himself and the city: providing for the good rooting and growth of the just, and for the bad a change as great as possible from ignorance and unrestraint and cowardice and altogether from every injustice, for all the wicked whose opinions are curable. (957d957e)

Unlike the observation mission, the judge's "antidote" seems to ward off anything that disagrees with the writings of the lawgiver. The practice of executing those with fixed opinion—as a method of "curing" them—suggests that the judge perpetuates the law by enforcing its commands. This would also imply that "intelligence" (νόος) is *not* a matter of interpreting or understanding the law but enforcing it correctly.[22]

As stipulated in Book 6 (766d), however, judges are required to go beyond what is said on either side of a dispute. In order to render judgment it is necessary to go *further* than the testimony of contending parties. In order to be a judge, one would have to be able to go beyond the writings of the written law to interpret what more it says, and precisely this is meant by "intelligence." The discussion of "Travel Abroad" (949e) and the process of becoming a judge demonstrate that the city needs citizens who are able to go beyond the law, so as to address the possibility of corruption and perversion that animate the laws at their core. A judge must take on, even internalize, the possibility not that one thing or another will be different in its particular interpretation, but that everything will be turned upside down and seen in a wholly different light. The work of internalizing the powers of corruption, detachment, and innovation, in the city will be performed at the highest level by the Assembly (σύλλογος), which is described by the Athenian as an anchor that will "preserve" (σῴζειν) all things we wish for (βουλόμεθα)" (961c).

The Assembly is the appropriate savior in each of the city's activities, just as in an animal it is the soul and the head, or sight and intelligence, that preserve the animal, and on a ship it is the pilot and the sailors that "nous-about-what mixed with senses would be preservation for ships in storms and in fair weather? On board, don't the pilot and sailors together save themselves and the other things on ship by mixing the senses with piloting-nous?" (961e).[23] According to the text, the Assembly (1) knows the city's goal, (2) knows in what way to attain the goal, and (3) gives advice. Furthermore, it performs these tasks in the face of the natural and necessary innovation. The Athenian says that legal customs wander (πλανᾶσθαι) because different parts of the legislated code address different aims (962d), and the Assembly must be able to re-found the laws in order to preserve the city. The role of intelligence is to guide, and the city is guided by the Assembly.

The final law, according to the Athenian, is whether the Nocturnal Assembly (νυκτερινὸν σύλλογον) is to become guard of the city, for the sake of safekeeping (σωτηρία) (968a–b). Cleinias cannot see this law passed quickly enough, but as eager as the Athenian is to follow suit, there is something standing in the way. Before this law can be established the Assembly must first be enacted in deed. At present, the Athenian can only go so far as to identify the necessary preparations for establishing this body, which include "teaching through prolonged companionship" (διδαχὴ μετὰ συνουσίας πολλῆς).[24] Even going this far poses problems: it is not easy to discover the proper subjects of education, or to find the person who can make this discovery, or indeed to become a student of that person. And then there is the difficulty of determining at what times and for how long a subject should be taken up (968d). The Athenian finally declares the core issue here:

> it is vain to say these matters in writings, for it wouldn't be clear to the learners themselves whether the subject were being learned at the right time, until knowledge of the subject had, doubtless, come into being within the soul of each. (968d–e)

The Athenian clarifies that things are not indescribable secrets, but neither are they capable of being described beforehand. Thus at the end of the laws the subject returns to "education and upbringing," and the Athenian refers for the first time to the "Divine Assembly" (ὁ θεῖος . . . σύλλογος) that is now their hope, and the risk they must undertake to bring their project to completion. The last thing the Athenian says is to extol the "Divine Assembly" to be for its unprecedented "virtue of safekeeping" (ἀρετὴ σωτηρίας) (969c).

Conclusion

The purpose of this essay has been to show that in spite of signs that Books 11 and 12 of the *Laws* are not edited, they are nonetheless unified as an important concluding study of institutional impiety that is an ineradicable material basis of life in the polis and a resource for its flourishing. Human beings are not gods, and they are not quite at home among things, property, money, etc. As such they are to a degree incapable of belonging to the gods or occupying their place and time completely. Placelessness has been in this essay attributed to an inexhaustible power of reversibility in things, but also in customs and the symbols of power, even in language itself, all of which tacitly support the impious view that body is "older than" the soul. Rather than doing away with this outlaw power of reversibility, I have suggested that these are the moments at which the soul gains distance from the received ways of doing things enough to embark on a philosophical project. This distance does not come without its risks, and the subsequent ambiguity entailed is what most of all marks this city as "second best."

The Athenian is only able to take the project at hand as far as the moment of its actual inception, at which point the Assembly would be founded. The end of the *Laws* is therefore not quite the beginning of Magnesia, insofar as the law governing that Assembly must wait for the establishment of that Assembly, which falls outside of their project. The finishing touch of "irreversibility" (Atropos) will be the establishment of an organ that will host the power of reversibility inherent to the material basis of existence, both internally in contracts, retail trade, etc., and externally in its relation to other cultures and norms. It is fitting then that the Assembly must consist of elders and young people rather than philosopher-kings, for a human city must draw on the power of dialogue, especially the dialogue between the old and the young, to preserve its soul.

Notes

1. Interestingly, this is simultaneously a process of arriving at a beginning, for in the process of the investigation the Athenian says that they are not yet lawgivers, but becoming lawgivers, so they are not only arriving at a conclusion but getting closer to the beginning of lawgiving.

2. Mitchell Miller suggests in this volume that *Laws* 11–12 seem unedited up to the introduction of the Nocturnal Council at 960c. I will be maintaining that the incompleteness Miller notices in the *Laws* should not be interpreted to imply that the final books do not serve a particular function of their own within the overall structure of the dialogue.

3. The translations in this chapter are mine, but I have received substantial assistance from Patricia Fagan.

4. Pangle translates δίκαι here as "procedures." There are at least two translations necessary to capture the meaning δίκαι carries in the *Laws*. On the one hand δίκαι can be translated as "penalties" or "a suit," which is the sense of the term adopted in *Laws* 9 when the speakers turn from the laws proper to the penalties enforcing them. But δίκαι can also refer to the "system of courts," which as we shall see is the sense of the term appropriate to the *Laws* 12 turn from contracts to the organization of the judiciary.

5. The sheer diversity of the topics intervening between the beginning of *Laws* 11 and the turn to the δίκαι in *Laws* 12 tends to undermine any single organizing principle. Laws governing abusive speech, slander, oratory (i.e., improper use of language) in Book 11 seem unrelated to laws governing military organization or those governing the city

auditors in *Laws* 12. It is not clear what any of these topics would have to do with laws governing poisoning and violent injury.

6. What I call "contracts" Miller limits to the first of four divisions of Books 11 and 12. In his essay in the present volume, Miller divides these books into the following parts: (1) movable property and commercial transactions, (2) family law, (3) personal injury, (4) agents of the state acting in official capacities. By contrast, I take everything from the beginning of *Laws* 11 (913a) to the middle of *Laws* 12 (956b), almost forty-three Stephanus pages, to be responding to the problem and necessity of contractual relations within the city, followed first by the discussion of the "system of courts" (δίκαι) (956b–960b) and the discussion of the Assembly (σύλλογος) (960b–end).

7. Miller takes the promised return to the δίκαι to occur in the *Laws* 9 discussion of "penalties," following the completed discussion of the offices and the laws. Although I see a few reasons why someone would interpret the text this way, I disagree with Miller on the grounds that the promise in *Laws* 6 is to continue the discussion of the courts of justice (δικαστήρια), which the Athenian characterizes as not quite ruling offices (ἀρχαί) and not completely different from ruling offices, and most importantly as some provisional outline given from outside (οἷον περιγραφή τις ἔξωθεν) that still needs to be filled out. Thus the promised return to the δίκαι cannot concern the circumstances of punishment, as it does in Book 9, but must rather concern "the parts of the entire city" (μέρη . . . τῆς πόλεως συμπάσης) (956b), as it does in *Laws* 12.

8. It seems the Athenian is referring to Hesiod. This reference to the many earlier things that were "sung beautifully" may be a reference (1) back to *Laws* 7, 799b where the sequence of regulations was interrupted by the "strange argument about laws" according to which anyone who fails to sing the songs ordained for each of the gods will be excluded or exiled, and anyone who refuses to abide exile can be charged with impiety by "anyone who wants to bring the charge." There the Fates were mentioned as those gods to whom the citizens sacrifice in common to sanctify the ordained songs. However, there is no mention here either of singing to the Fates or of their designations. It may also refer (2) back to *Laws* 3, 692a when the self-destruction of Argos and Messene is compared to the self-preservation of the Lacedaemonian system. There the Athenian mentions the "three saviors" of the Spartan regime, referring to the splitting of authority that lent that system its measure and cured its fever (692a). But here the Fates are not even mentioned by name. The "many earlier things" that were "sung beautifully" might also refer to (3) the identification of the three Fates in the closing sections of *Republic* 10—Lachesis, Clotho, and Atropos—who sing of what has been, what is, and of what is going to be (*Republic*, 617c). In *Republic* 10, each soul once having chosen its life goes forward in order first to Lachesis (dispenser of lots), who sends each away with the daemon he had chosen to act as a guardian of the life and a fulfiller of the choice; the daemon then leads the soul to Clotho (spinner), where the soul turns the spindle and ratifies the life it had chosen; then after touching her (i.e., Clotho) the daemon leads the soul to the spinning of Atropos (inevitable or unturnable), "making the threads irreversible" (620e). Here there is mention of the singing of the Fates and their designation, but there is no mention of anything being sung by the poet or philosopher. The reference might also be back to (4) Hesiod's *Theogony*, which is explicitly marked out as a song, and a song in which the three Fates are designated; although the only mention made at *Theogony* 905–906 is that Zeus of the Counsels gave the Fates the greatest

honor: "Clotho, Lachesis, Atropos, who release / to moral human beings good and bad (things) to have."

9. As Sara Brill remarks in her essay on *Laws* 10, the unity of the city will in some sense be founded on the institution of property and not, as in at least the case of the Guardians of the *Republic,* on the abolition of this institution. As Brill notes, the preservation of this institution is accompanied by an acknowledgement of the limitations of mortal nature and its distance from the divine, as mentioned in *Laws* 5 (739c–e).

10. Pangle comments that the lawgiver in question seems to be Solon.

11. In terms of the "image of our education and lack of it" in *Republic* 7, it is not possible to be in the cave if it were not for the impious act of Prometheus in which fire was stolen from Zeus and given to human beings. The abstract relationship to place and time is made possible by fire, by technology, and it is the condition for life in the cave.

12. John Sallis has pointed out that the gift exchange, referenced here in passing, seems to become untenable in Magnesia. It seems that the consequence of the laws governing property would be either to mandate gift-giving relationships in which services are traded for services, or to attenuate or even undermine the possibility of gift-giving in Magnesia. The status of the city as "second best" implies that it must withdraw its support for the very practices that would promote virtue and friendship in order to make room for a city that is unable to achieve virtue as a whole.

13. As Patricia Fagan makes clear in her chapter in this volume, the dangers of terrain, especially the sea, are reducible to the dangers posed by contact with other people and the "reversibility" that contact would introduce into the customs and character of Magnesia. Notably, it is not simply the encounter with different customs that would cause the problem but the introduction of money-making. Fagan expands this point with reference to the habits of cowardice and changeability that take root in people who are too dependent upon the sea, as evidenced in the very style in which marines wage war. This problem of instability in customs and character is at a rudimentary level solved by placing Magnesia away from the sea and protecting its citizens from the evils of retail and mercantilism. The lasting solution will involve the sending out of special observers who will be able to internalize and thereby master the forces of corruption, to which we will turn below.

14. As Mitchell Miller points out, the city under discussion in the Laws is "second-best" insofar as it can only imitate, but not achieve, the paradigm example of political life under the rule of Cronus. The cause of this falling short introduced in *Laws* 4 is the "birth, nurture, and education" (740a) of human being, and the proposals for land ownership and private property I have been examining are meant to approximate the divine to the extent possible for the human.

15. This final point regarding the effect of the terrain on the virtue of citizens is clearly elucidated in Patricia Fagan's chapter in this volume.

16. The natural imperfection of human beings is also characterized in *Laws* 5 as an excessive self-love that is a cause of all harms (731e) (also noted by Brill).

17. This echoes a point the Athenian made in *Laws* 4: "So Cronus was aware, just as we recounted, that no human nature is sufficient to human affairs, when managing all human affairs autocratically, without becoming full of arrogant violence and injustice" (713c). Human beings need something external to themselves in order to moderate their

natural tendency toward insolence, injustice, and impiety. Even if they have adequate knowledge as an expert, still they would need the law to prevent them from becoming corrupt. Mitchell Miller in his essay in this volume not only points out the human dependence upon law but also uses this characterization of human nature to clarify the horizons within which the conversation of the *Laws* takes shape. Miller reads the limitation of human nature to be the inescapable (perhaps because uneducable) claim that our own pleasures and pains make on us. Cf. Aristotle, *Politics* 3.1287a, for a discussion of the political climate of distrust in which abstract norms are preferred to individual expertise. Aristotle compares this climate to one in which people would rather use a book to heal themselves than trust a doctor.

18. The most impious of the impious persons is the one who maintains the argument that the gods can be "appeased by the unjust," i.e. turned, reversed willy-nilly. The argument that responds to this impiety is the third, in which the gods are shown to be impassive.

19. This is reminiscent of, but apparently the converse of, the discussion of Egyptian Art in *Laws* 2, 656d–657b: Egyptian Art is praised for introducing no innovations; literally for 10,000 years the paintings were made "in no way" more beautiful or ugly.

20. When the "perfect and permanent safeguard" is introduced, it is referred to as the "[Assembly (σύλλογος)] previously discussed" (961a). The Assembly mentioned here is most likely the Assembly mentioned at *Laws* 12.951d just ten pages earlier in the discussion of the procedures governing travel abroad (949e–954a). That Assembly consists of a mixture of young and elderly men. It meets every day from dawn until the sun has risen (crepuscule). It consists of the priests who have obtained the prizes of excellence, the ten Guardians of the Laws who are eldest at any given time, the new Supervisor of Education and all retired ones, each of whom attends with a young man of thirty or forty, chosen as they please. Its purpose is to re-found the laws of the city, placing the ones nobly laid down on "firmer footing" and correcting others if they are lacking something, for "without this observation and search a city will never remain perfect (τελέως)" (951c). Its purpose is to deal with innovation, deviation from the established norms. The discussion of "Travel Abroad" is situated in "Harms to the City" (and their redress). Because Magnesia does not engage in commerce, it must be prepared to deal with "innovations," which are the greatest of all injuries to cities governed by means of correct laws (949e–950a). There are other "councils" mentioned. In *Laws* 6 there is a council (βουλή) with 360 members consisting of four parts of ninety members elected in a way that strikes a mean between Monarchic and Democratic regimes (756b–757a). There are the few members (βουλευταί) of this council, divided into twelve parts, who will keep watch at night to give or receive information, and to keep guard against innovation (6.758a–d). And the Guardians described at *Laws* 6.769a–e seem to have a similar function to this council in *Laws* 12. At *Laws* 6.764a the same Greek noun is used as in *Laws* 12, but it is used to describe "the common assembly" (κοινὸν σύλλογον). At *Laws* 10.909a, those who are impious because of a lack of intelligence are to be kept in the Moderation Tank for no less than five years and have contact with no citizen except the Nocturnal Assembly (νυκτερινοῦ συλλόγου), who talk to him only for admonishment and salvation of the soul. At *Laws* 10.908a, the second of the city's prisons is to be built at the meeting place of "the assembly of the ones holding nightly assemblies" (τὸν τῶν νύκτωρ συλλεγομένων σύλλογον), and that is the Moderation Tank.

21. If this is an Athenian context, the word has the sense of a "juror" more than a "judge."

22. Continuing the above quote, we can see that the juror's judgment is not directed at the law as much as it is directed at the souls that are subject to the law: "... but to those whose opinions are truly spun out, prescribing death as a remedy to souls so disposed, which justly would be said, these sorts of jurors and leaders would become worthy of the whole city's praise" (957e–958a).

23. In armies it is generals who aim at victory and superiority over enemies; in the art of medicine it is doctors that aim at provision of health for the body.

24. Cf. Socrates' own references to specifically philosophical companionship in *The-aetetus* (150d–e).

Bibliography

Annas, Julia. *Platonic Ethics, Old and New.* Ithaca, NY: Cornell University Press, 1999.

Arends, Frederick. "Why Socrates Came Too Late for Gorgias' Epideixis: Plato's *Gorgias* as Political Philosophy." In *Gorgias—Menon: Selected Papers from the Seventh Symposium Platonicum,* edited by Michael Erler and Luc Brisson. Sankt Augustin: Academia Verlag, 2007.

Bearzot, Cinzia. *Focione tra storia e trasfigurazione ideale.* Milan, 1985.

Benardete, Seth. *Plato's "Laws": The Discovery of Being.* Chicago: University of Chicago Press, 2000a.

———, tr. *Plato's Sophist.* Chicago: University of Chicago Press, 1984a.

———, tr. *Plato's Statesman.* Chicago: University of Chicago Press, 1984b.

———. *Socrates and Plato: the Dialectics of Eros.* (German and English). Munich: Carl Friedrichs von Siemens Stiftung, 2000b.

Bertrand, J. M. "Du nid au pilori. Le clair et l'obscur dans la cité des Magnètes platoniciens." *Ktema* 23 (1998): 423–430.

Bloom, Allan, tr. *The Republic of Plato.* New York: Basic Books, 1968.

Boardman, J. *The Parthenon and its Sculptures.* Austin: University of Texas Press, 1985.

Bobonich, Christopher. "Persuasion, Compulsion and Freedom in Plato's *Laws.*" *Classical Quarterly* 41, no. 2 (1991): 365–388.

———. *Plato's "Laws": A Critical Guide.* Cambridge: Cambridge University Press, 2010.

———. *Plato's Utopia Recast: His Later Ethics and Politics.* Oxford: Clarendon Press, 2002.

———. "Reading the *Laws.*" In *Form and Argument in Late Plato,* edited by Christopher Gill and Mary Margaret McCabe. Oxford: Clarendon Press, 1996.

Boehringer, Sandra. "Comment classer les comportements érotiques? Platon, le sexe et erôs dans le *Banquet* et dans les *Lois.*" *Études Platoniciennes* 4 (2007): 45–67.

Brill, Sara. "Psychology and Legislation in Plato's *Laws*." In *Proceedings of the Boston Colloquium in Ancient Philosophy,* vol. 26, forthcoming.

Brisson, Luc. "Ethics and Politics in Plato's Laws." *Oxford Studies in Ancient Philosophy,* 28 (2005): 93–121.

Brown, Eric. "Justice and Compulsion for Plato's Philosopher-Rulers." *Ancient Philosophy* 20 (2000): 1–17.

Brun, P. "L'Île de Keos et ses cités au IVe s. av. J. C." *Zeitschrift für Papyrologie und Epigraphik* 76 (1989): 121–138.

Burger, Ronna. "The Thumotic and the Erotic Soul." *Interpretation* 32, no. 1 (2004): 57–76.

Burkert, Walter. *Greek Religion.* Translated by John Raffan. Cambridge, MA: Harvard University Press, 1985.

Bury, R. G., tr. *Plato: Laws with an English Translation.* Edited by T. E. Page, et al. Cambridge, MA: Harvard University Press, 1926.

Calame, Claude. *Choruses of Young Women in Ancient Greece: Their Morphology, Religious Role and Social Functions.* Translated by Dereck Collins and Janice Orlon. Lanham, MD: Rowman & Littlefield, 2001.

——. *Les choeurs de jeunes filles en Grèce archaïque.* 2 vols. Rome: Edizioni dell' Ateneo e Bizzarri, 1977.

Cargill, J. *The Second Athenian League: Empire or Free Alliance.* Berkeley: University of California Press, 1981.

Carone, Gabriela. "Theology and Evil in *Laws* 10." *Review of Metaphysics* 48 (December 1994): 275–298.

Clay, Diskin. *Platonic Questions: Dialogues with the Silent Philosopher.* University Park: Pennsylvania State University Press, 2000.

——. "Plato's Magnesia." In *Nomodeiktes: Greek Studies in Honor of Martin Ostwald,* edited by Ralph M. Rosen and Joseph Farrell, 435–445. Ann Arbor: University of Michigan Press, 1993.

Cohen, David. "Law, Autonomy and Political Community in Plato's *Laws*." *Classical Philology* 88, no. 4 (1993): 301–317.

Cook, Erwin F. *The Odyssey at Athens: Myths of Cultural Origins.* Ithaca, NY: Cornell University Press, 1995.

Cooper, John M., ed. *Plato: Complete Works.* Indianapolis: Hackett, 1997.

Cooper, Laurence. *Eros in Plato, Rousseau, and Nietzsche: The Politics of Infinity.* University Park: Pennsylvania State University Press, 2008.

Davies, J. K. *Athenian Propertied Families, 600–300 B.C.* Oxford: Clarendon Press,1971.

Denniston, J. D. *The Greek Particles.* Indianapolis: Hackett, 1996.

Despland, Michel. *The Education of Desire: Plato and the Philosophy of Religion.* Toronto: University of Toronto Press, 1985.

Detienne, Marcel. *Dionysus at Large.* Translated by A. Goldhammer. Cambridge, MA: Harvard University Press, 1989.

Dewey, John. *Democracy and Education*. New York: Free Press, 1944.

———. *Experience and Education*. New York: Touchstone, 1997.

Dorter, Kenneth. *Form and Good in Plato's Eleatic Dialogues*. Berkeley: University of California Press, 1994.

Dover, K. J. *Greek Homosexuality*. Cambridge, MA: Harvard University Press, 1989.

Duke, E. A., W. F. Hicken, W. S. M. Nicoll, D. B. Robinson, and J. C. G. Strachan, eds. *Platonis Opera*. Oxford: Clarendon Press, 1995.

Dusanic, Slobodan. "Les Lois et les programmes athéniens de réform constitutionelle au mileu du IVe siècle." *Revue Française d'Histoire des Idées Politiques* 16 (2002): 341–350.

England, E. B. *The Laws of Plato*. 2 vols. Manchester: Manchester University Press, 1921.

Follon, Jacques. "Note sur l'idée d'amitié dans les *Lois*." In *Plato's Laws: From Theory into Practice, Proceedings of the VI Symposium Platonicum Selected Papers*, edited by Samuel Scolnicov and Luc Brisson. Sankt Augustin: Academia Verlag, 2003.

Gaca, K. *The Making of Fornication: Eros, Ethics, and Political Reform in Greek Philosophy and Early Christianity*. Berkeley: University of California Press, 2003.

Garlan, Y. "La defense du territoire a l'époque classique." In *Problèmes de la terre en Grèce ancienne*, edited by M. I. Finley, 149–160. Paris, 1973.

———. *Recherches de poliorcètique grecque*, 66–82. Paris: Bibliothèque des écoles francaises d'Athènes et de Rome, fasc. 223, 1974.

Gernet, Louis. *Platon: Lois, livre IX, traduction et commentaire*. Paris: Ernest Leroux, 1917.

Gerson, Lloyd. "*Akrasia* and the Divided Soul in Plato's *Laws*." In *Plato's Laws: From Theory into Practice, Proceedings of the VI Symposium Platonicum Selected Papers*, edited by Samuel Scolnicov and Luc Brisson, 149–154. Sankt Augustin: Academia Verlag, 2003.

Görgemanns, H. *Beiträge zur Interpretation von Platons Nomoi*. Munich: Zetemata, 1960.

Harding, P. *Translated Documents of Greece & Rome*. Vol. 2, *From the End of the Peloponnesian War to the Battle of Ipsus*. Cambridge: Cambridge University Press, 1985.

Herington, Jon. *Poetry into Drama: Early Tragedy and the Greek Poetic Tradition*. Berkeley: University of California Press, 1985.

Howland, Jacob. "Re-reading Plato: The Problem of Platonic Chronology." *Phaenix* 45 (1991): 189–214.

Jones, Nicholas F. "The Organization of the Kretan City in Plato's Laws." *CW* 83 (1990): 473–492.

Kahn, Charles. *Pythagoras and the Pythagoreans*. Indianapolis: Hackett, 2001.

———. "From Republic to Laws." *Oxford Studies in Ancient Philosophy* 26 (2004): 337–362.

Klosko, George. *The Development of Plato's Political Theory*. Oxford: Oxford University Press, 1986.

Krämer, H. J. *Plato and the Foundations of Metaphysics*. Translated by John Catan. Albany: State University of New York Press, 1990.

Laks, André. "In what sense is the city of the *Laws* a second best one?" In *Plato's Laws and Its Historical Significance: Selected Papers of the I International Congress on Ancient Thought, Salamanca 1998*, edited by Francisco Lisi, 107–114. Sankt Augustin: Academia Verlag, 2001.

———. "The *Laws*." In *The Cambridge History of Greek and Roman Political Thought*, edited by C. Rowe and M. Schofield. Cambridge: Cambridge University Press, 2000.

———. "Legislation and Demiurgy: On the Relationship Between Plato's 'Republic' and 'Laws'." *Classical Antiquity* 9 (1990): 209–229.

Lee, E. N. "Circular Movement as the Model of Mind (*Nous*) in the Later Plato." In *Facets of Plato's Philosophy*, edited by W. H. Werkmeister, 70–102. Amsterdam: Van Gorcum, 1976.

Liddell, Henry George, Robert Scott, and Sir Henry Stuart Jones. *A Greek-English Lexicon*. Oxford: Clarendon Press, 1940.

Lisi, Francisco Leonardo, ed. *Plato's Laws and Its Historical Significance. Selected Papers of the International Congress on Ancient Thought*. Salamanca: Akademia, 2001.

Mayhew, Robert, ed. *Plato: Laws 10*. Oxford: Oxford University Press, 2008.

Menn, S. "On Plato's ΠΟΛΙΤΕΙΑ." In *Boston Area Colloquial in Ancient Philosophy*, edited by J. J. Cleary and G. M. Gurtler, 21, 1–55. 2005.

Miller, Mitchell. "Beginning the 'Longer Way'." In *The Cambridge Companion to Plato's* Republic, edited by G. R. F. Ferrari, 310–344. Cambridge: Cambridge University Press, 2007.

———. "Figure, Ratio, Form: Plato's Five Mathematical Studies." In *Recognition, Remembrance and Reality: New Essays on Plato's Epistemology and Metaphysics*, edited by Mark McPherran, 73–88. (=*Apeiron* 32 no. 4 [Dec. 1999]).

———. "A More 'Exact Grasp' of the Soul? Tripartition in *Republic* IV and Dialectic in the *Philebus*." In *Truth*, edited by Kurt Pritzl. Washington: Catholic University of America Press, 2010.

———. *The Philosopher in Plato's* Statesman, including "Dialectical Education and Unwritten Teachings in Plato's *Statesman*." Las Vegas: Parmenides Publishing, 2004.

———. "The *Timaeus* and the 'Longer Way': Godly Method and the Constitution of Elements and Animals." In *Plato's* Timaeus *as Cultural Icon*, edited by Gretchen Reydams-Schils, 17–59. Notre Dame: University of Notre Dame Press, 2003.

———. "'Unwritten Teachings' in the *Parmenides*." *Review of Metaphysics* 48, no. 3 (March 1995): 591–633.

Monoson, Sara. *Plato's Democratic Entanglements.* Princeton, NJ: Princeton University Press, 2000.

Morrow, Glenn. *Plato's Cretan City: A Historical Interpretation of the* Laws. Princeton, NJ: Princeton University Press, 1960.

Munn, M. "Agesilaus' Boiotian Campaigns and the Theban Stockade of 378–377 B.C." *Classical Antiquity* 18 (1987): 106–138.

———. *The Defense of Attica: The Dema Wall and the Boiotian War of 378–375 BC.* Berkeley: University of California Press, 1993.

———. "The Nike Balustrade and the Erotic Attraction of Victory," presented at the Archaeological Institute of America Annual Meeting, Philadelphia, January 8–11, 2009.

———. *The School of History: Athens in the Age of Socrates.* Berkeley: University of California Press, 2000.

Nagy, Gregory. *Pindar's Homer: The Lyric Possession of an Epic Past.* Baltimore: Johns Hopkins University Press, 1994.

Nails, Debra and Holger Thesleff. "Early Academic Editing: Plato's *Laws.*" In *Plato's* Laws: *From Theory into Practice, Proceedings of the VI Symposium Platonicum Selected Papers,* edited by Samuel Scolnicov and Luc Brisson. Sankt Augustin: Academia Verlag, 2003.

Newell, Waller R. *Ruling Passion: The Erotics of Statecraft in Platonic Political Philosophy.* Lanham, MD: Rowman & Littlefield, 2000.

Nightingale, Andrea. "Plato's Lawcode in Context: Rule by Written Law in Athens and Magnesia." *Classical Quarterly* 49, no. 1 (1999): 100–122.

———. "Writing/Reading a Sacred Text: A Literary Interpretation of Plato's *Laws.*" *Classical Philology* 88, no. 4 (1993): 279–300.

Nikulin, Dmitri, ed. *Plato's Inner-Academic Teachings.* Albany: State University of New York Press, forthcoming.

Ober, J. *Fortress Attica: Defense of the Athenian Land Frontier, 404–322 B.C.* Leiden: Mnemosyne supplement 84, 1985.

O'Brien, Michael. "Plato and 'Good Conscience': Laws 863e5–864b7." *Transactions of the American Philological Association* 88 (1957): 81–87.

Ostwald, Martin. *Nomos and the Beginnings of the Athenian Democracy.* Oxford: Oxford University Press, 1969.

Palagia, O. *The Pediments of the Parthenon.* Vol. 7, *Monumenta Graeca et Romana.* Leiden: Monumenta Graeca et Romana, 1993.

Pangle, Thomas L. "The Political Psychology of Religion in Plato's *Laws.*" *The American Political Science Review* 70, no. 4 (1976): 1059–1077.

———, tr. *The Laws of Plato.* New York: Basic Books, 1980.

Parry, R. "The Soul in *Laws* X and Disorderly Motion in *Timeaus.*" *Ancient Philosophy* 22 (2002): 289–302.

Post, L. A. "The Preludes to Plato's Laws." *TAPA* 60 (1929): 5–24.

———. Review of Des Places edition. *American Journal of Philology* 75 (1954): 202.

Pradeau, Jean-François. *La Communauté des Affections: Études sur la Pensée Éthique et Politique de Platon.* Paris: J. Vrin, 2008.

Reinmuth, O. W. *The Ephebic Inscriptions of the Fourth Century B.C.* Leiden: Mnemosyne supplement 14, 1971.

Robins, Ian. "Mathematics and the Conversion of the Mind, *Republic* vii, 522c1–531e3." *Ancient Philosophy* 15 (1995): 349–391.

Roy, Jim. "The Threat from Piraeus." In *Kosmos: Essays in Order, Conflict and Community,* edited by Paul Cartledge, Paul Millet, and Sitta von Reden, 191–202. Cambridge: Cambridge University Press, 2002.

Russon, John. *Bearing Witness to Epiphany: Persons, Things, and the Nature of Erotic Life.* Albany: State University of New York Press, 2009.

———. *Human Experience: Philosophy, Neurosis, and the Elements of Everyday Life.* Albany: State University of New York Press, 2003.

Sachs, Joe, tr. *Aristotle's On the Soul and On Memory and Recollection.* Santa Fe, NM: Green Lion Press, 2002.

Sallis, John. *Chorology: On Beginning in Plato's Timaeus.* Bloomington: Indiana University Press, 1999.

Saunders, Trevor J., tr. *The Laws.* Harmondsworth, UK: Penguin, 1975.

———. "Plato's Later Political Thought." In *Cambridge Companion to Plato,* edited by Richard Kraut. Cambridge: Cambridge University Press, 1992.

———. *Plato's Penal Code: Tradition, Controversy, and Reform in Greek Penology.* Oxford: Clarendon Press, 1991.

———. "The Socratic Paradoxes in Plato's *Laws.*" *Hermes* 96 (1968): 421–434.

Sayre, Kenneth. *Plato's Late Ontology: A Riddle Resolved.* Las Vegas: Parmenides Publishing, 2005.

Schofield, Malcolm. *Saving the City: Philosopher-Kings and Other Classical Paradigms.* London: Routledge, 1999.

Schöpsdau, Klaus. "Syssitien für Frauen: eine platonische Utopie." In *Plato's Laws: From Theory into Practice, Proceedings of the VI Symposium Platonicum Selected Papers,* edited by Samuel Scolnicov and Luc Brisson. Sankt Augustin: Academia Verlag, 2003.

Scolnicov, Samuel and Luc Brisson, eds. *Plato's Laws: From Theory into Practice, Proceedings of the VI Symposium Platonicum Selected Papers.* Sankt Augustin: Academia Verlag, 2003.

Seaford, Richard. "Dionysus as Destroyer of the Household: Homer, Tragedy, and the Polis." In *Masks of Dionysus,* edited by Thomas H. Carpenter and Christopher A. Faraone, 115–146. Ithaca, NY: Cornell University Press, 1993.

Solmsen, Friedrich. *Plato's Theology.* Cornell Studies in Classical Philology, 27. Ithaca, NY: Cornell University Press, 1942.

Stallbaum, G. *Platonis Leges et Epinomis.* Gotha: F. Hennings, 1859–60.

Stalley, R. F. *An Introduction to Plato's Laws.* Indianapolis: Hackett, 1983.

Strauss, Leo. *The Argument and the Action of Plato's* Laws. Chicago: University of Chicago Press, 1975.

Taylor, A. E. *The Laws of Plato.* London: J. M. Dent & Sons, 1934.

———. *Platonism and Its Influence.* New York: Longmans, Green, 1924.

Thesleff, Holger. "Studies in the Styles of Plato." *Acta Filosofica Fennica,* fasc. 20, 1967.

Tod, M. N. *A Selection of Greek Historical Inscriptions.* Vol. 2, *From 403 to 323 B.C.* Oxford: Clarendon Press, 1948.

Tritle, L. A. *Phocion the Good.* London: Routledge, 1988.

Voegelin, Eric. *Plato and Aristotle.* Vol. 3, *Order and History.* Baton Rouge: Louisiana State University Press, 1957.

Weiss, Roslyn. *The Socratic Paradox and its Enemies.* Chicago: University of Chicago Press, 2006.

Wohl, Victory. *Love Among the Ruins: The Erotics of Democracy in Classical Athens.* Princeton, NJ: Princeton University Press, 2002.

Yunis, Harvey. *A New Creed: Fundamental Religious Beliefs in the Athenian Polis and Euripidean Drama.* Göttingen: Vanderhoeck & Ruprecht, 1988.

———. *Taming Democracy: Models of Political Rhetoric in Classical Athens.* Ithaca, NY: Cornell University Press, 1996.

Zuckert, Catherine H. "Plato's *Laws:* Postlude or Prelude to Socratic Political Philosophy?" *Journal of Politics* 66 (2004): 374–395.

———. *Plato's Philosophers.* Chicago: University of Chicago Press, 2009.

Contributors

Sara Brill is Associate Professor in the Department of Philosophy and the Classical Studies Program at Fairfield University. She is the author of articles on Plato, Greek tragedy and ancient Greek medicine; currently, she is completing a monograph on the political dimensions of Plato's psychology.

Patricia Fagan teaches Greek and Roman Studies in the Department of Languages, Literatures and Cultures at the University of Windsor in Windsor, Ontario. She is a specialist in Homer and Ancient Greek Literature.

Francisco J. Gonzalez is Professor of Philosophy at the University of Ottawa. He is the author of *Dialectic and Dialogue: Plato's Practice of Philosophical Inquiry* and *Plato and Heidegger: A Question of Dialogue*, as well as numerous articles on Ancient Greek and Contemporary Continental philosophy.

Robert Metcalf is Associate Professor and Chair of the Department of Philosophy, University of Colorado Denver. He is translator, along with Mark Tanzer, of Martin Heidegger's *Basic Concepts of Aristotelian Philosophy* (Indiana University Press, 2009), and the author of numerous articles on topics in ancient Greek philosophy.

Mitchell Miller is the Dexter M. Ferry Jr. Professor at Vassar College. He is the author of *Plato's* Parmenides: *The Conversion of the Soul* and *The Philosopher in Plato's* Statesman. In recent years he has been concentrating on "the longer way" declared by Socrates at *Republic* 435c–d and 504b–e and on the problem of the "unwritten teachings." For more on his work, go to http://blogs.vassar.edu/mitchellmiller/.

Mark Munn is Professor of Ancient Greek History and Greek Archaeology in the Department of Classics and Ancient Mediterranean Studies at Pennsylvania State University. He is the author of *The School of History: Athens in the Age of Socrates*.

Gregory Recco is a tutor at St. John's College in Annapolis, Maryland.

David Roochnik is Professor of Philosophy at Boston University. He is the author of four books and forty articles on various topics in Ancient Greek Philosophy. His most recent work is *Retrieving the Ancients: An Introduction to Greek Philosophy*.

John Russon is Professor of Philosophy at the University of Guelph, in Guelph, Ontario, Canada. He is the author or editor of various works of original philosophy and various studies in the history of philosophy, including *Retracing the Platonic Text* (2000), *Human Experience* (2003), *Bearing Witness to Epiphany* (2009), and *Reexamining Socrates in the Apology* (2009).

Eric Salem has been a tutor at St. John's College since 1990. He and two of his colleagues, Eva Brann and Peter Kalkavage, have just finished their third joint-translation project, a translation of Plato's *Statesman*.

John Sallis is Frederick J. Adelmann, S.J. Professor of Philosophy at Boston College. He is author of *Force of Imagination, On Translation*, and *Topographies*.

Eric Sanday is Assistant Professor of Philosophy at the University of Kentucky.

Catherine Zuckert is Nancy Reeves Dreux Professor of Political Science and Editor-in-Chief of *The Review of Politics* at the University of Notre Dame. Her books include *Plato's Philosophers: On the Coherence of the Dialogues* and *Postmodern Platos: Nietzsche, Heidegger, Gadamer, Strauss, Derrida*.

Michael P. Zuckert is Nancy Reeves Dreux Professor of Political Science and Director of the Tocqueville Program for Inquiry into the Place of Religion in American Public Life and the Potenziani Program in Constitutional Studies at the University of Notre Dame. He has published extensively on early modern political philosophy and modestly on ancient philosophy.

Index